WHAT EVERY SMALL BUSINESS
OWNER *HAS* TO KNOW

- How to attract an investor and woo a banker
- How to screen a résumé to spot a gem or a fake
- How to sell your products or services to minority markets
- How to attract new clients to your consulting practice
- How to collect the money people owe you
- How to expand sales overseas
- How to decide who will take over when you step down
- How to revamp your marketing program without spending a bundle

This is just a small sampling of what you will learn quickly and easily in the most user-friendly guide ever written for anyone who runs a small business or is thinking of starting one. If time is money, reading this book will be the best time you have ever spent.

JANE APPLEGATE is a nationally syndicated newspaper columnist with 10 million weekly readers. Her radio and television reports on small business reach millions more each week. A popular lecturer, she writes a column for *Working Woman* magazine, owns a national media communications firm, The Applegate Group, and was named 1994 Media Advocate of the Year by the Small Business Administration. Her first book, *Succeeding in Small Business*®, is also available in a Plume edition.

Also by Jane Applegate

SUCCEEDING IN SMALL BUSINESS®

Jane Applegate's Strategies for Small Business Success

A PLUME BOOK

PLUME
Published by the Penguin Group
Penguin Books USA Inc., 375 Hudson Street,
New York, New York 10014, U.S.A.
Penguin Books Ltd, 27 Wrights Lane, London W8 5TZ, England
Penguin Books Australia Ltd, Ringwood, Victoria, Australia
Penguin Books Canada Ltd, 10 Alcorn Avenue, Toronto, Ontario, Canada M4V 3B2
Penguin Books (N.Z.) Ltd, 182–190 Wairau Road, Auckland 10, New Zealand

Penguin Books Ltd, Registered Offices: Harmondsworth, Middlesex, England

First published by Plume, an imprint of Dutton Signet,
a division of Penguin Books USA Inc.

First Printing, May, 1995
10 9 8 7 6 5 4 3 2 1

 REGISTERED TRADEMARK—MARCA REGISTRADA

LIBRARY OF CONGRESS CATALOGING-IN-PUBLICATION DATA:
Applegate, Jane.
Jane Applegate's strategies for small business success / Jane Applegate.
p. cm.
Includes bibliographical references and index.
ISBN 0-452-27352-8
1. Success in business—United States. 2. Small business—United States—
Management. I. Title. II. Title: Strategies for small business success.
HF5386.A625 1995
658.02'2—dc20   94-46123
                                                        CIP
Printed in the United States of America

This book is dedicated to my husband and best friend, Joe Applegate. Without his love and sense of humor, I couldn't do what I do. And to John Lennon, whose words and music fill me with inspiration as I write.

Contents

Acknowledgments

Thanks, first, to the hundreds of entrepreneurs around the country who agreed to be interviewed and who filled out my quirky surveys. Without your generosity and wisdom, this book would not exist.

I couldn't have found the strength and inspiration to write this book without the good humor, unswerving love and support from my husband, Joe Applegate. I appreciate the patience of my daughter, Jeanne, and my son, Evan, who missed out on many hours of my time while I was traveling around the country researching this book and then locked away in my office writing it.

Thanks to Cheryl Sarfaty, an energetic and skilled writer and research associate; Bob Howard and Jennifer Pendleton, freelance writers who helped me interview some of these wonderful entrepreneurs; Josette Crisostomo, my office manager, for managing my business so I could keep writing. I especially want to thank Brooke Halpin, my public relations consultant who made me famous and is the executive producer of our television show. Brooke can always make me laugh when I feel like crying.

I'm fortunate to have terrific editors to thank as well: Steven

Seiler, at the *Los Angeles Times*, Valerie Marz, formerly at the Los Angeles Times Syndicate and Susan McHenry at *Working Woman*. I also want to thank the scores of business editors across the country who subscribe to my column.

Thanks to my parents, Martin and Sherrie Weisman, for their unflagging love and support, and to my grandparents, George and Jean Coan, for being my biggest fans. Steve and Carol Coan also deserve special thanks for their loving enthusiasm and encouragement, as do my sisters, Amy Berger and Andrea Weisman.

Thanks to Deborah Dakin, my makeup artist, Tracee Nillson, my hairdresser, for making me look great in public, and to Sarah Novack and Martin Nuñez for keeping me in shape.

I also appreciate the counsel I receive from Jerry Gottlieb, my brilliant business and legal adviser, and to Dominick Abel, my elegant and ethical literary agent. Special thanks to Deborah Brody, my editor at Plume who liked this book enough to convince her bosses to publish it.

Introduction

Much has changed in the world since my first book, *Succeeding in Small Business: The 101 Toughest Problems and How to Solve Them,* was published in 1992.

With the help of millions of entrepreneurs, the country has pulled itself out of a major recession. Interest rates have fallen. We have a president who understands and appreciates small-business owners. The United States has opened its economic borders to embrace the North American Free Trade Agreement (NAFTA). International horizons for entrepreneurs have expanded as the Asian Pacific economy booms, South Africa embraces majority rule, and Vietnam and China become entrepreneurial havens.

Many of the millions of white-collar workers laid off in the painful corporate contractions of the late 1980s and early 1990s are working for or establishing their own small businesses. Best of all, the terror many associate with becoming an entrepreneur has subsided.

Why? Because there are so many affordable resources available. Computer, software, and telecommunications prices are dropping about 10 percent a year, plummeting to the point where even the tiniest, home-based business can appear big and sophisticated. Although access to capital is not universal, banks are seeking out successful entrepreneurs to lend to, venture capital is flowing, and government programs are easing the so-called credit crunch.

Much has changed in my personal and business life as well. While *Succeeding in Small Business*® was based primarily on my syndicated newspaper column of the same name, and the wisdom of others, this book goes beyond a compilation. While featuring some of my most popular columns, it includes advice from scores of successful entrepreneurs as well as my own experiences in founding and running a successful national media and communications company, The Applegate Group.

We are one of the smallest companies in America doing business with some of the largest corporations in the world—including IBM. IBM and Ameritech Corp. sponsor my one-minute "Succeeding in Small Business"® radio reports. Together, we organize educational events and seminars aimed at helping America's entrepreneurs prosper.

In the past two years, I've reaffirmed my personal mission: to provide affordable, inspirational, and practical information to all small-business owners. To do this, I had to diversify. In addition to writing and producing the radio reports, I produce small-business reports for various television shows. And, by the time this book is in your hands, my television show *The Power of Women in Business* will be reaching even more people.

Making the transition from covering small business at the *Los Angeles Times* to running my own business required a tremendous leap. But now, when people ask me, "What do you know about running a business?" I can honestly say, "A lot." I've hired and fired employees. I've negotiated major contracts, grappled with payroll-tax issues, dealt with dishonest business associates, and handled tricky personnel problems.

This book is rich in geographical diversity. Thanks to speaking tours sponsored by the U.S. Small Business Administration, Ameritech, US WEST and IBM, I have visited about fifty cities and met with thousands of entrepreneurs. Everyone I've met has generously shared their experiences and knowledge, contributing their answer to this simple question: What sets a successful entrepreneur apart from someone who just never seems to get it together?

I can't say I have the perfect answer, but I have a few.

The secret of success has several elements:

First, successful entrepreneurs admit they don't know everything and move quickly to get the help they need. When egos are set aside and resources are assembled, great things happen.

Second, successful entrepreneurs invest time and money to obtain the best information on which to base important business decisions. With the plethora of accessible and affordable information resources out there, there is no excuse for making an uninformed business decision. On-line data bases, seminars, peer counseling, and consultants are all out there to serve successful entrepreneurs.

My belief that more businesses fail from lack of information than lack of money is stronger than ever. Without the right information, I can guarantee you'll lose money by making poor decisions.

Third, successful entrepreneurs surround themselves with good people; people much smarter than themselves, people who make them laugh and feel energized rather than exhausted at the end of the day.

The greatest lesson I've learned from owning my own business is that when you have the freedom to choose whom to do business with, never, ever work with people who give you a headache.

Fourth, successful entrepreneurs buy and use the best technology available. There is no excuse for lagging behind just because you are afraid of the modern age. Computers have gone far beyond being user-friendly. They can help you succeed. One caution here: If you don't know what technologies you need, hire someone who can help you make decisions.

Finally, successful entrepreneurs are open to new ideas and especially to collecting them from their employees. If you love and appreciate the people you choose to work with, they will reward you with much more than loyalty and productivity. They will think of better, cheaper, and faster ways to run your business.

For the rest of the secrets and strategies I've collected, read on.

I've worked hard to make this book as readable and accessible as possible. You can read it from start to finish or dip into it for a quick answer or dash of inspiration. Everything in this book is tested, tried, and true. There are no fancy management theories or formulas.

Why? Because the collective wisdom of America's 15 million entrepreneurs is worth more than all the expensive business consultants put together. You'll meet experts, like yourselves, from all over the country. People like cost-containment consultant Doug Arbuckle from Louisville, Kentucky. People like advertising expert Dan Zadra from Woodinville, Washington, and turnaround consultant Ward Wieman of Santa Monica, California.

Like *Succeeding in Small Business*, this book is packed with tip boxes, checklists, and bits of inspiration. I've made it as lively and informative as possible. It also features excerpts from a national survey of business owners I conducted in the spring and summer of 1994.

If you like it, tell your friends about it. Let me know what you think. I would appreciate your comments. Write to me at P.O. Box 637, Sun Valley, CA 91353.

To your success!

Jane Applegate
Sun Valley, California

People: First, Take Care of Yourself

Someone once told me, "Business is great, except for the people."

It sounds funny, but if you think about it, your stickiest problems are probably people-related. Your customers and clients can be difficult to please. Your employees may be late, sick, flaky, upset, or unmotivated. Your partner may be a crook or a tyrant or both. If you work with your kids, your brothers, or your spouse, you deserve a medal.

The truth is, unlimited amounts of money, technology, creativity, and persistence will not solve your people problems. That's why this book begins with ways to solve and avoid people problems. If you run a big company, you can have a few duds on your payroll. Not so in a small business. You absolutely can't afford to have any problem people sapping your time and budget.

Once you've learned how to cope with difficult people, and get the hopeless ones out of your life, your pathway to business success will be clear.

In this section, you'll meet business owners creatively solving all sorts of people problems: finding honest workers, ferreting out dishonest employees, maintaining a safe workplace, coping with office romances, and counseling employees who refuse to dress for success.

Before tackling these perplexing problems, let's start with the most important person in your business:

You.

If you don't take care of yourself and solve your own problems, your business will suffer. While entrepreneurs are famous for having massive egos and big hearts, entrepreneurs are notorious for neglecting themselves. There is no harder job than running your own business. It requires tremendous stamina and energy to meet the daily demands of entrepreneurship.

Yet wherever I go, I meet exhausted, unhappy, and unhealthy business owners. I know it's tough to balance the demands of a growing business with your personal needs, but it is imperative if you are to experience true success.

The most successful business owners I know work hard and play hard. They are selfish about their personal time and take good care of themselves.

One of the wisest people I know is Martin Nuñez, owner of Nice to Be Kneaded, a heavenly health spa and massage therapy center in Burbank, California. Martin is the only person I know who can unkink my neck when it's nearly paralyzed with tension.

As a gentle way of chastising me for not taking better care of my body, Martin quietly told me about a high-powered, talented attorney he knew. The man lived on whiskey, coffee, and not much else. At the peak of his law career, he was rushed to the hospital for emergency abdominal surgery. The problem: He had literally worn out his intestines with his caustic liquid diet. He survived the surgery, but didn't live much longer.

That's a graphic and grisly example of what happens when you don't take care of yourself, but it is meant to get your attention. In fact, scores of entrepreneurs who responded to my survey said the thing they regretted most was not taking good care of themselves, spending enough time with their families, or having enough fun.

When I asked the question, "If you could do one thing over in your life, what would it be?" these were some of the most common answers:

"Have more than two children."

"Take better care of myself. The bad times take a lot out of you."

"Learn to play without guilt."

"Lead a more balanced life."

People who know me will say I'm as guilty as anyone reading this book when it comes to working myself into a frazzle. My husband, Joe, once said I'm like a Ferrari—either racing at full throttle or in the shop for major repairs.

I know it's tough to justify taking a day off when things are falling apart, when the truck breaks down, that big order falls through, or everyone else's kids have the chicken pox. But sometimes the best thing you can do for yourself and your business is get away and get some perspective on your problems.

While it's incredibly tough to break the cycle of working too hard, collapsing and then dragging yourself back into the office, it can be done.

TIP

The first step to recovery is simple: Set aside just one hour each day to take care of yourself and your needs. One hour isn't too much to ask. Spend part of that time eating well, drinking lots of water, taking a "power nap" (see the story about sleep deprivation on page 6) or walking around the block. Buy a mini-trampoline for your office if you can't get to that health club you joined.

Everyone has a favorite way of cheering themselves up. A brisk walk, a strong laugh, and a chunk of Cadbury Fruit and Nut chocolate will do it for me.

Take Action

You know what makes you feel better, so do it. You also know how lousy you feel if you don't pay attention to your body.

My personal "feel better" formula is based on the four M's: Meditation, Massage, Manicure, Movement.

The first M, Meditation, can be any kind of quiet thought. You don't have to follow a certain program, although it helps to set aside twenty minutes in the morning and afternoon to clear your mind. Some of my most brilliant business solutions come to me after a quiet meditation in the middle of a frantic day.

The second M, Massage, intimidates some people, but if you are lucky enough to find a skilled massage therapist, you will count the hours until your next appointment. A trip to a good massage therapy center is better than going on a vacation—and a lot cheaper. Combine a long sauna with a massage and you are on the road to recovery.

The third M, Manicure: This isn't for everyone, but plenty of men, including supermacho actor Chuck Norris, enjoy manicures. (He frequents my nail salon.) I learned the hard way to take better care of my hands. One infected hangnail landed me in the emergency clinic and in a finger splint for a week. My bitten-down fingernails made writing painful and miserable. Two years ago, I started visiting Oriental Nails every week or two. The visits help my mental health, as well as my hands. Michelle Trinh, my manicurist, is better than any psychiatrist, and a visit is a bargain—$12 for a manicure and pedicure. While I'm up to my ankles in warm bubbles, we solve the world's problems.

The fourth M, Movement: Everyone needs to move, no matter how busy or unathletic you are. Walking is the easiest and most available form of movement. We have a mini-trampoline that we drag into the living room from the front porch. If someone has ticked me off or the check was *not* in the mail, there is nothing better than jumping through five or six rousing Bob Seger rock-and-roll tunes. It's a tremendous tension reliever.

Whether you enjoy bungee jumping, kung fu, kayaking, water-skiing, yoga, or jogging, promise me you'll spend some time doing something good for yourself every day.

If you absolutely can't get away from your office, here's something terrific you can do for yourself right in your office every day.

Forget the power lunch.

Take a power nap.

This afternoon, instead of gulping coffee or caffeinated soda, tell your secretary or assistant to hold your calls for fifteen minutes so you can catch a few Zs. When you awake, you'll be refreshed, energized, and more creative, according to sleep expert Dr. James Maas.

"Take a power nap to get you through the rest of the day," advises Maas, a Cornell University psychology professor and a documentary filmmaker who specializes in sleep research.

Maas says entrepreneurs and executives are among the most sleep-deprived group of Americans. Most busy people sleep seven hours a night, missing out on the crucial eighth hour of productive, dream-filled sleep.

"The last hour of the night is the most essential for learning, memory, and problem solving," says Maas. A good night's sleep can also protect you from illness. "When you only get six hours (of sleep) a night you are 50 percent more vulnerable to coming down with a viral infection."

Maas asks audience members if a heavy meal, warm room, boring meeting, or one alcoholic drink has ever made them feel sleepy. When every hand goes up, he declares that none of the above will cause sleepiness in a well-rested person. He suggests if you want to slip something by someone or gain the upper hand in a negotiation, conduct the meeting between two and four p.m. in a dark room—and show slides.

You can be sure that the sleepy participants won't put up much of a fight.

Although much of Maas's presentation is humorous, sleepiness in the workplace is dangerous. If your business runs a night shift, make sure that your workers are not exhausted and "microsleeping" on the job. Microsleeping is when you take a short nap, although your eyes are open and you appear to be awake.

"America has 20 million night-shift workers," says Maas. "According to research, 56 percent of them fall asleep at least once a week on the job."

He cautions business owners to prohibit tired workers from driving company cars or trucks because several companies have been successfully sued by exhausted workers who killed or injured people on their way home from work.

SLEEP TIPS

Dr. Maas has these tips for improving your sleeping habits:

1. Sleep in a cool room.
2. Wear comfortable pajamas, or nothing at all. (About 25 percent of men and 40 percent of women sleep in the nude.)
3. Read a boring, nonbusiness book before bedtime.
4. Keep a set of index cards by your bed and use them to jot down your worries. Once you write down what's bothering you, set the cards aside and go to sleep.
5. Exercise regularly, but not early in the morning when your body temperature is lowest and you are most prone to injury.
6. Keep sunlight out of your bedroom. Install heavy draperies or light-blocking shades.
7. If you can't sleep, get up, drink some warm milk, and try to work or read for a while. Don't toss and turn.
8. Throw away your alarm clock. Go to bed earlier and try to get the eight hours of sleep you need to be healthy and productive.
9. Be patient. It may take four to six weeks to change your bad sleeping habits and make up a long-standing sleep deficit.

"Driving drowsy is the same as driving drunk," says Maas, adding that there are an estimated 10,000 fatal accidents every year attributed to drivers falling asleep at the wheel. How do traffic investigators know someone fell asleep? There are no skid marks on the highway.

Finding Good Employees:
How to Avoid Hiring Bad Apples

"A good entrepreneur takes advantage of opportunity. Difficult people take advantage of people."—Dr. Mark Goulston

Dr. Mark Goulston, founder of the Direct Conflict Resolution Group in Santa Monica, California, got into helping business owners in an unusual way. As a psychiatrist, he counseled dying patients and their families.

"I wondered why they had to wait so long to say I'm sorry," says Goulston. That's when he began working with other management consultants who had reached their wits' end in dealing with intractable family-business owners.

Goulston believes business owners can save themselves a lot of grief if they spend more time choosing the people they work with.

"I think people come in three categories: those with a core of hate, those with a core of hurt, and those with a core of health," Goulston explains.

"People with a core of hate—if you upset them, they will retaliate rather than get into a discussion. They see your comments as an enemy assault and their reaction tends to be frightening, so you tend to avoid them."

People like this thrive on emotional blackmail, Goulston says. "They can make you dread coming into work. It's also demoralizing if other people see you, their leader, being undermined by a juvenile delinquent."

Goulston continues:

"People with a core of hurt are different. When you upset

them, they attack themselves and fall apart. They make you feel guilty for hurting them."

The problem is "You feel so sorry for them, you don't hold them accountable."

"People with a core of health have realistic expectations of themselves and others," Goulston says. "They see disagreement as a difference of opinion rather than as an assault. They can ask for help but are not helpless. They don't feel they are bad people if they feel bad about something."

Now that you know about these three different kinds of people, how do you toss out the bad apples with the hateful cores?

Make sure you can answer these four questions after interviewing a prospective employee:

1. Can this person listen with an open mind?
2. Can he or she make decisions?
3. Can he or she take responsibility for his or her decisions? Is he or she willing to pay the full consequences if the decision doesn't work out?
4. Will he or she give the same effort to something he or she disagrees with as something he or she agrees with? In other words, is he or she a good team player?

Goulston says one good way to test someone's mettle is to deliberately disagree about something during the interview to see how defensive that person gets.

Then, ask about a blowup at the interviewee's former job and find out what happened. "You want to get a sense of whether someone is a blamer or not," Goulston says.

"Ask about a regret or bad decision she made in her previous job and how she handled it."

The reason you want to spend so much time finding good people is obvious: Firing people is hellish, and everyone hates to do it. "Next time you fire someone, say 'I will never do this again.' "

Ask people how they feel after firing a bad employee, Goulston says, and they'll tell you they feel relieved and wish they'd done it sooner.

If you remember how awful you felt after firing the last person, you'll be more careful when hiring the next person.

There's another important reason to rid your life of hateful people: Hateful people drain your energy. After meeting with them, you need a lunch break or a smoke.

"Pay attention to your gut feelings," says Goulston. "You shouldn't underestimate the corrosive impact of difficult people on you and your business."

Another great tip:

Be sure to meet with all new employees two weeks after they start their jobs. Ask them if they think the priorities are the same ones you outlined to them at the start. If not, make some adjustments so your expectations will match.

"A good person will say it's not working and fix it," says Goulston.

TIPS

Cast a Wide Net for Good Employees

Many entrepreneurs, too busy to look for good employees, make the mistake of hiring the first person who walks in the door. It doesn't take much to expand your search for competent people.

1. Place classified ads in your local or regional newspaper and be very specific about the skills you need.

2. Ask your customers, vendors, and suppliers if they know anyone who is qualified for the job.

3. Offer employees a bonus or gift for referring someone you end up hiring.

4. Tell people you know who belong to trade or professional associations what kind of people you want to hire. Word of mouth can often bring in the best candidates.

Don't be afraid to "test market" employees, to see if they are right for the job.

To contact Dr. Goulston, write to Direct Conflict Resolution Group, 606 Wilshire Boulevard, Suite 405, Santa Monica, CA 90401-1505. Phone: (310) 451-7171.

William L. Ayers, president of The Ayers Group, a Manhattan-based executive recruiting and outplacement firm, routinely puts résumés to the "acid test" before recommending candidates to clients. He offers these tips on flagging the fictitious résumé.

1. Correlate employment dates with company names. Look for incorrect use or spelling of a company name or a preponderance of employment that cannot be verified.
2. Look for unexplained gaps in job history.
3. Question degrees from foreign, defunct, or unrecognizable colleges.
4. Check for any legal or disciplinary actions when contacting a previous employer for references.
5. Look for inflated salary history. Some candidates may state salaries that include the value of benefits, not their base compensation. Ask for a copy of W-2 forms or pay stubs to verify compensation.
6. Question titles that seem incongruous with responsibilities and experience.
7. Check whether foreign nationals have proper work visas.
8. Check facts regarding a recent termination. Ask the candidate to sign a release authorizing you to contact the previous employer for details.
9. Look for signs of instability such as frequent changes of employment, place of residence, or career.

Ayers says the five most common misrepresentations on résumés are:

1. Salary history
2. Education
3. Experience level
4. Budget and supervisory responsibilities
5. Actual dates of employment

Dealing with Problem Employees

It's a subject so painful that no business owner wants to talk about it. And, if they will talk, they don't want to be quoted by name.

The subject: dishonest and violent employees.

"One in three employees steal and it's rising by 5 percent a year," says K. C. Bettencourt, a former undercover investigator turned consultant and author of *Theft and Drugs in the Workplace*. Bettencourt works with large and small employers to help them thwart employee theft.

"Many employees believe that stealing from their company isn't really stealing," says Bettencourt. "Their philosophy is: 'Everyone does it and no one cares if you take a few things.'"

A consultant who agreed to share her shocking experience with a dishonest employee on condition that she not be identified lost more than a few things. In the course of a year, her assistant stole $70,000 from her business and savings accounts.

"She said she was a Sunday school teacher," says the consultant, who is still recovering from the financial, emotional, and psychological trauma caused by the theft. "All her references seemed to check out."

However, there was a puzzling, six-month gap on the woman's résumé, which she explained by saying she took some time off to make jewelry at home.

Impressed with her references, the consultant hired her for the $26,000-a-year job. The seemingly competent, efficient assistant did everything: scheduled appointments with clients, handled the daily bookkeeping chores, made bank deposits, paid the bills, etc. Confident that everything on the business side was taken care of, the consultant focused on serving her clients.

It wasn't until the end of the year, when checks started bouncing, that she realized there was a serious problem. The checks were bouncing because the assistant periodically forged $5,000 checks made out to cash and blatantly cashed them at the bank branch in their building. She apparently did it by befriending the tellers and telling them she had authority to cash checks, even though her name was not on the account.

When the forged checks weren't enough, she introduced herself to her employer's stockbroker at a major brokerage house and began requesting cash withdrawals from the family's investment accounts.

"She would request a check made out to cash and then send a courier to pick it up," recalls the business owner. "The broker, who I've known for years, never called me to ask why we were emptying our account."

With twenty-twenty hindsight, she sees now that the crooked assistant cleverly covered her tracks by "losing" important checks, bank statements, and records. The embezzler went a step further and fired the bookkeeper so she could doctor the books and show revised statements to her employer.

When the assistant was finally arrested, the district attorney handling the prosecution told the consultant that the woman was already on probation for stealing $70,000 from a local contractor. The assistant served a two-year state-prison sentence for theft. The bank settled for a few thousand dollars and the brokerage house denied any liability.

"This was the most devastating experience of my life," says the consultant, who was ill for months after the thefts came to light. "I don't wish it on anyone."

Her advice to you?

"Have your bank statements and other important records sent to your home so you can look them over before bringing them to the office," she says.

Bettencourt says a better background check would have turned up the missing information. (A good check by an investigator can cost between $100 and $400, well worth the grief it can save you.) Hiring people based on your gut instinct or "chemistry" is too risky in today's business world.

Check for these danger signs around your business:

- Employees who regularly violate company policies
- Frequent tardiness or absenteeism
- Overall poor attitude and constant complaints
- Frequent customer complaints about certain employees
- Inventory shrinkage or losses
- Finding products hidden in the employee lunchroom or rest rooms
- Voids, credit slips, or gift certificates issued without authorization
- Missing receipts, invoices, or checks
- Consistently lower net sales on certain shifts

No matter what business you are in, you can tighten security immediately by posting loss-prevention rules, locking the safe, verifying cash deposits with a second signature, and returning any out-of-place products to the selling floor.

Always ask more than one person to close your store, and don't lend anyone your keys for more than a few minutes because most keys are easily copied. It's also a bad idea to have the same person making bank deposits and writing checks on your business account.

If your employees don't steal from you, they may still be upset enough to kill you or other employees, according to S. Anthony Baron, author of *Violence in the Workplace* and founder of the Scripps Center for Quality Management in San Diego, California.

"Murderers have included fired employees, disgruntled employees still working, and, in remote cases, irate customers," says Baron, who teaches seminars on how to identify and deal with potentially violent employees.

The United States averaged 760 on-the-job murders each year throughout the 1980s and early 1990s, according to a report issued by the Centers for Disease Control and Prevention. According to the directors of the National Safe Workplace Institute, about 111,000 acts of violence occur at American businesses each year. They believe if you count the unreported incidents, the number might be triple that.

Rape and sexual assaults are also on the rise. In fact, assaults and violent acts account for 43 percent of women's workplace fatalities, compared with only 18 percent for men, according to the 1992 Census of Fatal Occupational Injuries by the Bureau of Labor Statistics.

Baron says most of the problems are usually caused by employees who have been fired or laid off.

He often counseled employees who had threatened to harm their former employers or made bomb threats.

After they were caught, some workers told Baron the bomb threats gave them a sense of power. "They would tell me, 'This was the only time I felt like God,' " Baron says.

Although business owners should be concerned about workplace violence, especially among terminated employees, Baron says fewer than 5 percent of the workers who threaten to harm their employers actually do.

To order the books mentioned: *Theft and Drugs in the Workplace* is published by R&E Publishers, P.O. Box 2008, Saratoga, CA 95070. Phone: (408) 866-6303. The 138-page paperback book costs $14.95, plus $2.50 for shipping and handling, for a total of $17.45.

Violence in the Workplace is published by Pathfinder Publishing, 458 Dorothy Avenue, Ventura, CA 93003. Phone: (805) 642-9278. The price is $22.95 for the 164-page hardcover edition, $14.95 for the paperback, plus $2.50 shipping. California residents must include sales tax.

Coping with an Office Romance

One of the prickliest problems a small-business owner has to deal with is an office romance, especially if your business is very small and your employees have to work closely together.

Business owners, big and small, say that whether or not you have a policy forbidding office dating, you'll probably have to deal with employees falling in and out of love.

Here's a true story. In a small office, which relied heavily on outside consultants, one consultant began dating a key staffer. They were discreet for weeks, and the owner probably never would have found out about the relationship except that one day an associate dropped into the office and felt the sexual tension.

Once their relationship was out in the open, the owner was forced to discuss the situation privately with each person. They were told that although the owner couldn't stop them from dating, he didn't want their personal lives interfering in any way with their business goals. The owner said he never wanted to take sides in a dispute between them, especially if it was not work-related.

Well, at first, when things were going well between them, it was happiness and bliss around the office. Their gentle kidding around was fun and harmless. But when things began to go awry, there were tears, sarcastic comments, hostility, and signs of a broken heart all over the place.

The tension escalated to the point where the owner told the consultant that the disintegrating relationship was taking its toll on the company.

The best solution was for the owner to work with the consultant outside the office. This kept the lovers apart and alleviated some tension. But as the romance chilled, it became apparent they could not work together at all anymore. This was a serious problem, since they were working as a team on several key projects. The projects ended and things eventually settled down, but there is still a bit of unease between them.

Here's some advice from the owner who dealt with this office romance:

- Deal with it openly, and clearly outline your expectations of both parties.
- If job performance begins slipping, begin documenting it carefully. Clearly warn the employee that his or her job is in jeopardy if the relationship continues to interfere with productivity or performance.
- If possible, physically separate the people and don't assign them to work on the same projects.
- Face the fact that you may have to choose one person over the other. Base the decision on who is more productive or valuable to your operation.

If you do have to fire someone, be very careful to consult your attorney about the do's and don'ts of terminating employees. Carefully document the problem and offer counseling throughout the process.

Dressing for Success

Small-business owners frequently complain to me that they can't get their employees to dress appropriately. It's a tough problem because dressing well is a matter of taste, and what seems appropriate to your employee may be totally wrong as far as you are concerned.

I interviewed several veteran managers for their help on this. One marketing executive told me she had to deal with a young, inexperienced saleswoman whose tight, short skirts were causing a flap around the office.

"I asked her to come into my office for a private chat," she said. "I began talking to her about our company image and how we were trying to project a professional image to our customers.

Then I worked the conversation around to the way she was dressing and gently explained that her outfits were causing a stir."

What was the employee's reaction?

"She said she hadn't realized that her short skirts were inappropriate. She quickly agreed to wear longer ones to work in the future."

The next day, she wore a more conservative suit and never caused any more problems with her short skirts.

That was easy enough, but not every employee will take your counseling with such goodwill. One good approach is to establish a clear dress code for new and old employees. If you carefully spell out what's acceptable and what's not, and set a good personal example, it may be easier to handle the problem of maverick dressers.

The key, though, is to practice what you preach. If you like to work in a sweatshirt and Levi's, don't expect your employees to dress up for you every day. The way you dress depends on the kind of business you're in. If you are in investment banking, you have to wear a certain costume. If you are a graphic artist, you have more leeway in what you wear around the office.

Another thought is to invite a local fashion consultant, personal shopper, or clothing-store owner to conduct a workshop about proper business attire. By presenting the information to the whole staff, you won't be singling out one particular person. Tracee Nillson, my hairdresser, tried this group approach in her Encino, California, salon, but still couldn't seem to get through to a few of her chameleon employees.

The day we discussed this problem, one woman was wearing a sheer, white, baby-doll minidress and black cowboy boots. As she clumped by in her boots, the beautifully dressed Tracee sighed. "I don't know what else to do with her," she said. "I've even offered to take her out shopping for clothes. The problem is, she doesn't have good taste."

After investing in a total salon remodeling, Tracee tried again to establish an informal dress code prohibiting very short skirts and blue jeans. That seemed to take care of the problem.

Other than imposing a strict dress code or insisting that your employees wear uniforms, you will have to work diligently and diplomatically with employees who embarrass you by the way they dress.

Leasing Your Staff

One way to share the responsibility of hiring the best people is to lease them from another company. Leasing, or coemployment, as it is sometimes called, means you select, train, and supervise the workers, but another, much larger company is legally responsible for providing them with payroll checks, benefits, and insurance.

The upside is that you, the small-business owner, don't have most of the headaches faced by employers. The downside is that you pay for the service. Coemployment companies' fees are usually based on a small percentage of the employee's salary. This can mean hundreds of dollars a month in fees for coemploying a few employees, depending on where your business is located.

Even if you have only one employee, staff leasing may be a logical alternative to putting people on your payroll. Why? Because the government regulations and paperwork applicable to small businesses today are so complicated.

"Leasing is actually a coemployment relationship, where we become the employer for the human-resources function and for the administrative tasks an employer is saddled with," says Mark Stein, executive vice president of Your Staff Inc. in Woodland Hills, California. "Our client is the employer for the day-to-day supervision and direction of the workers."

Your Staff, a subsidiary of Kelly Services, serves about 500 California companies that employ more than 5,000 workers. The staff-leasing company employs the workers and administers all health-care and insurance policies, pays the premiums on the policies, ensures that employment practices and safety measures conform to all government regulations, and furnishes employee handbooks.

According to the National Association of Professional Employer Organizations, based in Arlington, Virginia, in 1994 there were about 2,200 staff-leasing firms in the United States employing about 1.6 million workers.

"Staff leasing is designed for small businesses," Stein says, "because small businesses typically can't afford to establish a separate personnel department or devote the time required to learn all of the complicated rules and regulations required to employ someone in today's regulatory environment."

Staff leasing began in the 1970s when tax laws made it advantageous. Those advantages disappeared with the Tax Reform Act of 1986, but the industry has flourished anyway and has enjoyed successive periods of growth for various reasons. In the last several years, the business has been growing at about 30 percent per year.

"When I joined the firm in 1987, we had under 500 employees," Stein says. "Today we have over 5,000. That type of growth is pretty much representative of the industry." Such growth is one reason bigger players have entered what was traditionally the realm of small and midsize enterprises. Your Staff, for example, is owned by Kelly Services.

One attraction of staff leasing for small companies has been that a staff-leasing company, because it employs hundreds or thousands of workers, can offer a benefits package comparable to that offered by a large corporation. Although that's still an advantage of staff leasing, Stein explains that with health insurers and other types of benefit providers offering more policies aimed at the small-business market, the benefits package isn't always the primary reason that companies choose staff leasing. Instead, according to Stein, the primary reason for choosing staff leasing today is often the increasing government regulations that small businesses face.

"Issues like workers' compensation are becoming too complex for the average business owner to cope with," Stein says. "The motivating factor today is that it has become so onerous to be an employer because of all the compliance issues. Every day there are about fifteen pages of legislation, regulation, or interpretation being dropped on the doorsteps of small businesses, and they are expected to comply regardless of their size."

According to Stein, staff leasing almost always saves money, either directly by reducing personnel-administration costs or indirectly by freeing more time for the owner to concentrate on the core business.

"The hardest thing for small-business owners to realize is the value of their time," he says. "If they can quantify that value, staff leasing will always save money. About a third of the time, we can actually bring hard dollar savings to our clients. A third of the time we break even. A third of the time it costs them a little more."

Even if it costs a little more, Stein believes staff leasing is worthwhile.

"As a business owner you're not in the business of being a personnel director and becoming an expert on the regulations pertaining to the human-resource function," he says.

Hiring through a staff-leasing firm "allows you to concentrate on the productive side of your business."

Stein, who formerly was the public-relations chair for the National Association of Professional Employer Organizations (NAPEO), offers these tips for choosing a staff leasing company:

- Assess your personnel needs so you can talk knowledgeably about them when you meet with a staff-leasing firm.
- Look for a company that has special knowledge of your industry. For example, if you own a light manufacturing company, you want to look for someone who has expertise in workers' compensation and risk management, claims administration, and safety services.
- Make sure the company is financially sound, because it's going to be taking your money to pay for health insurance and other benefits. Ask for banking and credit references. Ask the leasing company to demonstrate that payroll taxes and insurance premiums have been paid. A NAPEO-accredited member can show you a verification statement prepared by a certified public accountant.

- Ask for client and professional references.
- Find out how the employees' benefits are funded. Are they fully insured or partially self-funded? Who is the third-party administrator or carrier? If your state requires a third-party administrator or carrier to be licensed, does the administrator or carrier have the necessary license?
- If your state requires staff-leasing companies to be licensed, make sure the company you are considering has such a license.
- Review the agreement carefully and ask for a provision that permits you to cancel on short notice, such as thirty days.

To find a staff leasing company in your area, contact:

The National Association of Professional Employer Organizations, 1735 North Lynn Street, Suite 950, Arlington, VA 22209-2022. Phone: (703) 524-3636.

Mark E. Stein, executive vice president, Your Staff Inc., 20300 Ventura Boulevard, Suite 150, Woodland Hills, CA 91364. Phone: (818) 999-4100; Fax (818) 593-5447.

Training Your Workers

Mention "government program" to most small-business owners and watch them shudder. But thousands of business owners across the country are taking advantage of state-funded job-training programs aimed at helping companies maintain a competitive edge.

Instead of bemoaning the aerospace industry's persistent slump, Huck International, based in Irvine, California, applied for $500,000 in state funds to improve and upgrade the skills of 200 Huck aerospace workers.

"We decided to use this downtime to retrain our employees so we will be really strong when the boom comes," says Gary Hegenbart, director of human resources for Huck International. "Huck University" classes in office automation, English, Total Quality Management, math, welding, and metallurgy have been

so successful, Hegenbart says, that the company wants to train another 200 workers at its Lakewood, California, plant.

In 1993, forty states budgeted $339 million for customized
worker training, according to a survey by training industry consultant Steve Duscha.

"I think states are becoming more sophisticated in their understanding of business and the notion of helping business," says
Duscha, who works in Sacramento, California.

"Training has become an important way to protect employment."

California's twelve-year-old Employment Training Panel (ETP)
program is considered a model for the nation. Last year, the panel
handed out $90 million in training funds, more than any other
state program.

Other states are jumping on the training bandwagon. Texas, for
example, earmarked $50 million for worker training in 1993. That
same year, New Jersey and Hawaii imposed new training taxes as
part of their unemployment-insurance programs. New Jersey's
worker-training budget increased from $2 million to $50 million
after the change. However, some states, including New York,
Michigan, Ohio, and Wisconsin, cut state training funds due to
overall state budget cuts, according to Duscha's survey.

Dennis Sienko, chief executive officer of the Prairie State 2000
Authority in Chicago, said his agency focuses on helping train
workers at small and medium-size businesses.

"It's not unusual for the company president to come in here
with a letter in his or her hand from a major customer, saying you
will do this or you will lose the contract," says Sienko, whose
group has about $6 million to spend on helping businesses cover
the cost of hiring trainers.

Most companies Sienko helps have been in business an average of thirty-seven years and have been able to make money without investing in upgrading the jobs skills of their employees. Now,
with many big companies reducing the number of suppliers they
deal with and demanding higher quality, small businesses are
forced to retrain workers or go out of business, Sienko says. "With

the new people coming into the workforce having so many problems, it makes a lot of sense to upgrade the people you have,"
Sienko said. For information, write to the Prairie State 2000 Authority, State of Illinois Center, Suite 4-800, 100 W. Randolph
Street, Chicago, IL 60601. Phone: (312) 814-2700.

If you would like to apply for state training funds but are afraid
of the paperwork, there are consultants who specialize in working
through the bureaucracy. "We are surprised that so many people
don't know about it [state-funded training]," says Bill Parker, vice
president of National Training Systems, based in San Juan
Capistrano, California. The company, which also has offices in
Newark, New Jersey, and Arlington, Texas, helps business owners
apply for funds, find trainers, and keeps track of the paperwork required for reimbursement. Many state programs require companies to prove that retrained workers remained on the job for at
least ninety days before they will reimburse training costs.

"It's fairly easy to apply for the money," says Parker. "But actually getting paid is often a bit harder." For information, call:
National Training Systems, Inc., (800) 530-3554.

Gerald Geismar, executive director of California's Employment Training Panel, says the number of small businesses applying
for training dollars increased from 800 in 1990–91 to 2,300 in fis-
cal 1992–93. He expects the numbers to increase in 1994 and
1995.

"About 60 percent of our money went to small businesses last
year," Geismar says. "And 50 percent of the money went to businesses with under fifty employees."

(The ETP considers businesses with 250 employees or fewer to
be small.)

Geismar says many smaller businesses can take advantage of
ETP funds without doing a lot of paperwork by sending workers to
classes at training sites operated by community colleges. Glendale
Community College in Glendale, California, is a leader in the
field, having received about $10 million in state training funds,
Geismar says.

States try to make contributing to training funds relatively painless. For instance, California employers pay about $7 per employee per year into the unemployment-insurance fund. "Sometimes we are referred to as the best-kept secret in the state," Geismar says.

For information on how to apply for training funds, write to: State Employment Training Panel, Marketing Dept., 800 Capitol Mall, MIC-64, Sacramento, CA 95814.

TRAINING TIPS

- Don't wait for your biggest customers to insist you retrain your workers. Figure out how you can upgrade skills today.
- Contact your industry trade association for information about industry-specific training programs. Many states work with trade groups to get the word out about available funding.
- Join with other small-business owners to share the cost of hiring trainers.
- Ask other business owners to recommend effective trainers. Trainers range in quality from terrific to awful.
- Ask your major corporate customers if your employees can attend any of their training sessions. (Very large companies spend between $27 billion and $30 billion a year to train and retrain their workers, according to the American Society for Training and Development.)

Using Contract Workers to Save Money

One way to keep your overhead costs low is to contract out special projects. Many business owners are not aware that Goodwill Industries operates workshops across the country filled with skilled workers ready to give you a hand.

When Keepers International, a Chatsworth, California, hosiery manufacturer, needs extra help getting a big order out the door, company president Steele Davidoff often turns to a team of workers located about twenty-five miles from his office.

"With salaries and workers' compensation insurance, it's very expensive for us to hire and train extra people," said Davidoff, who instead relies on Goodwill Industries' contract-services division to help meet tight shipping deadlines.

"We are very pleased with the work," says Davidoff. "It's a good way to contribute to the community, and they do an excellent job."

Goodwill, best known for its thrift stores, operates 160 contract-services divisions across the United States, according to Nicholas Panza, president of Goodwill Industries of Southern California. Goodwill's contract-services division recruits and trains disabled or economically disadvantaged people, providing them with job skills and experience, while helping local business owners.

"Our ultimate goal is to get these folks back into the real world," says Panza.

Los Angeles contract-services manager Kathleen Moore divides her time between attracting new clients and performing time-and-motion studies so she can bid on new projects. One morning, I visited the workshop where about ninety employees were busy packing, sorting, and wrapping things.

One team of workers were carefully assembling boxes, inserting video tapes, and affixing mailing labels to thousands of cassettes for a Disney resort promotion. Others were sorting thousands of hangers for return to Robinsons-May department stores, re-packing bottles of salad dressing for a food importer, and sorting reply cards for a philanthropic organization. While most workers work in teams, one man was carefully inspecting and sorting drill bits before they could be returned to a major aerospace company for sharpening.

Most months, there is plenty of work for everyone on the contract-services division payroll.

"We can't hire people fast enough," said Moore as she surveyed the spacious work area.

Upstairs in another part of the building, Steve Golden's video cassette duplication and recycling company was keeping dozens of Goodwill workers busy. Golden, who owned a film company in Europe, came out of retirement at the urging of his friends to start Quest Services.

Every year, he said, 300 million video cassettes flood the market and millions end up in landfills. Today, companies like his recycle and sell millions of used cassettes to consumers for home use.

"Last year, we recycled 6 million cassettes," said Golden. "In 1994, we'll do 12 million."

Quest's Goodwill workers are also trained to duplicate tapes by loading tapes into 1,000 industrial-quality video-cassette recorders. Most people would be surprised to learn that to maintain high quality, video tapes are duplicated one at a time and must be loaded and unloaded by hand.

"The Goodwill workers are just as capable as anyone else," said Golden. "They have problems, but they are willing to work hard and willing to learn."

As soon as new machines are installed, Quest's workers will be trained to load raw video tape into the plastic cases. This will save money and boost Quest's profits.

Golden said that the tape recycling and duplication business is growing so fast, he will eventually have to operate two shifts a day, seven days a week.

TIPS

For information on Goodwill's Southern California contract-services division, contact Kathleen Moore at (213) 223-1211 ext. 102. Be prepared to provide a sample of the work you want done. Although Goodwill can meet tight deadlines, Moore says they prefer to have two to three weeks to complete a job. Outside Southern California, contact your local Goodwill office.

Goodwill's Panza says that as his workers become more skilled, they move into more challenging positions. Eventually, they are encouraged to quit and move into the mainstream work world.

"We purposely try to lose our best employees," he says.

Keeping Your Workers Safe

Luis Mendez, a pressman at Sun Litho Inc. in Van Nuys, California, spent $35 of his $75 safety bingo jackpot on lottery tickets. He was feeling lucky after winning the company's fiftieth consecutive bingo game.

Robert Valenzuela, president and chief executive of the thirty-two-year-old commercial printing company, has relied on a popular safety bingo game to encourage safety and awareness among his 250 employees.

"We've been very fortunate the momentum has lasted as long as it has," says Valenzuela. "The safety bingo has been very well received."

Employees are divided into teams and are eligible to play as long as no one misses a day of work due to a work-related accident. Since they began playing bingo in 1985, the company has given away tens of thousands of dollars in cash prizes and has substantially reduced its workers' compensation insurance premiums. One year, there were no accidents at all, which is almost unheard of at a printing plant.

Games, drawings, and prizes are among the incentives offered by big and small companies as a way to reduce workers' compensation insurance premiums, which are based, in part, on the number of workplace accidents. Some critics contend the games discourage workers from reporting legitimate injuries or delay reporting them until after they win the prizes. But, overall, employers and insurance company executives say a well-managed incentive program, backed by a sincere effort to reduce accidents, can really cut costs.

"There is a lot of controversy and skepticism around these games, contests, and incentives," says Chuck Mitchell, executive vice president of risk management for C. E. Heath Compensation and Liability Insurance Co. in San Francisco. "I'm convinced an incentive program will not work unless top management at the company demonstrates they really care about employees."

SAFETY TIP #1

While most business owners cringe when they hear "OSHA," the Occupational Safety and Health Administration actually has a great program to help you fix problems before they turn into major nightmares. OSHA has about 425 health and safety consultants who will visit your business free of charge and make suggestions on how to clean up your act. Better yet, the consultant won't turn you in to the enforcement side unless you refuse to fix the problems.

Every year, these consultants get to about 30,000 companies. For information, contact the federal OSHA office nearest you.

Mitchell, who works closely with clients to develop workplace-safety incentive programs, collects and shares novel ideas with his clients. For example:

• The president of an upscale outdoor-furniture maker holds a monthly safety drawing, awarding the lucky winner a piece of furniture.

• A food-processing company involves workers and their spouses in the company's safety-awareness program. Every month, the safety officer posts a new safety message on the bulletin board and encourages workers to read it. Then a company representative randomly calls a few spouses, asking if they know the current message. If the spouse knows it, the family wins a prize.

• A ready-mix concrete company having trouble getting workers to a monthly safety meeting rewards attendees with a chance to enter a drawing for dinner at a classy local restaurant.

• A small supermarket sponsored a safety poster contest for workers and their families, awarding cash prizes for the winners and displaying the posters throughout the store.

At Sun Litho, between 10:00 A.M. and 10:30 A.M., Valenzuela's secretary, Cheryl Martinson, picks two or three numbers from a deck of bingo cards and announces them over the public-address system.

"If you have an accident, you can't play, so we are much more conscious of accidents," says Mendez, the most recent winner, relying on Valenzuela to translate from Spanish to English. "We also know most accidents are due to doing something dumb."

SAFETY TIP #2

About four years ago, Seth Marshall, founder of Santa Monica Seafood, developed a bingo-based program that was so popular among his seventy employees he decided to sell it to other business owners. Marshall, who has retail and wholesale operations in Santa Monica and Orange, California, now devotes most of his time to selling "Safety Pays" nationwide.

Joie Valentino, Safety Pays director of marketing, says the toughest challenge is convincing business owners that they need some type of incentive program.

"There are still managers out there who think 'I already pay my employees a salary, why can't they do their job and be safe?' " says Valentino.

The company's basic program costs about $800 and comes with a quarterly customer newsletter. "Most companies see results in thirty to sixty days, and it also builds teamwork," says Valentino. For information, call Safety Pays at (800) 942-1022.

What to Do When You or an Employee
Has a Serious Illness

Every day, successful entrepreneurs cope with lack of cash, fickle customers, and broken equipment, but battling cancer while trying to keep a business going is another story.

When Judi Firestone, founder of Computer Related Services North in Solon, Ohio, was told she had breast cancer, the first dilemma she faced was whether to tell her clients.

"A gallbladder problem is one thing, but when you say cancer, it's a different feeling," says Firestone, a computer-software consultant with clients across the United States.

Firestone was, and still is, the primary income-producer for her small business, which provides software for IBM midrange computer systems. Like many entrepreneurs who are the brains behind their ventures, she had no one to turn the business over to when she fell ill in 1990.

Today, Firestone, who feels she's beaten the disease, says she wanted to share her story because too many entrepreneurs think they are invincible and immortal. Yet all business owners should have a plan to keep their business going if they can't work, in addition to adequate disability insurance.

"A heart attack or something serious like that can really throw your business into a wingding," she says.

Arlene Robinovitch, director of rehabilitation and support services for the American Cancer Society in Atlanta, says business owners and employees have to deal with the issues related to cancer because "most cancer care today is oriented toward helping the person function as fully as possible."

"Some people can't work if their treatment is vigorous, but others work without a blip on the screen," says Robinovitch.

Once Firestone decided she wanted to keep her business open, she had just ten days before major surgery to inform all her clients about her situation. She called each client, explained what was going on, and asked for their support and flexibility. "I didn't ask for sympathy," said Firestone, who founded CRS North in 1986. "I just wanted to let them know that things would be different for a while."

After undergoing a bilateral mastectomy and breast reconstruction in April 1990, Firestone scheduled all her chemotherapy sessions on Thursday afternoons, giving herself long weekends to recover. During ten months of treatment, she combated the nausea and side effects of the treatments by eating cottage cheese and drinking lots of vanilla milkshakes.

"I received cards, flowers, plants, and support from everyone," says Firestone. "I can only think of one incident in a year when someone sheepishly asked me if there was another company they could call if something happened to me."

In the midst of chemotherapy and keeping clients happy, Firestone found out her secretary was taking advantage of her long absences by sneaking out of the office the minute Firestone left for treatments. When confronted, the woman quit. Today, Firestone relies on a more ethical secretary, a bookkeeper, and outside consultants to run the business.

Firestone's clients say they were impressed by her strength and determination to keep her business going.

"She never pitied herself," says Nancy Spencer, controller at Encore Manufacturing Corp., a machine-parts maker in Cleveland. "She was willing to work around everything that was happening to her."

Spencer says she was amazed at Firestone's open approach to dealing with her recovery.

"One day, while we were waiting for software to be loaded, she was on the phone ordering a wig," says Spencer. (Chemotherapy patients often lose their hair as a side effect of the treatment.)

At times, Spencer admits wondering how Firestone's illness would affect her performance. "I have to admit, I did think 'How is this going to affect me and what the future might hold as far as dealing with her?' " says Spencer. "But her being totally up front with us was the key to maintaining our working relationship."

TIP

Dealing with Illness in the Workplace

The Americans with Disabilities Act protects workers with cancer and other illnesses. Business owners with fifteen employees or more are required to make "reasonable accommodations" to allow ill employees to keep working as long as they can. These accommodations include restructuring jobs, modifying work schedules, and reassigning employees to other locations. Building wheelchair ramps and providing assistants also fall into the accommodation category. Small businesses can qualify for exemptions if they can prove that the changes constitute an "undue hardship." But you must prove that the changes are "excessively costly, substantial or disruptive" or that they "fundamentally alter the nature or operation of the business."

It's against the law to fire an employee who tells you he or she has cancer, AIDS, or any other life-threatening illness. Don't be tempted to demote someone or give him or her a less desirable job at another location, because this could be considered discriminatory.

Do what you can to educate and involve coworkers. Make sure everyone understands what is happening and whether they have to take any precautions around the ill worker. At several companies, coworkers have donated vacation time to sick colleagues and shared the workload to help the sick person remain on the job as long as possible.

One final note: Juries across the country have awarded large cash settlements to workers who have sued their employers under the ADA. The first case was filed by Charles Wessel, who was fired by AIC Security Investigations Ltd. in Chicago when he was diagnosed with terminal brain cancer. In March 1993, a jury awarded him $572,000 in punitive damages and back pay. A federal judge later reduced the award to $272,000. Wessel died in December 1993 at age sixty.

Ken Uveges, vice president of Enterprise Group Planning Inc., a managing general agent for a health-insurance company in Solon, says his first reaction when Firestone told him she had cancer was "fear and concern for her."

"But when she made it clear that she expected to work, I never questioned or doubted that she'd be able to do it," says Uveges.

Once in a while, employees complained that Firestone wasn't available to answer their questions as much as she had been before, but they worked around her schedule and kept going. "She had a million and one reasons to pack it up and take it easy," says Uveges. "But she loves her work—it's a big chunk of her life."

Does Firestone regret keeping her business open while she was so ill?

"To sit at home and feel sorry for yourself doesn't make sense to me," she says. "I could be just as uncomfortable at work as I was at home."

Her advice to entrepreneurs dealing with a major crisis:

Maintain your sense of humor. "I have a theory: You can laugh or cry. It doesn't take as much effort to laugh."

RESOURCE

Mainstream's National Survey of Disability Service Providers is a one-of-a-kind, computerized directory that puts employers in touch with organizations and individuals in their local communities that can provide them with technical assistance in complying with the Americans with Disabilities Act (ADA) as well as with qualified applicants with disabilities. And it connects disability service providers with their peers around their region or across the country. To order *Mainstream's National Survey of Disability Service Providers* on computer disk, send a check or money order for $39.95 (which includes shipping and handling costs) to Mainstream, Inc., 3 Bethesda Metro Center, Suite 830, Bethesda, MD 20814. Questions, please call (301) 654-2400 (Voice/TDD).

Marketing

You may have the most incredible new product or service on the planet, but if no one buys it, your business will fail. Everyone thinks developing a marketing strategy is easy. In fact, it's often the biggest obstacle to success.

We all recognize marketing genius. Think about Ben & Jerry's wild-flavored ice creams. Or the media hype surrounding the cigarette-smoking Joe Camel character.

You don't need a multimillion-dollar marketing budget to get noticed. In fact, some of the most spectacular campaigns I've covered have been rich in creativity and poor in dollars. (See My Fortune's story on page 60.)

In my search to figure out why one company flourishes while another flops, I've collected scores of clever, low-cost marketing tips. My only requisite: It has to work.

Some examples: Ron Hawley of FCD Corp., a drafting and design support company in El Grove Village, Illinois, passes out jumbo packs of Wrigley's spearmint gum with his business card stuck on the back. It's cheap. It's downscale, but it works.

Or how about John Baraona, owner of the Fussy Cleaners in

Akron, Ohio? During the worst of the early 1990s recession, he offered free dry-cleaning services to unemployed customers. When
they landed new jobs in the clothes he cleaned, they became his
most loyal customers.

Another Akron marketing legend, Russ Vernon, president of
the 25,000-square-foot West Point gourmet market, offers kid-size
plastic shopping carts and a treasure map so kids can wend their
way around the store and end up at the bakery for a free cookie.

Sometimes a small company gets lucky and lands a celebrity to
build a marketing campaign around. Lion Brand Yarns in New
York City signed a promotional deal with spokesmodel Vanna
White, who just happens to love crocheting with Lion Brand
Yarns. Vanna and Lion's "Jamie" and "Jiffy" brand yarns have appeared on the covers of *Workbasket*, *Hooked on Crochet*, *Crafts*,
and *McCall's Needlework* magazines, among others. Vanna signed
autographs at a trade show, wowing Lion's toughest customers.

"One guy, a big buyer, was floored by her," says David
Blumenthal, one of the firm's owners. "He was a pussycat after he
got her autograph."

You'll find many more marketing tips in this section, but just
passing along creative tips isn't going to help your particular product shoot off the shelves.

First, you need to determine exactly where your products and
services fit into your market, what your competition is doing to attract your customers, and then make some changes if your current
plan isn't working. Once you craft a strategy, it's easy to integrate
your marketing plan into your business plan and revise it monthly,
quarterly, and annually. The key to marketing success is carefully
tracking the results and tweaking or dumping the campaign if it's
not working.

The following "Stop, Look, and Listen" marketing strategy
came to me when I was teaching my five-year-old son, Evan, how
to safely ride his bike around the neighborhood. We all remember
learning how to cross the street—our hand tightly gripped by our
mother or father. As we timidly approached the corner, they told

us to "stop, look, and listen" so we wouldn't be run over by a passing car.

While this approach taught us how to cross a street, it can also work to create a truly "market-driven" business.

The first part takes an hour or two, but requires no special tools or experience.

Step One: STOP

Schedule some time with yourself on a quiet Sunday afternoon, maybe after church or before the football or baseball games begin on television. Go to your office and gather up all the marketing material you've produced. Collect business cards, letterhead, flyers, catalogs, direct-mail pieces, advertisements, Yellow Page ads, trade publication listings, etc.

Put it all in a pile and take a long, careful look at everything. Ask yourself:

Are we presenting a coherent business image to the public?
Does the material look like it goes together?
Does it tell people exactly what our company does?
Is it fresh and creative, or old and tired?
Is it confusing?

Be objective. I know it's your stuff, but it still may be awful and the sooner you admit it, the better. If you think some of the material is okay, set it aside. If you feel a few pieces need work, put them in another pile. The "redo pile" can be shared later with your marketing director, other employees whose opinions you respect, and possibly an outside marketing consultant.

Step Two: LOOK

Before you leave your office, flip through all those trade journals stacked behind your desk or in your bookcase. I know it takes time, but you can really gain competitive information just by reading your industry publications every month. If you don't want to do it, assign a staff member to read the magazines and pass along copies of a few key articles. If you don't belong to a professional society or trade association that produces an industry publication, join one.

(Make time, too, to read the *Wall Street Journal*, even if you read a week's worth on the weekend. And of course, read my column in your local newspaper.)

If you commute by car or train, listen to business books on tape or executive summaries of business journals. If you attend a good conference, buy the tapes and listen to the speakers you missed hearing in person.

The purpose is to be aware of your market and the fickle nature of consumers. What's worked for the past twenty years will not necessarily work this year.

Step Three: LISTEN

It's easy to manage your business in the eye of a hurricane. It may feel safe and calm in your office, but most days storm clouds are blowing in from your competition. Instead of hiding, buy a raincoat and get outside.

The listening process is critical to developing an effective marketing strategy. Listening means collecting important competitive intelligence firsthand.

If your product is sold in stores, prowl the aisles and watch what people are buying. If they don't buy your product, ask them why. You may think you are too busy or too important to get out, but the most successful entrepreneurs I've met are constantly out visiting with and listening to customers.

Here's how one of my favorite entrepreneurs collects streetwise marketing information.

I call Barbara Rodstein the plumbing queen of North America. Rodstein took over Harden Industries, her husband's Southern California plumbing business, after his death a few years ago. By keeping a keen eye on a fickle home improvement and new-construction market, Harden has kept pace with much bigger brass-bathroom-fixture makers.

One of my most memorable mornings was spent riding in her champagne-colored Rolls Royce to a donut shop near Los Angeles International Airport. You might wonder why we were driving through a drive-in donut joint in a Rolls Royce.

Well, it's because the owner of Randy's Donuts was one of the best sources for worldwide competitive intelligence. Customers coming and going to the airport from every country left tidbits of marketing intelligence along with their donut crumbs. We heard about trade missions going to Russia and arriving from China. We heard about the strength of the dollar against the yen, and so on.

Think about the people you see every day who see many other business owners. Befriend your friendly postman, Federal Express or UPS driver. Who better knows which businesses are busy, which are slowing down, and which might be moving into your neighborhood?

Befriend the man or woman who runs the catering truck that feeds workers in your area. Who else knows better which companies are hiring and which are laying off workers than the guy who sells everyone their Cokes, coffee, and candy bars?

Think of other people who are in contact with many people every day. In our neighborhood, Sandy Burns, the owner of Glenwood Cleaners, is a fountain of information and serves as the neighborhood clearinghouse for news and friendly gossip.

Sandy sells candy bars for every school fund-raiser and sells gift items and pot holders made by her friends.

Next on your listening list: Call your key vendors and suppliers. Why? Because they are on the phone talking to your competitors every day and are much more aware of the big picture than you can ever be.

For example, by reading trade magazines and talking to his major chemical suppliers, my father learned that the Environmental Protection Agency was about to ban the use of toluene in nail polish. By being one of the first private-label cosmetics manufacturers to develop a toluene-free nail-polish formula, Sher-Mar Corp., my dad's company, gained a competitive edge.

Next: Include your employees in the research process. If they feel safe and appreciated, they will tell you exactly what your customers are telling them about your company. It may be painful, but you should know what's going wrong before it hurts your bottom line.

Depending on how big your company is, meet with employees individually or in groups. Ask them what people like and don't like about doing business with your company. Create a customer survey. Pass it out or mail it out, but get it out the door and carefully study the results.

Offer an incentive for filling it out, such as a discount coupon or free product sample. If possible, get people to fill it out while you wait. While checking out of the tony Adolphus Hotel in Dallas, the clerk asked me to fill out a customer survey while she printed out my hotel bill.

It took only a few minutes and they had my immediate feedback.

TIPS

Smart Surveys

Use descriptive cover letters.
Do surveys on company time.
Ask selected workers to edit your drafts.
Keep surveys short, and do them frequently.
Make surveys user-friendly.
Broadcast the results—and act on them.

The point of collecting all this information is to create a base on which to build your new marketing strategy. Remember, Francis Bacon said: "Knowledge is power."

After you've stopped, looked, and listened, you will be ready to revamp your marketing strategy. While you are working on yours, read on for some great ideas from other successful business owners and some top marketing consultants.

MARKET TIPS

Survey Finds Public Distrusts Company Spokespeople in Business Crises

A consumer study recently conducted by Porter/Novelli Public Relations reveals that American companies are doing far worse in handling business crises than many would like to believe.

In fact, during a crisis, the public finds company spokespeople to be the least believable source of information, with the media doing only slightly better.

Naming Your Business

Choosing a great name for your business is one way to insure its success. Every year, just for fun, I organize a Great and Not-So-Great Small Business Name contest. My last contest brought in more than 650 entries from across the country. Our dining room was filled with boxes and boxes of entries, product samples, and letters begging for recognition.

It was extremely tough to narrow the field, especially since a few readers like Ruth Anne "Catnip" Mariano of New Brunswick, New Jersey, sent in twenty-six nominations. In a bizarre twist, several people sent in names for businesses that don't exist, like Shades of Envy, a sunglass or paint store nominated by a guy named Frank from Tenafly, New Jersey. Mark Jachec, of Thousand Oaks, California, said that if he ever owned a restaurant on Oak Street, he'd name it That Place on Oak. Arlene Delaney's sixth graders at Oxnard Street Elementary School in North Hollywood, California, submitted fantasy business names: To Bee or Not to Bee Syrup Co. and Rip-Off Airlines.

Wag & Brag, a Los Angeles maker of wind-up novelty items that slip onto the bill of a baseball cap, was high on the list for cleverness. So was Absolute Rubbish, a rural waste-disposal and recycling company in Oregon. Low Dough Tow in Sacramento is pretty cute. So is Latte Dah, an espresso cart in St. Paul, Minnesota. Andrea Polevoi, an Oakland, California, greeting-card maker, calls her company Hannah's College Fund, and included a picture of her little girl with her entry.

Michael Mann, vice president of Totally Twisted Inc., a Rockville, Maryland, pretzel company, came very close to winning this year. So did Sharon Wyckoff of Vienna, Virginia, who nominated her husband's computer-consulting firm, Rent-A-Nerd. Michael Cathey of Bethesda, Maryland, entered two great names, Hogs on the Hill, a Washington, D.C., barbecue restaurant, and Now Showing, a movie theater turned lingerie shop in Oklahoma.

There were terrific entries in the financial services category. The Phelan Bank (pronounced "failin'") in St. Paul, Minnesota, and The Fudge Factor, a Southern California bookkeeping firm. Best of all is Cheatham Tax Service, a thirty-year-old Oceanside, California, company. "Believe me, we make an honest living at this work, with some 800 individual clients," wrote Dean Cheatham, whose father, Bill, was still working in the business in his eighties.

"Many clients originally came to us because they liked the name and they love to tell their friends that Cheatham Tax Service does their returns."

Ellen Lieber, of Mill Valley, California, might be the first to compete in both the best- and worst-name categories. Her Access/Abilities firm helps people with disabilities—and has a clever name. But her other business, Humpty Dumpty Seminars, is not so great. Charlie King of Atlanta, Georgia, likes Haul American, a moving company in his city. Two women who recently left a major advertising agency founded their own firm, the Free Range Chicken Ranch, in Campbell, California.

Enough suspense. Here are the finalists in the great name category:

Substitoothes, a temporary-employment agency for dental hygienists and assistants owned by Loree Lee in El Sobrante, California.

Holy Cow Vegetarian Foods in Eugene, Oregon.

The 1994 winner was:

Wreck-A-Mended, a family-owned auto-body shop on Grant Street in Orlando, Florida.

Owner Bill Farmer says he came up with the name a few years ago and most people like it. "They remember it," says Farmer, whose two sons also work in the business. "But we are so far back in the Yellow Pages that most people have already found a body shop before they get to us." Farmer takes this chance, though, as he likes the name too much to change it.

Choosing the worst name was extremely tough. There were two great airlines this year: Kiwi International, named after a bird that can't fly, and Coffin Air Service. The Amigone (pronounced "am I gone") funeral homes in upstate New York were nominated by several readers. Big Bill's Plumbing, in Pachecho, California, is also pretty bad. The Pluck U chicken shop in New York City and Bland Farms, a mail-order food company in Glennville, Georgia, could use some work.

There were also businesses with impossible-to-pronounce names: Anatomorphex, a special-effects company in North Hollywood, and the mNemoDex Group, the trademarked name for Robert Gordon's information management company in Los Angeles. Luckily, Gordon pointed out the name is pronounced "knee-mow-decks."

Drumroll, please. Despite hours of deliberation by me and my daughter, Jeanne, two businesses tied for a recent Not-So-Great-Name Award:

The Poo-Ping Palace Restaurant, a Thai restaurant on Foothill Boulevard in Tujunga, California, was nominated by Ben and Patty Coats of Los Angeles. "We stopped and bought a disposable camera to take a picture of their sign," said Patty Coats. "We couldn't believe it."

(The manager of the restaurant says she is tired of people making fun of their name. "Poo Ping is the name of the royal palace in Thailand," she says.)

Poo-Ping Palace tied with The Electric Fetus, a popular chain of music stores based in Minneapolis.

"The company name has met with mixed responses over the years, so we leave the category decision (best or worse name) up to you," wrote Dawn Jeche, Electric Fetus's advertising coordinator. "While we feel the name is great (once people are familiar with our business, they never forget it!), others may not feel the same way."

If you have a great or not-so-great name to nominate send it along with your name and address on a postcard to: Jane Applegate, P.O. Box 637, Sun Valley, CA 91353-0637.

Tapping New Markets: Gays and Hispanics

The Gay Market

Savvy business owners, big and small, are waking up to the buying power of gays.

"It's the market of the decade," says Michael Kaminer, a New York City marketing and public-relations consultant who specializes in gay promotions. Many gay households have double incomes and no kids, which dramatically increases their disposable income, Kaminer says.

America's gay population is in the limelight now. While President Clinton and the Pentagon are grappling with the issue of gays in the military, major advertisers including Giorgio Armani, Banana Republic, Virgin Atlantic Airways, and New Line Home Video purchased ads in the May issue of *Out* magazine for the first time.

CBS/Fox Video issued a press release urging gay and lesbian consumers to ask the owners and managers of local video stores to buy copies of *The Lost Language of Cranes*, a British Broadcasting

Corporation–produced drama about a father and son who both admit their homosexuality.

"It benefits everyone if video stores carry more gay and alternative titles," says Mindy Pickard, vice president of marketing for CBS/Fox. "The stores win, consumers win, distributors win. This market offers true growth potential if its needs are addressed."

Although the debate rages on exactly how many Americans are gay, marketing consultants estimate the total could be as high as 10 percent of the U.S. population or about 18.5 million people. Gay couples have an average annual household income of about $50,000 a year and are avid travelers and buyers of everything from personal computers to camping equipment, according to Rick Dean, senior vice president of Overlooked Opinions, a Chicago-based polling and market-research firm specializing in the gay market.

Overlooked Opinions launched its own business venture, a national long-distance-telephone service for gay and lesbian consumers. Thousands of people signed up for the Community Spirit phone service, which donates 2 percent of all long-distance charges to the gay, lesbian, or AIDS organization of the customer's choice.

The company also purchased advertising space on 2 million Washington, D.C., Metro subway tickets bearing the Community Spirit logo and a welcome to the 1993 "Gay and Lesbian March on D.C."

Mainstream companies are also tapping into the gay market. Paper Moon Graphics, a West Los Angeles greeting-card and stationery company known for its humorous cards, launched a line of gay greeting cards. The cards are flying out of stores, according to founder and copresident Fred Zax.

"We're simply offering a product for the gay market which is about gay people," says Zax. "We were pretty sure the cards were going to be a hit."

Paper Moon's gay-oriented cards feature 1950s and '60s stock photographs that are colored by a computer. Copywriters add humorous dialogue dealing with friendship, flirting, and romance. "We try not to be too insulting," says Zax.

While Paper Moon added a gay line to its diverse mix of cards, Chicago-based Cardthartic creates cards exclusively for the gay market. Six gay and straight founders started the company in 1993 because they believe the $5.3 billion greeting card industry has ignored gay consumers.

"We are really passionate about creating cards to curl hair at Hallmark," says Jodee Stevens, Cardthartic's president.

Stevens says the small company's greatest challenge is distribution. "We need retailers to recognize that the needs of this market are distinct and important so they will add a 'gay interest' section to their stores."

Cardthartic's "Through Our Eyes" line features adoption announcements for lesbian couples, humorous cards, and a serious "Passages" line featuring paintings by William Trotter and original poetry by Dwight Okita.

Okita wrote this poem for a card designed for men with AIDS:

> You can't leave one place
> without arriving someplace else.
> Here's to a safe arrival—wherever that is.
> Here's to a universe that
> gave me you for such a short time.

The Hispanic Market

Small businesses, just like large businesses, need to be aware of population shifts transforming the culture. If your business is ignoring the Hispanic market, you are making a costly mistake.

"It used to be okay not to target this market, but no longer," says Anita Santiago, owner of a Santa Monica, California, ad agency that helps companies sell to Hispanics.

Hispanics are not only growing in numbers but in earning power, she says. According to U.S. Census Bureau projections,

Hispanics will become the majority population in California by 2020. The Census Bureau predicts that Hispanics will make up 36.5 percent of the population in twenty-six years; non-Hispanic whites, 34 percent.

Santiago describes the growth in the Hispanic market as "explosive." If you don't go after the Hispanic market now, you will have to play catch-up with your competitors later.

In Los Angeles County, for example, Garcia was the most common surname among new-home buyers in 1993, according to Dataquick Information Systems, a real-estate database in La Jolla. In that same year, there were two to three times more Latino home buyers in L.A. County compared to the levels of five years earlier.

What sets the Hispanic market apart?

- They are brand-loyal. Hispanics don't switch brands as easily as other groups. There is a sense of tradition unlike other cultures. If your mother bought a brand, you're likely to buy the same brand, says Santiago.
- Hispanics are extremely family-oriented. "Everything revolves around the family," says Santiago.
- Hispanics have a high regard for goods that are made in America based on a faith in Yankee quality.
- They're hard-working. Santiago said Hispanics are the largest employed minority in the United States, sometimes holding two or three jobs. "They're motivated by the American dream," says Santiago.
- It's not a race, it's a multifaceted culture.
- Hispancs look to media as an information source, less as an intrusion or entertainment vehicle.

But be careful: Advertising and promotional messages aimed at Hispanics must be on target—or the effort can backfire.

"You must be extremely culturally appropriate," says Santiago. "You can't just take a campaign from the general market and translate it."

As an example, she points to a campaign for the California Milk Advisory Board. For the general market, the organization, which promotes milk consumption, was using a humorous campaign that made jokes about milk deprivation. It talked whimsically about the dangers of running out of milk.

TIPS

Here are Santiago's tips regarding the creative content of campaigns aimed at Hispanics:

- Be sensitive to cultural differences among various Hispanic groups. Avoid using slang.
- Be aware that Hispanic cultures have their own holidays and traditional foods. The celebration of the Virgin of Guadalupe on December 12 is a Mexican holiday not celebrated in other Hispanic cultures, for example.
- *Hispanic* is a comprehensive term for people whose ancestors hail from Spain, Mexico, Cuba, Puerto Rico, Central and Latin America. The common bond is the Spanish language; each people has its own distinct culture.

Anita Santiago is president and creative director of Anita Santiago Advertising, Santa Monica. The seven-year-old independent ad agency specializes in creating Spanish- and English-language advertising for Hispanics, a fast-growing population segment. Major corporate clients include First Interstate Bank, Home Base, See's Candies, Miller's Outpost, Blue Cross of California, California Milk Advisory Board, California Department of Health and Human Services, and Caltrans.

Santiago advised the Milk Board not to take this tack in advertising to Hispanics. She felt that translating the English-language campaign into Spanish would have been insensitive. The Milk Board listened. "Milk deprivation is not funny to us," she said. "If you're a first-generation Hispanic and you're struggling to feed your family, you're not going to think it's funny not to have milk. This is a hard reality of life."

Instead, the Santiago agency produced a campaign designed with Hispanic sensibilities in mind. It played on the Hispanic tradition of passing down family recipes with a campaign promoting recipes with milk as an ingredient. The emphasis was on health and families, and promoted mothers as heroines. This played on the more traditional concept of womanhood and motherhood held by many Hispanics, says Santiago.

One big difference among Hispanic groups is language, says Santiago. For example, the term *baby bottle* is expressed in different ways in different Spanish-speaking countries. A company could inadvertently end up offending one group by using the term from one culture in advertising messages to another.

Another example: In parts of Latin America, if you wanted to say "Give me a ride," you'd say *"Vame la colita,"* but in Mexico that phrase has sexual connotations, translating roughly into "Give me the little tail."

In Puerto Rico, there's a slang phrase, also roughly meaning give me a ride, *"Dame pom."* It makes no sense in any other Hispanic culture.

Santiago cites other examples of general-market ad campaigns that bombed when directly translated into Spanish:

- The now-defunct Braniff airline, for example, had a general campaign urging customers to "fly on leather." When translated directly into Spanish, it used a slang word for leather that meant naked, says Santiago. So Braniff was urging would-be customers to "fly naked." When there was a furor over it, Braniff compounded the error. It answered critics with the retort, "Hispanics have dirty minds."
- Raid insecticide's "Kills Bugs Dead" campaign worked for the mainstream, but in Spanish it read "Kills dead bugs."
- Eastern Airline's "The Wings of Man" campaign, when translated into Spanish, had the connotation that you'll die, become an angel, and go to heaven.
- Budweiser, the King of Beers, ended up being the Queen of Beers in Spanish-language ads. The slang "queen"

means the same thing in Hispanic culture that it does in the general culture.

Cashing In on a National Trend

It's the kind of phone call everyone dreads. Someone from a hospital calling to tell you that your spouse passed out on the sidewalk and was rushed to the emergency room.

On October 27, 1992, Dan Tepper, a sportswear buyer from Edison, New Jersey, collapsed in front of Macy's department store on 34th Street in New York City. A few days later, Tepper underwent successful heart surgery and joined the ranks of Americans whose doctors strongly encourage them to eliminate all fat from their diets—forever.

Tepper's wife, Pat, says she was surprised at how tough it was to buy tasty fat-free foods for her husband. Her time spent grocery shopping tripled as she searched gourmet and health-food stores for healthy, flavorful low-fat foods.

"Dan couldn't feel like he was being deprived," says Tepper. "He had to lead a normal life. If he wanted to sit in front of the television and snack, the snacks had to taste good."

Unfortunately, many of the fat-free crackers and cookies she brought home tasted like Styrofoam.

Frustrated by the lack of flavorful products available, the Teppers attended a food industry trade show and were inspired to create *Fatwise*, a catalog featuring only fat-free foods.

Having run a small, mail-order needlecraft business out of her home for fifteen years, Pat Tepper believed she had the expertise to get the company off the ground. In January 1994, she began by sending letters to thirty fat-free-food manufacturers. When all but two said they would like their products to be included in the catalog, she was convinced it was a good idea.

The Teppers quit their jobs and invested about $100,000 of their own money to launch *Fatwise*. They mailed out the first thirty-six-page issue of the colorful *Fatwise* catalog. They stocked a

Linden, New Jersey, warehouse with fat-free pasta sauces, cereal bars, dried noodle soups, cookies, rice cakes, and candies. Prices range from ninety-nine-cent fruit bars to a "Sauce Lover's Package" of pasta sauces for $26.99, plus shipping and handling charges.

So far, Tepper says orders are streaming in from around the country, mostly based on word-of-mouth recommendations from happy customers and publicity. A second, fifty-two-page catalog, featuring detailed nutritional information about each product, is out. Dan Tepper, who handles the finances, projects first-year sales will hit $250,000.

For a free *Fatwise* catalog, call: (908) 862-3886, or write to Fatwise, P.O. Box 25, Dept. LAT, Colonia, NJ 07067-0025.

"We would not have gotten into this if we thought it was a fad," says Pat Tepper. "It's not a fad. It's a healthy way of eating."

Dr. David Heber, director of the nutritional medicine program at the UCLA School of Medicine, agrees.

"In 1988, the surgeon general said that next to stopping smoking, cutting out dietary fat was the number-one thing you can do for your health," says Heber.

Heber, who works mainly with obese patients, says obesity is a major health problem because it causes heart disease, high blood pressure, and many common forms of cancer.

"Cutting out fat is going to be a major concern of the American people," Heber says. "The problem is, fat enhances the taste of many foods. The challenge is finding new and creative ways to enhance taste while using less fat."

Richard Freedman, founder of Gratis, a trendy Brentwood, California, restaurant featuring fat-free cuisine, is convinced he has found the secret to making fat-free food taste good.

After failing to find a restaurant that offered good-tasting, fat-free food, he recruited a team of experts to come up with pizzas, burritos, salads, and desserts, among other things.

"It took us four months to get a good chocolate cake and one year to get a fat-free cheese cake," says Freedman. "I spent a year and a half being unreasonable and persistent."

Freedman, who sold his clothing business in 1989, never planned to open a restaurant. But when he began gaining weight a few years ago, "I found that if I ate no fat, I could eat just about anything else and lose weight."

Like the Teppers, he went shopping and found that most fat-free food tasted awful.

"I tried a pizza with grilled vegetables that tasted terrible," says Freedman. "Where is it written that you need fat to make something taste good?"

His persistence in developing new recipes has paid off. Today, Gratis, located on San Vicente Boulevard, is a bustling place with a loyal clientele.

"The fat-free muffins are incredible," enthuses John Taylor, a mergers-and-acquisitions specialist who frequents the busy restaurant.

Freedman, who invested about $500,000 in the research, recipe development, and the restaurant itself, said he's planning to open new locations and expand his concept.

"People leave here feeling full, but they feel very good," he says. "It's guiltless eating."

Gratis: 11658 San Vicente Boulevard, Brentwood, CA 94513 Phone: (310) 571-2345.

One-Trick Ponies:
Managing a One-Product Business

In this age of diversity and variety, some savvy small-business owners stand out by specializing in just one product. 100% Rocking Chair is a small business that is very happy to be a one-trick pony.

Step inside Matt Bearson's spacious, inviting store on the corner of Third Street and La Brea Avenue in Los Angeles, and there is no question that 100% Rocking Chair sells only rockers. There are Mexican wrought-iron rockers, cowboy rockers, Shaker rockers, gliding love seats, and a menagerie of rocking sheep, birds, and other beasts.

"A lot of people have always wanted a rocker and we just make it easy to find one," says Bearson, a former assistant film director in Hollywood.

Bearson said he got the idea to open a rocking-chair store after searching around town to buy a rocker for a friend. "There are tons of places with a couple of rockers," Bearson says. "Generally, the rockers are ugly or tucked away in the corner of a furniture shop."

So, tired of 100-hour work weeks and the gypsy lifestyle that accompanied his show-business career, Bearson borrowed $35,000 from family and friends and opened the 3,000-square-foot store in July 1992.

The planning and budgeting skills he learned from the movie business serve him well as an entrepreneur.

He saved money on rent by waiting until the last minute to sign the lease. He conserved cash by arranging for his first batch of rockers to be delivered a few days after he moved in. He saves money by having only one full-time employee and a few part-timers.

Despite a lack of off-street parking, Bearson says his store has been profitable from day one.

When Chris Kruysman and his pregnant wife, Renee, dropped in to shop for a rocker, Bearson's assistant, Ayessa Rodies, handed Renee an eleven-pound burlap bag of rice nicknamed Pilaf.

Cradling Pilaf in her arms, Renee tested a variety of rockers she intended to share with their baby. A sleek, black-leather gliding rocker topped her wish list.

Baby Pilaf isn't the only special touch that sets Bearson's store apart from other furniture retailers. Instead of banning refreshments from the showroom, everyone who stops in is offered tea, coffee, spring water, or a soft drink. The refreshments and soft music playing in the background encourage shoppers to sit and rock for a while, whether or not they intend to buy.

"People come in and share their rocking-chair memories," says Rodies. "Our store is a nice place to hang out."

100% Rocking Chair has been so successful, Bearson is thinking about expanding to another location.

While Bearson focuses on cornering the rocking-chair market, Sharon Jones is hoping to become the snow-dome queen of North America. Her small mail-order business, Global Shakeup, opened in 1991, born out of her love for snow domes, the liquid and flake-filled domes that create a trickling snowfall when shaken.

Jones says she was completely taken by a snow-dome book she once browsed through. "It was just the most delightful book," Jones says. "I never owned a snow dome as a child. My parents wouldn't have bought me something like that."

So she created a whole company that sells nothing but snow domes. "I thought if I liked them so much, maybe others would feel the same way."

Global Shakeup offers a wide selection of snow domes through its mail-order catalog. Some are sentimental, featuring a bride and groom or a big teddy bear inside the dome. Others are religious. And of course, there's the Elvis dome for a whole lot of shakin'.

Global Shakeup's customers are mainly business travelers who previously bought snow domes in airport gift shops, Jones says.

She recommends them as a great pick-me-up for busy people. "It's like having a mental break in your office," she says. "They are inherently wonderful."

Snow domes range in price from $4.99 to $75. For a catalog, send your request to Global Shakeup, 2265 Westwood Boulevard, #618, Los Angeles, CA 90064.

One More One-Trick Pony

You can't eat rocking chairs or snow domes, but you can eat a gooey, chocolate-and-marshmallow confection that's guaranteed to drip down your chin. It's called Valomilk, and it's the only product produced by Russell Sifers, the Merriam, Kansas candy company.

Sifers, a former General Motors production worker, resurrected the family's flagship candy, Valomilk, in 1987.

If you grew up in the Midwest, you'll remember Valomilk as the chocolate-cup candy that dribbled creamy marshmallow down your chin. Created by Harry Sifers in the early 1930s, Valomilk was known for its delicious "flowing center," made from corn syrup, sugar, egg whites, salt, water, and vanilla. Sixty-plus years later, the sweet, gooey stuff still flows out of a delicious milk-chocolate cup.

Hoping to increase production and expand distribution nationwide, the Sifers sold the company to Los Angeles–based Hoffman Candy Co. in 1970. "In the 1970s, we were in a merger mania," says Russell Sifers. "The big candy companies were gobbling up the little guys."

For a while, Valomilk seemed compatible with Hoffman's other candies, including Cup O' Gold, a similar filled-chocolate-cup confection. "The sale sounded good to us, but it just didn't work out," Sifers says.

The Sifers resisted Hoffman's desire to cut production costs by using less-expensive ingredients. Hoffman stopped making Valomilk around 1980. A few years later, Sifers obtained the rights to the Valomilk brand name from Hoffman. He began making Valomilk again in 1987, using the original copper pots his grandfather did.

Richard Hoffman, who sold his trademarked candy lines and machinery to Adams and Brooks Candy Co. in Los Angeles, agrees with Sifers that older brands of candy are gaining popularity. "There was a period when I thought Mars and Peter Paul and Nestlé were going to buy us all out of the market, but I believe we are coming back," says Hoffman, who oversees production of Cup O'Gold at Adams and Brooks.

Meanwhile, back in Kansas, Sifers said he's happy that Valomilk is back on the shelves after disappearing for nearly a decade. Sales are still under $1 million a year, but he's signing up new distributors every year.

Today, ten employees help Sifers produce about 700 cases a

month. Although distribution is still limited to the Midwest, sales are growing and Sifers will fill mail orders if it's not too warm outside. Valomilk has a low melting point and doesn't like to travel on airplanes because the chocolate cups spring leaks at high altitudes.

(Depending on the weather, Sifers will ship you twenty-four packages, each with two Valomilks, for $21.95, which includes UPS shipping across the continental United States. The address is: 5112 Merriam Drive, Merriam, KS 66203.)

Doing Business with a Giant

You may think your business is too small to do business with a major corporation, but that's probably not true. Look at my company: With three people, we may be the smallest company in the country doing business with IBM, Ameritech, Ford, and US West.

Corporations are turning to entrepreneurs because entrepreneurs usually get the job done cheaper and faster. Selling your products or services to a major corporation has never been easier. Downsizing and outsourcing provide tremendous opportunities for small companies. The secret to making a deal is twofold. First, figure out what a big company needs to boost sales or improve customer service. Then, find the right person to pitch your idea to.

"Large companies realize that the world has changed," says David Poole, technical director of corporate-industry marketing at Digital Equipment Corp. in Marlborough, Massachusetts. "A lot of the new innovations are coming out of small companies. If a large company wants to survive, it has to be open and receptive to the ideas small companies have."

Poole said DEC works with many small companies, including Corollary Inc., an Irvine, California, company that describes itself as a "computer company's computer company." Poole credits Corollary with not only helping DEC quickly bringing a new computer system to market, but accelerating DEC's entry and success in the personal-computer marketplace.

"The relationship with Corollary saved us time and the systems made us money," says Poole. Unlike some big high-tech firms, DEC is very open to signing nondisclosure agreements before taking a look at new ideas.

"Big companies have wide distribution, a reputation for quality, and all the other things consumers want, but at the same time, the new ideas are likely to be dreamed up by small companies," Poole says.

Corollary, a pioneer in multiprocessor computer technology, which links several central processing chips together, does business with a Who's Who of computer giants including IBM, Unisys, Zenith, and Hewlett Packard. One major advantage of dealing with a deep-pocketed corporation is that the smaller company can ask for advance payments to help finance product development or meet payroll. DEC, for example, paid Corollary several hundred thousand dollars up front as an advance against future royalties.

George White and Alan Slipson founded Corollary in 1985 after leaving Texas Instruments. While White says working with big companies has fueled Corollary's growth, it feels like he's riding an "emotional rollercoaster."

"We often walk a tightrope between fulfilling our responsibilities to our big customers while making sure our smaller customers are happy, too," says White, whose company employs about sixty-five and projects 1994 sales of $16 million.

Because big corporations tend to move people into new jobs frequently, White says key people he's dealt with at many big companies are "no longer there or in bigger jobs." He says it's essential to have one or two contact people to shepherd a project along.

While very big customers generate about 50 percent of Corollary's revenues each year, Santa Monica–based Self-Cleaning Environments Inc., which makes a patented self-cleaning public rest room, is courting major corporations to serve as strategic partners as well as customers.

Amoco, a major oil company, tested the company's novel, self-contained rest room at two gas stations in the Midwest. Self-Cleaning Environments Inc. approached another major oil company and a fast-food chain to see how the companies might benefit by installing the low-maintenance bathrooms.

The $16,000 unit, featuring a standard size sink and toilet, closes up like a refrigerator and works like a dishwasher. Twenty-four minutes after an attendant flips a switch, the bathroom is sparkling clean from ceiling to floor. Instead of doing a dirty job, employees have only to mop up excess water from the floor.

Inventor and architectural planner Glenwood Garvey had been dreaming about a self-cleaning rest room for more than twenty years, ever since he was asked to help a major oil company brainstorm about the "rest room of the future." The patented rest rooms were tested at an Amoco station along Interstate 55 in Bolingbrook, Illinois, and in Indianapolis.

"We've had nothing but good reviews from customers," says John Jordan, who previously managed the busy Bolingbrook station. "As long as everything keeps going the way it is, eventually it should be everywhere you could have it in gas stations, restaurants, and bus stations."

Jordan, now the manager of two company-owned stations in Aurora and Warrenville, Illinois, said employees flip the switch to clean the bathroom three times a day. "I'd love to have one for my house," he said.

Garvey, with fewer than a dozen employees, hopes to bring the cost down to $5,000 once they go into full production. He admits working with big companies has its pitfalls. Amoco, for instance, shelved plans to buy additional units after going through a major downsizing and cost-reduction period. American Standard, which provides the bathroom fixtures, was a potential strategic partner, but put off making a decision while it cut expenses.

Frustrated but not defeated, Garvey and his marketing director, Liz Taylor, are focusing on new corporate relationships and trying to raise money through a private placement offering.

TIPS

Dealing with Major Corporations

Here's some advice from George White and Glenwood Garvey:

1. Hire an attorney who has experience negotiating with big corporations.

2. Try to sign a letter of intent to get the project going and the cash flowing while the actual contract is being completed.

3. Draft your own contracts whenever possible. This saves time and headaches in the long run.

4. Find one person at the corporation to champion your project.

5. Maintain good communications with your corporate partners via memos and frequent telephone conversations.

6. Bring extra people to meetings with your corporate partners. If they plan to have four people, you should have at least two.

7. Call the company's marketing department to find out who might be interested in your product or service. Do your homework and be very familiar with the company's existing product lines.

8. Ask the corporation to sign a nondisclosure agreement to protect your trade secrets.

9. Be patient and persistent. It may take twelve to eighteen months to hammer out an agreement, but a solid corporate relationship can last for years.

10. Watch out for middle managers who may sabotage your project because it was "not invented here."

11. Be responsive. Corporate partners demand attention and action.

12. Attend industry trade shows to meet potential corporate partners.

"Even as a one-product company, Self-Cleaning Environments has long legs potential," says Brian Foley, senior vice president of The Chicago Corporation, an investment-banking firm working with Garvey. "Our firm is always on the lookout for small, emerging companies with a unique product or service with long legs. Long legs means many, many years of profitability."

Tiny Messages: One-Line Gems

"There are single thoughts that contain the essence of a whole volume, single sentences that have the beauties of a larger work."—Joseph Joubert

Tiny, one-line messages may be the secret to cutting through advertising clutter, according to two successful entrepreneurs who have built their businesses around the concept.

Brad Edwards and Dan Zadra have never met, but both rely on pithy thoughts presented in a unique manner to get their messages across. Edwards packages custom one-liners in acrylic fortune cookies. Zadra's messages appear behind the pop-up windows of unique paper cards.

Zadra, a veteran advertising expert, opened his first advertising agency in Seattle twenty years ago. From research and experience, he found that simple messages, relayed one at a time, cut through advertising clutter and were remembered.

Today, Compendium, Zadra's small Woodinville, Washington, company, creates messages and customized campaigns for big and small companies.

"You don't find our window cards in the street because people save them," says Zadra, who writes many of the messages featured on the pop-up cards and perpetual calendars. "Our cards have been to the top of Mt. Everest, in Polaris submarines, and in space with a NASA astronaut."

The pop-up cards, about the size of a matchbook, can be packaged in boxes of twenty-eight with a theme like "Brilliance," featuring inspirational quotes for women. Other sets feature popular business themes such as quality and customer service.

U.S. Forest Service employees passed out Compendium's cards to create goodwill between the agency and residents in the Southwest. Miles Laboratories, Bank of America, and Nordstrom are among Zadra's bigger clients. Many smaller businesses, like the Palomino restaurant chain, have purchased the cards.

Palomino, with restaurants in Minneapolis, Palm Desert, San Francisco, and Seattle, passes out the cards to customers as a way to say thank you. Palomino's red-and-purple cards feature quotes from famous people, including Marlene Dietrich who said, "It's the friends you can call up at 4 a.m. that matter."

Patty Howard, Zadra's Corona del Mar, California, representative, says the tiny messages offer big and small companies a way to set themselves apart from the competition.

For as little as $500, Compendium can customize a set of pop-up cards by adding a company logo or insert. The cards cost between five and ten cents each, depending on the quantity ordered. The company designs and manufactures all the cards at its Washington headquarters. For a copy of its first catalog or card samples, write to: Compendium, 13125 N.E. 175th Street, Woodinville, WA 98072.

Brad Edwards, founder of San Francisco–based My Fortune, started working for his family's printing company when he was thirteen. But a crippling industrial accident and a desire to thank his fortune-cookie-loving girlfriend for her support thrust him into a new, fast-growing business. His new venture, My Fortune, makes acrylic fortune cookies featuring customized messages.

"Every time my girlfriend, Jennifer, and I went out to eat Chinese food, she would ask for about ten fortune cookies," says Edwards. "She loves keeping the messages—they are all over her house."

Edwards's life changed drastically two years ago, when his left hand was crushed in a die-cutting press. Despite several surgeries to cosmetically reconstruct his hand, it will never work again.

To thank Jennifer for her support, Edwards asked a glassblower to make a glass fortune cookie as a gift. When the glassblower couldn't do it, Edwards found a plastic company that crafted a fortune cookie from a flat acrylic disk in less than a day.

"When Jennifer opened up the box and saw the fortune cookie, she started to cry," Edwards recalls.

Soon, family members and friends all wanted Brad's acrylic fortune cookies. Edwards invested $48,000 of his own money to launch My Fortune in 1993. The company, which now contracts with skilled fortune-cookie benders to form the cookies, is looking at buying new machines to boost production.

Edwards sells more than 15,000 cookies a month to companies, including wedding planners who use them as party favors. The cookies are cleverly packed in a tiny paper Chinese food container, complete with a wire handle.

Although Edwards started out selling boxes of sixty cookies to gift and card shops, he's now focusing on producing big orders for major clients like *Fortune* magazine. One message *Fortune* ordered for a batch of acrylic cookies was "Innovate or Evaporate."

Edwards says his next big move is into the lucrative specialty-advertising market, which makes customized giveaways for businesses. The fortune cookies are perfect for the market because they can be turned into refrigerator magnets and key-chain ornaments.

My Fortune has also generated business for A. W. Stern Paper Box Co., Edwards's family business. The company stamps company logos on the paper boxes and ships out the packaged fortune cookies. My Fortune cookies retail for about $5.

"When I got hurt, I thought it was the end of my life," said Edwards, who spent most of his time before the accident fixing cars, motorcycles, and printing equipment. He admits that he was so depressed after his accident that he once contemplated suicide.

Edwards credits the success of My Fortune with pulling him out of his slump and giving him a reason to live.

For information call: (800) MY FORTUNE [693-6788] or write to: 5990 Third Street, San Francisco, CA 94124.

TIPS

Tiny Messages

Advertising expert Dan Zadra says the best way to convey your company's message is with intensity, repetition, and duration. "Intensity doesn't mean loud, pushy, phony, insecure, or exaggerated. Repetition refers to frequency rather than redundancy. Duration refers to the length of time in which you repeatedly deliver your intensely meaningful messages.

"You want to be careful about the content," he cautions. "The quality of the message is very important."

Every marketing or advertising campaign should meet these goals:

- Break patterns
- Cut through the clutter
- Open up people's minds
- Be remembered

Make Your Company Market Driven

In a highly competitive industry, being creative and market driven can set you apart. Here are two small-business owners who have figured out how to make money caring for people who are recovering from illness or injury at home.

Heart to Home in Great Neck, New York, provides transportation for its nurses' aides, while Sacramento Home Care carefully matches caregivers with homebound elderly and others needing long-term care.

One of Heart to Home's greatest challenges was making sure its nurses' aides showed up for work on time. Many aides, who earn less than $7 an hour, can't afford cars and are dependent on public transportation. That's when founder Arlene Weis decided to invest in vans to transport workers from local bus and train stations to their patients' homes.

"We have vans that pick up our aides and deliver them to their jobs," says Weis. "It's very expensive, but very good in the long run, because everyone shows up for work."

The clients feel secure that they will be cared for, while the employees enjoy the benefit of free, reliable door-to-door transportation.

Weis, former vice president of a New York hospital workers' union, became an entrepreneur after a change of union leadership about twelve years ago.

"The home-health-care business was a natural for me," she says. "I had all the connections necessary to open the business. Plus New York state was about the last state in the country to regulate the home-care industry."

A few years ago, however, the state established stringent regulations for home-health-care providers, Weis says.

"Now, I don't take care of patients anymore, I take care of the paperwork."

Heart to Home has about forty full-time employees and another sixty per-diem nurses and nurses' aides. The company, which posts revenues of $2 million a year, is licensed to serve patients in ten New York counties.

"Home care makes it possible for the frail elderly to remain at home," says Weis. "It's far cheaper than being in a nursing home, and people like staying in their own homes."

Heart to Home's success has freed Weis to start another health-care business: Workplace CPR. That two-year-old venture provides cardiopulmonary-resuscitation (CPR) and first-aid training to employees of businesses and schools. Weis, who runs the company with Cecilia Carroll, says they encourage employers to provide the training because if someone has a heart attack, you have only four minutes to restore oxygen to the brain before permanent damage occurs.

Jerri Anderson, founder of Sacramento Home Care, became interested in providing home-care services in the late 1980s when she volunteered to find caregivers for homebound members of her church. When she saw how tough it was to find competent, honest, and reliable workers, she said, "There's got to be a better way to do it." Instead of putting caregivers on her payroll, Anderson acts as a matchmaker, interviewing and screening workers for her homebound clients. Her clients pay the workers directly.

"Most agencies place their own employees in a home, and that can cost thousands of dollars a month," says Anderson. "We screen the people and place them to work in a client's home for less than half the cost."

Clients pay Anderson a one-time placement fee based on the caregiver's salary. The fee includes a six-month follow-up period and Anderson's promise that the caregiver will be replaced if she doesn't work out. "For the first two years, I was charging way below normal rates and running the business like a charity," says Anderson. "Then a friend told me that if you're the best, you don't have to be the cheapest."

While Heart to Home provides a range of services from homemakers to skilled registered nurses, Anderson's company provides companions and homemaking services, calling on other companies if her homebound clients require medical care.

CUSTOMER SERVICE TIPS

Treating Employees and Customers Right

Treating your employees right is the first step toward improving customer service. "Customer satisfaction is built on employee satisfaction," according to Thomas Connellan and Ron Zemke, authors of *Sustaining Knock Your Socks Off Service* (Amacom Books, $19.95). "No company can satisfy its customers if it can't satisfy its employees.... Research shows that there is a direct relationship between people who feel good about the work they do and customers who feel satisfied about the way work is performed on their behalf."

Connellan and Zemke also emphasize the importance of rewarding your employees for quality service. "Companies that preach quality service but reward something else get something else."

Here are their eight common barriers to customer service:

1. Inadequate communication between departments
2. Employees not rewarded for quality service or quality effort
3. Understaffing
4. Inadequate computer systems
5. Lack of support from other departments
6. Inadequate training in people skills
7. Low morale, no team spirit
8. Bad organizational policies and procedures

One of my favorite customer-service books is *Crowning the Customer,* by Feargal Quinn, a successful Irish entrepreneur who owns eight shopping centers and thirteen stores in Ireland. His lively writing style and practical suggestions will inspire you to solve your customer-service problems as well as boost employee morale.

Distributed by Raphel Marketing, $19.95, plus $3.50 for shipping. To order, write to: Raphel Marketing, 12 S. Virginia Avenue, Atlantic City, NJ 08401. Phone: (609) 348-6646.

Consulting Success: Marketing Yourself

With thousands of consultants out there all competing for the same clients, how do you set yourself apart from the competition? Let's meet Shelly Porges, a respected marketing consultant with a specific niche business.

Shelly Porges regularly serves as a marketing consultant to Visa and to other banks and financial-services organizations that are among the country's largest issuers of credit cards. Yet Porges and her partner, Patricia Hudson, have only a handful of permanent employees: mainly themselves. How do they do it?

They specialize, they always find time to prospect for new business no matter how busy they are, and they hire independent contractors for each project.

Porges specializes in providing marketing-consulting services to the financial-services industry: banks, credit-card issuers, and others are her customers. Her advice to anyone who wants to market to big companies is twofold: First, identify a niche in which you can help the big firms. Next, after you have identified a general category (in her case, financial-services marketing), narrow your specialty down to a very specific niche. The more specialized, the better, because you can always add new specialties later as your business builds.

For example, when Porges started her business in 1990 she decided to concentrate on financial-services marketing because that was her background as a senior-level marketing executive at Bank of America. However, she knew that she also had to identify, very precisely and specifically, what marketing problem she could solve for the big companies if she wanted to gain an audience.

After finding out that customer retention was one of the biggest issues facing Visa and the banks and other organizations that issue credit cards for Visa, Porges approached Visa's marketing executives with a pitch: She would create a customer-retention program, along with a seminar to teach the program. Visa could sponsor the seminar and offer it to the company's credit-card issuers. The first seminar was such a success that Visa asked her to repeat it in other cities throughout the United States, so she wound up conducting the seminar in San Francisco, Atlanta, New York, Philadelphia, Chicago, and Washington, D.C. The seminars produced more business for Porges because some of the credit-card issuers who attended the Visa-sponsored seminar asked Porges to come to their companies and conduct the seminar for their staffs. She quickly became known as an industry expert on customer retention.

"Besides getting a big piece of business by developing the seminar, we got fantastic exposure in the credit-card community and we got the credibility that comes of being associated with a big company like Visa. We started getting calls from publications about the subject, which added to our credibility when we were quoted in the publications," Porges says.

Porges's advice to others: "Pick a niche in which you can become a specialist. This is true not only for a startup business but also for an ongoing business. The more specifically you can tell a big company what kind of a problem you are going to solve for them, the better chance you have of doing business with them."

Porges also advises being flexible in modifying your niche as the marketplace changes. After building her business as a customer-retention expert, she found companies that needed help in breaking into new markets, such as the Hispanic and other ethnic markets. She developed marketing-consulting programs for that specialty, thus adding a second niche to the types of services she can offer to financial services companies. Lately she has developed yet another niche, promoting cobranded credit cards. At the same time, demand for customer-retention programs is picking up again, so her company is busier than ever.

A big part of niche marketing is making it very clear to people what you can do for them. "Although I was already known to a number of people within retail banking and the credit-card industry because of my background at Bank of America, I still found that we had to tell people what we were all about, what kind of a problem we were going to solve for them," she says. She noted that this is especially important for consultants.

"Obviously, if you're a manufacturer producing a tangible product, it's much easier to explain what your product is. But in the consulting business your product is often intangible," she says. Among her tips for success:

- Listen to whatever source of market information you have. This is not the same as doing formal research. This means listening to executives or others who work in the industry to find out what they need. It ties in closely with the next tip.

- Stay in touch with people you have worked with, former clients, people who leave one job to go to another, and anyone else who is a potential client or source of information.

Says Porges: "Don't hesitate to reach back into your past. I call this networking, but it doesn't mean going to cocktail parties and chatting. It means contacting people you've known and worked with. People who were junior product managers with me when I began my career are now senior executives with client companies or potential client companies. It is overwhelming to do a cold call on someone, but it's less overwhelming if you know them.

"For example, a woman who had been a consultant to me and called on me when I was in corporate life has recently entered a corporate job herself, so I have become a consultant to her."

Porges advises not to despair when a client leaves a job to go to another company. Yes, it means you have to work on establishing rapport with the new executive who replaces your client, but it also means you now have a former client whose new company is a potential new client.

Reading trade journals is important too, because you need to stay informed about who is moving where. "I send congratulations to people who change jobs or get promoted, and I just generally try to stay in touch. When people are in transition is a good time to reconnect with them and find out if they might need you."

Further advice from Shelly Porges:

- Don't be intimidated by senior management at large companies. "You have to realize that these are just people with business problems to solve, and they'll usually listen to you if you can solve a business problem for them." For example, Porges happened to hear a speech by a senior-level marketing executive at a large company who was describing a marketing problem the company was trying to solve. "I went up to her after the meeting and explained how a cobranded credit card would be perfect for her marketing problem," Porges says. That company is now a Porges client.

- Court the press. "Establish relationships with the key journalists in your trade. You can meet them at conferences or you can simply pick up the phone and call them," Porges says. "My experience has been that journalists are happy to have an experienced source that can give them good, valid information about a subject." But you have to understand that journalists work on tight deadlines and you must respond quickly. "My priority for returning phone calls is No. 1, clients, and No. 2, the press," she says. Porges doesn't advertise much because "I just happen to think that PR and personal referrals are the best ways for small businesses to promote themselves as consultants, although that might be different if you're a retailer or a manufacturer."

- Package what you do so you don't have to reinvent the wheel every time you do it. "That's both a marketing suggestion and a practical management suggestion for a small company," Porges says. "If you continually reinvent the wheel for every project, you haven't leveraged the investment you made in the last project. The work needs to be customized, but the approach can be standardized and then modified."

- Keep looking for new business, even when you're at your busiest. "One of the biggest challenges for small business is ensuring that the work gets done in excellent fashion while you continue to develop new business," Porges says. She handles new-business development while her partner makes sure all the existing work gets done.

- Call attention to speeches you make or other appearances or accomplishments that will remind clients and potential clients of your capabilities. For example, when Porges speaks at a prestigious credit-card-industry conference, she sends notices to existing and past clients to let them know she'll be there. Afterward, she sends copies of her speech to those who don't attend.

K. Shelly Porges, chief executive officer of Porges/Hudson Marketing Inc., 44 Montgomery Street, Suite 500, San Francisco, CA 94104. Phone: (415) 955-2738; fax: (415) 397-6309.

Eight Brochure Don'ts

1. Don't focus on facts instead of benefits. For example, don't go into detail about the kind of equipment you use. Talk instead about the end product readers will see and buy.
2. Don't use jargon, formal words, or stilted language.
3. Don't use dates. They make your brochure obsolete.
4. Don't confuse your prospect with too much information. Simple, well-organized information is better.
5. Don't forget to include yourself and the personality of your company in your brochure. Otherwise, it will be dry and boring.
6. Don't use an expository style exclusively. Bullets are much easier to read.
7. Don't send it to anyone cold, especially if it's expensive to produce. Most people throw away the first thing you send them. Some feel they have to keep something that looks really expensive. Then they become resentful because they have to find a place to put it.
8. Don't carry your brochure around or give it out at trade shows. People often take too much information at events and then it ends up in a pile unread. Instead, hand out something small—your card or postcard—get their card, then follow up with your brochure.

From *The Art of Self-Promotion*. For a year's subscription (four issues) to their newsletter, please send a check for $25 to The Art of Self-Promotion, P.O. Box 23, Hoboken, NJ 07030-0023. Phone: (201) 653-0783.

Persistent Marketing Pays Off

Ron Safier, a marketing consultant, specializes in turning around troubled products and launching new products. His toughest challenge has been marketing his own product, the Brush-Ette, distributed by Brush-Ette Inc., in Menlo Park, California.

A Brush-Ette is a thick-bristled plastic brush that dispenses insecticides or medication through small holes in the bristle.

Invented by Charles Wilkeson, the brushes languished until Wilkerson hooked up with Safier. Safier eventually bought the rights to license and distribute Brush-Ette.

But bringing this product to market has proved much harder than Safier anticipated.

Here's what he's done to launch the product:

Before he even bought the rights to Brush-Ette, he visited seventy-five supermarkets around the country. He stood in front of pet-products counters with his prototype and asked customers, "Would you buy this product?" He interviewed about 1,200 people and got thrown out of ten stores.

But, 92 percent of those he interviewed said yes, they'd buy something like the brush.

Next, he trekked to twenty dog and cat shows around the country to see if there were similar products on the market. Finding none, he concluded that Brush-Ette filled a niche no one else was filling. He also spent another two months visiting about thirty veterinary practices.

Safier's initial strategy was to sell Brush-Ette to veterinarians through veterinary pet-care distributors. He felt that if he found acceptance in the professional market, Brush-Ette could achieve the credibility it needed. That would provide a foundation for a broader launch into the mass market at a later date.

Brush-Ette gained professional credibility by gaining the endorsement of veterinary medicine professors. Getting your product accepted by professionals is a great way to increase its credibility with the public. To get the product out, Safier sends professors free samples.

Next, he tried mail-order sales, with the brushes represented in twelve different pet catalogs in the United States.

He also expanded the product line from one brush to four. On the advice of his wife, Safier introduced new colors—teal, purple, and pink in addition to the original blue—to appeal to Brush-Ette's primary customers, women.

He introduced a supersoft brush designed for cats, a large brush for horses or field animals, and he has designed a Brush-Ette for humans as well.

The brushes sell from $8.95 to $9.95 at retail; the larger brushes sell (at retail) for $13.95 to $14.95.

Thinking global, Safier is now selling Brush-Ette's product line in about a dozen foreign countries.

Although he remains convinced of the merits of Brush-Ette products, his marketing efforts have been hampered by a lack of funds. For all his meticulously crafted marketing plans, he doesn't have the capital to fund his dreams.

He's trying to raise money to create new packaging, put sales reps on the road, and pay for more advertising and public-relations support.

"Everything I have in the world is in the business," says Safier, who hopes one or two major orders will help him secure bank financing.

Although he's helped many others succeed, his toughest challenge is his own product. "If you stay around long enough, then customers will feel they better look into this product. You've got to stick around. You've got to last," says Safier.

His advice: "Go after many markets and go after them with a vengeance."

Because Safier sells the brushes so many ways, "people think we're a much bigger company than we are. They see us in the catalogs, at trade shows."

He believes how others perceive you is very important to gaining acceptance. "If they think you're big and successful, you get respect. Otherwise, they won't talk to you," says Safier.

Do-It-Yourself Events

While big companies spend hundreds of millions of dollars to exhibit their products at industry trade shows, some small-business owners who were disappointed by sales generated at the shows are hosting their own events.

In past years, Joel Lefkowitz, executive vice president of Hoboken Wood Flooring Inc. in Wayne, New Jersey, exhibited the company's wares at floor-covering-industry trade shows. But after a lackluster response at a regional show two years ago, Lefkowitz decided to host an old-fashioned carnival for customers and their families in 1993.

About 1,000 people played carnival games, rode amusement-park rides, and ate carnival food. They cheered floor-covering installers competing in a speed-nailing competition and, between events, met with sales representatives from leading floor-covering manufacturers.

The next day, Lefkowitz hosted a golf tournament for 144 golfers at his country club, followed by a barbecue. Hoboken's events were such a hit, people who weren't invited were offended.

"One guy wouldn't do business with me because he wasn't invited to play golf," says Lefkowitz, whose stepfather's father founded the business about fifty years ago. "This year, he's invited."

The next year, Hoboken hosted a glitzy casino-night party. Debbie Tighe, Lefkowitz's assistant, hired a caterer, rented a tent, hired a band, and installed a temporary dance floor. The casino night is aimed at "keeping our customers close to the manufacturers and salespeople." Between the casino night and golf tournament, the company will spend close to $100,000, but they believe it will be money well spent.

"Casino nights are getting more popular with companies than

they used to be," says Al Corrado, founder of Great Neck Games and Amusements in Lawrence, New York. "People like it because they want to participate in an event."

Corrado brings in casino-quality roulette wheels, black jack and crap tables. His dealers wear tuxedos and he prints up fake $100 bills with Hoboken's company logo.

"There's no question companies are looking for alternative ways to reach the market," says Lee Knight, publisher of *Exhibitor* magazine based in Rochester, Minnesota. He says small-business owners who have been disappointed by trade shows are producing their own sales and marketing events.

Make the Most of a Trade Show

While many business owners are producing their own events, participating in a successful trade show is still a great way to bring customers and sellers face-to-face. According to Lee Knight, publisher of *Exhibitor* magazine, the trend is toward trade shows serving very specific niche markets.

In fact, one of the fastest-growing shows is the three-year-old Silk Flower Show, according to Darlene Gudea, editor of *Tradeshow Week*, based in Los Angeles. The trade journal tracks the trade-show industry worldwide. In the United States alone, there are 4,400 trade shows each year, according to Gudea.

"Although attendance was on the decline for a while, trade-show growth is the highest it's ever been," says Gudea. "Even when companies host their own events, a lot tend to go back to the shows after a few years."

A 2.5 percent increase in the price of exhibit space last year may have deterred smaller exhibitors, she says. But businesses are saving money by using lighter, modular exhibits that cost less to ship and require fewer people to assemble.

Bill Whitely risked $30,000 to introduce his ten-employee Charlotte, North Carolina, multimedia company to the nation's leading corporate-meeting and exhibit planners in February 1994.

About 240 potential clients visited his twenty-by-twenty-foot booth at *Exhibitor* magazine's lively Las Vegas show.

"We put on a multimedia presentation about making presentations," says Whitely, who offered prospects a show-stopping deal: a full day of brainstorming for only $875 plus travel expenses.

Did the Whitely Group's major investment in the trade show pay off?

"We've already closed five projects valued at over $35,000 each," he says. His biggest coup: landing high-tech leader Unisys as a client.

"Here's this little old Charlotte company that became a national company by going to a three-day trade show," Whitely says.

TRADE SHOW TIPS

In 1992 and 1993, 1.2 million companies participated in trade shows, a substantial increase from the 660,900 companies that exhibited their products at shows during the 1991 recession. About 73 million people attended some sort of trade show in 1993; the number is expected to reach 85 million in 1994.

"Companies have to understand the trade show company is responsible for getting the audience to the show, but you have to give people a reason to go from the door to your booth," says Lee Knight, publisher of *Exhibitor* magazine.

Knight says a good trade show can reduce your sales cost and cut the sales cycle in half by prompting buyers to make decisions at the show.

Some tips:

1. Find out all you can about the show, including past attendance figures.
2. Find out exactly how the promoter intends to promote the show.
3. Choose a show that's within 400 miles of your major customers and personally invite them to meet with you at the show.

4. Staff your booth with experienced, enthusiastic people. Bored people who can't sell will create a negative impression and scare people away.

5. Carefully track results and follow up with every lead generated by the show.

Other resources:

The Trade Show Bureau is a nonprofit trade group that supports the industry. For information, write to: 1660 Lincoln Street, Suite 2080, Denver, CO 80264-2001. Phone: (303) 860-7626; fax: (303) 860-7479.

Exhibitor magazine, 745 Marquette Bank Building, Rochester, MN 55904. Subscriptions are $68 a year.

The Ernst & Young Complete Guide to Special Event Management, by Dwight Catherwood and Richard Van Kirk, John Wiley & Sons, $24.95.

Don't forget to contact reporters who cover trade shows for trade publications. "Most trade shows have some sort of press facility and allow exhibitors to place press kits, etc. in them," says Neal Rosen, with Kalt, Rosen & Associates, a San Francisco public-relations firm. "These are often good places to meet with editors and reporters and, in fact, there are often opportunities to set up interviews before the show."

Rosen says you can also host a press party if you have a new product and money to spend.

Working with the Media: A Primer for Enterprises

by Michael Owen Schwager

Public relations/publicity is an excellent vehicle for entrepreneurs of fast-growing companies.

Some Basic Assumptions

1. *Always* tell the truth. Make sure your product or service does what you say it does, and your information is accurate. If you're asked a question that sounds unfavorable to your organization, try to respond or get back to the reporter with the information. Remember, if you don't, the info will come from someone else—and not necessarily from a source that will help your organization. Also remember, candor usually equals *credibility*.

2. *Know* your outlet before you call. Have you read the magazine or newspaper in advance? Moreover, do you know the specific beat of the editor or reporter you intend to make contact with? Have you read his/her stories? It's fine to "cold call"; but don't call blindly [unless there really is vagueness about that person's turf]. Same principle applies to TV or radio.

3. *Attitude.* Make sure that whoever approaches a journalist has enough life experience under his/her belt *and* sufficient self-confidence so as not to be intimidated by an editor or producer. Be warm and polite, professional . . . and clear. See that individual as a peer and colleague. If they're brusque at the moment, they may be having a bad day. Simply ask if there's a better time to get back to them.

4. That said, *believe in your story.* The best PR people see themselves as resources of news and information who work with journalists to fill valuable time and print space.

5. *Don't waste their time.* When you call, communicate, in sharp and crystallized fashion, the essence of the story. Keep it

brief, respect deadlines, and ask in advance if the moment is clear for that editor/producer. NEVER call when you know an editor is under deadline pressure.

6. *Personalize.* I've seen too many impersonal, photocopied pitch letters. If you send something in advance to a call, or as a follow-up to a call, personalize. Keep your cover note as brief as possible.

7. *Listen to the editor.* It's as important to listen as it is to talk. Be sensitive to any verbal feedback, cues or clues that can assist you in fine-tuning your pitch. Keep your antennae fully extended.

8. *Respect the "no" and be prepared for it.* Ask quick, important questions: "What is it about this story that doesn't seem right for you?" "Is there anyone else for whom this story might work better?" Suggest how the story can be adapted to the outlet's needs. Best of all, suggest three to five different angles in advance. This reduces chances for rejection.

9. *But* when you get your final "no," let it go and release it. YOU haven't been rejected; just your story. And if you've handled the approach professionally and cordially, you'll always be able to come back with another story at another time. Regard your list of cultivated contacts as resources and investments for the long haul, not for "quick fix" purposes.

10. Occasionally, pass along an item of interest that lies outside your own sphere of self-interest. Be someone who's not always out to "get something." Also, supply your most important contacts with your home phone number.

11. Get out from behind your desk. The better you get to know the journalist on a one-to-one basis, the better your chance of a receptive ear.

12. *Getting beyond voice mail.* Leave a succinct, provocative, targeted message. If you don't hear from them in two days, try calling well before 9:00 a.m., or leave a message with an editorial assistant or colleague. Call back that other person to learn if your message was received and if there's a return message. Sometimes, you can ask the switchboard for the department that person works in, rather than specific voice mail.

13. REMEMBER THAT AN EDITOR OR PRODUCER IS BUYING YOU AS WELL AS YOUR STORY. THE BOTTOM LINE IS TRUST. IT'S UP TO YOU TO EARN IT.

"Creative Formating"

Controlled Messages

A controlled message is a message that you prepare in advance and place with various media as a finished project. Three examples of this technique are the video news feature, matted columns for suburban newspapers, and by-lined articles for specialized trade publications.

A **video news feature** is simply a ninety-second to two-minute news piece that gets scripted, shot, and distributed to TV newscasts around the country. The local newscast incorporates the piece as part of its news coverage, and the average viewer has no idea these stories are supplied by outside sources.

A **matted column** is simply a one-column or two-column story that is sent to suburban news weeklies as camera-ready copy. They don't have to edit it or prepare it for print. The column usually offers some kind of consumer advice, with a discreet yet effective plug within the story.

Vertical trade publications are magazines that are published for a specific audience or industry. Hundreds of them are published each month. Years ago, we ghosted by-lined articles for the president of a company that analyzed utility rates for other companies, showing them how to save thousands of dollars every year. These articles were placed with dozens of magazines that catered to a variety of industries. This campaign was the company's sole marketing vehicle for many years.

Trends

When one of our clients, a major photography magazine, needed to increase its exposure, we designed a segment on the *Today* show in which one of the magazine's editors brought the very latest equipment to the program. For seven minutes, he demonstrated the most current camera technology to millions of viewers. He also achieved some substantial awareness for his magazine.

Another client, the Magazine Publishers Association, was interested in increasing recognition. They wanted to establish the fact that magazines are at the leading edge of creative advertising communication. We designed a segment on the *Today* show that displayed the latest in "pop-up" ads in various magazines.

Positioning Your Message(s) for Television

Lesson 1: How to Take Control

- Carve out communications objectives or copy points.
- Plan the timing of the copy points.
- Develop and anticipate key questions.
- Turn negatives into positives ("turn lemons into lemonade").
- Rehearse out loud.
- Preview the interviewer and the program.

Lesson 2: How to Achieve Credibility

- Establish rapport.
- Communications: Use short words and simple sentences, convey poise in body language and dress, use high energy but modulated based on interviewer's style.

Lesson 3: How to Confront Crisis and Hostility

- Keep the problem in perspective.
- Pay attention to company positioning.
- Show compassion for victims.
- Be consistent, be as candid as possible.
- Admit mistakes.
- Avoid "no comment" 's.

Tackling Tough Problems

The Small-Business Owner's Checkup

You would never leave on a cross-country trip without a road map, yet you are probably running your business without a clear strategic plan.

A business plan is not something you just write when you are looking for investors; it is a living document that helps keep your business on course. Because there are many topnotch business-planning books, I'm not going to tell you how to write a business plan, but I've asked some experts in the field to share some of their best suggestions.

Before you think about your plan, spend some time with my Business Owner's Checkup outlined on the next few pages. This is a quick way to take the pulse of your business, to spot troubled areas, and to begin searching for solutions. Successful business owners constantly monitor the progress of their businesses. They look at daily, weekly, monthly, and quarterly financial reports. They meet weekly with key staff members and monthly with key customers and suppliers.

If things aren't going well, it's tempting to hunker down and withdraw, but this is a sure way to sink your business further into the mire.

Grab a pencil and answer the questions in Part One of the checkup. Part Two requires a meeting or telephone conversation with your advisers. Part Three is designed to be completed with the help of your employees. There are no pat answers to the checkup. Your responses will point you in the right direction and clarify your thoughts before you move on to the next section on how to revise your business plan.

The checkup is divided into three parts. The first part is for business owners or managers to complete. The second part includes questions for your banker, accountant, and insurance agent. The third part includes questions to share with your employees.

While there are no right or wrong answers, your responses will help determine the strengths and weaknesses of your particular business and pinpoint areas where action is needed.

To complete Part One, all you need is a quiet place to work, preferably without interruptions from telephone calls, pagers, or fax machines. You'll also need a blank, lined notepad and a pen or pencil. Don't labor over the answers; the first thought that comes to mind is usually the most truthful.

Part One

Ask yourself:

1. Is my business doing better or worse financially than it was at this same time last year?

2. Have we gained any new clients or customers in the last three months?

3. Have we lost any clients or customers in the last three months?

4. Have we hired, fired, or laid off any employees in the last three months?

5. When was the last time anyone on my staff met with our major clients or customers?

6. When was the last time we called on any prospective clients or customers?

7. What would happen to my business if our major client or customer went bankrupt, died, or took his business elsewhere?

8. Do we have any new products or services to offer?

9. Do customers owe us more than $1,000? $5,000? $10,000? $50,000?

10. What are we doing to collect the money we're owed?

11. What have we done recently to attract attention to our business? Have we advertised? Sent out a newsletter? Hosted a charity event? Spoken at a professional meeting?

Part Two

Here are some questions to ask your banker:

1. Do you have any new products or financial services to help my business run more smoothly?

2. Can I increase my commercial credit line?

3. If I need one, where can I obtain a commercial credit line?

4. How can the money I have on deposit in your bank work harder for me? Do you have sweep accounts? Higher interest money-market accounts?

To your accountant:

1. What new tax strategies can we work on for the coming year?

2. Can I take advantage of the increased office-equipment deduction? (It increased from $10,000 to $17,500 a few years ago.)

3. If we're not using a computerized bookkeeping system, what software do you recommend for my business? Can someone

at your firm help select the software, install it, and train my employees to use it?

4. What can I do to minimize my state and federal taxes this year?

To your insurance agent:

1. Is my business and inventory adequately covered against fire, theft, and earthquakes?

2. Should I purchase a business-interruption insurance policy?

3. What kind of personal-disability policy is best for me?

4. How much life insurance do I have? Should I buy more? Do we need "first-to-die" coverage for multiple owners?

5. If I rely heavily on a top manager, should I purchase a "key person" insurance policy to cover them?

6. What can we do to reduce our workers' compensation insurance premiums?

7. Are my business vehicles adequately covered? Can we reduce the coverage on older vehicles or ones that never leave the property?

Part Three

Based on the answers and responses you've collected from yourself and your key advisers, it's time to sit down with your employees. If possible, get away from your business for a few hours. Reserve a private dining room at a local restaurant, find a picnic table in a nearby park, or reserve a room in a club or recreation center.

If you absolutely can't get away, hire a temporary worker to answer the telephones for a few hours. If your business is too big to close down for a few hours, create a committee of representatives from every department to participate in this quick checkup.

Begin by asking everyone what could be done to make their particular jobs easier.

Who could help them do their job better or more efficiently?

What kinds of office equipment, computers, or communications equipment are needed to boost productivity?

What's going wrong that we can fix right away?

List a few short- and long-term goals. Short-term ones can be as simple as cleaning up the office, painting the lunchroom, or beginning a simple office recycling program.

Long-term goals might be landing new clients or customers, renegotiating the prices paid for major supplies, setting up a new training program, or moving into a new building.

Ask your employees to tell you what your customers are saying about your business. Remember, your employees are on the front lines every day. They have the best solutions to your toughest business problems.

Is Your Business in Trouble?

With your checkup answers fresh in your mind, it's time to think about revising your business plan. Read on for more insights into the strategic-planning process.

TIPS

Randy Patterson, owner of Turnaround & Crisis Management Inc. in Oakbrook, Illinois, helps small manufacturing and distribution firms solve all kinds of problems.

Patterson says to watch out for these warning signs of an impending business crisis:

1. Have tax liens been filed against your business?
2. Have you failed to pay all required payroll withholding taxes?
3. Is your bank asking for more collateral to secure your loans?

4. Has your banker sent you a letter expressing concern over your current losses?
5. Has your business lost money for five or six months in a row?
6. Is your controller's or treasurer's desk stacked high with messages from creditors or suppliers complaining about unpaid bills?

If you are experiencing any of the above, stop what you are doing and get some help quickly.

The Turnaround Managers Association, with 1,500 members, sells its national membership directory for $150. For information on finding a turnaround consultant in your area, contact the association at (312) 879–2124, or write to the TMA, Sears Tower, P.O. Box 06105, Chicago, IL 60606.

Here are two good books: *Crisis Marketing: When Bad Things Happen to Good Companies* by Joe Marconi, Probus Publishing, Chicago, IL, and *The Turnaround Prescription* by Mark R. Goldston, The Free Press, New York.

Refocusing Your Business Plan

If the thought of writing or updating your business plan brings back depressing memories of term papers and long nights at the library, don't despair. Instead of dreading the project, think of it as a way to figure out what's working and not working for your business. And know that a well-researched business plan is your road map to financial success.

Most business owners don't realize there are actually two types of business plans.

"There are financing plans and focusing plans," according to Molly Thorpe, a business-plan consultant based in Canoga Park, California.

Financing plans are designed to attract investors to your business and should include detailed sections on your product, marketing plan, and management team. But a focusing plan is designed to help you diagnose and solve tough business problems. Because it's for internal use, it doesn't have to be as elaborate or detailed.

Thorpe, who has over twenty years' experience in planning, marketing, and financing big and small businesses, says that during the recession years of the early 1990s, 95 percent of her clients revised their business plans to refocus their businesses and boost profitability—not raise money. "Now, I see more and more companies getting back into the market to raise money because they see the light at the end of the tunnel," she says.

Although it's tempting to hire someone to write your business plan, don't. It's fine to have help with the editing, but do the research and analysis yourself.

According to Thorpe, most plans are weak on marketing information. "Many businesses don't focus on who their real customers are because they are afraid to turn away business. But it's important to identify whom you don't want to sell to, so you don't squander your resources."

Begin your market research by asking everyone in your company to write down everything they know about your competitors. Your sales staff will probably have an entirely different perspective from your technical people.

"Then, look at your product from the customer's standpoint," advises Thorpe. "Focus on the value you provide to the customer, not all the bells and whistles."

Once you've put together a competitive analysis, you'll need sections on your management team, a brief company history, financial information and projections. The most important section is a two- to three-page executive summary, designed to be read quickly. "The summary should capture the essence of your company," says Thorpe, who hosts workshops on the basics of business planning.

Kipp Lykins, general partner of Lake Shore Capital Partners

Inc. in Chicago, helps his investment-banking clients create plans aimed at potential investors.

"But writing a business plan is a good exercise for everyone, whether or not you are trying to secure financing," Lykins says.

Like Thorpe, Lykins emphasizes the importance of knowing your competition and where your products or services fit into the market. He says too many business plans emphasize the products rather than the people running the company.

"Most transactions are based on trust and belief in an individual," he says. "People do transactions with people, not companies."

BUSINESS PLANNING TIPS

Kipp Lykins offers these business-plan tips:

1. Know your audience and the purpose for the plan.
2. Do your homework.
3. Remember, the business-planning process should lead people to take some sort of action. Invest money? Buy your company?
4. Ask people whose opinions you respect to review a draft of your business plan.

For information on Molly Thorpe's business-planning workshops, write to her at: 18 Colt Lane, Canoga Park, CA 91307. Phone: (818) 704-1548.

Here's a list of business-planning books to get you started:

The Successful Business Plan: Secrets and Strategies by Rhonda M. Abrams, Oasis Press, $21.95.

How to Really Create a Successful Business Plan by David E. Gumpert, Inc. Publishing, $19.95.

The Ernst & Young Business Plan Guide by Eric Siegel, Brian Ford and Jay Bornstein, John Wiley & Sons, $14.95.

Self-Help Groups

Entrepreneurs, especially successful ones, often have a tough time admitting they need help. Reluctant to discuss serious management problems with employees, friends, or colleagues, they may hire a consultant to help solve business problems, but this is expensive and often ineffective.

Many small-business owners can't afford one-on-one help or say they've been disappointed by the results in the past. As an alternative to traditional consulting, thousands of entrepreneurs across the country are joining high-level, self-help groups. The groups, sponsored by a variety of organizations, provide safe and confidential settings for managers to help solve each other's common but perplexing problems.

The Executive Committee (TEC), based in San Diego, is considered the granddaddy of the entrepreneurial self-help movement. TEC, which has about 3,000 members in the United States, Canada, Australia, England, and Japan, was founded in 1957 by Milwaukee businessman Robert Nourse. To join, a business owner must have at least twenty-five employees and $2 million in sales. (TEC members participated in my survey in the last chapter of this book.)

Two Southern California groups, the CEO Group and Breakthrough Partners, serve small-business owners with fewer employees and much smaller revenues.

Jennifer Freund, owner of Corporate Impressions in Van Nuys, California, credits Breakthrough Partners with helping her boost her company's sales by 40 percent last year. Corporate Impressions provides advertising specialties and printing services to businesses.

"The Breakthrough Partners group lets me explore ideas versus just letting them sit in my mind," says Freund.

The program encouraged her to invite a group of customers to tell her what they really thought about her business. "I was terrified," admits Freund. "We spent a half day with our customers. It was really fabulous. When it was over, they felt closer to us and it solidified the relationship."

Based on other suggestions she received from group members, Freund asked her employees to revise the company's mission statement. Her employees also decided to do away with a weekly production meeting that everyone dreaded. Now they hold a postproduction meeting to evaluate all the work they've done and discuss how to improve it.

"It's great to have your people moving along with you instead of fighting you," Freund says, adding that the changes they've made "freed me up to be a chief executive officer as opposed to the guy with the whip."

Bill and Maryella Pegnato, co-owners of Pegnato & Pegnato, a West Los Angeles roofing-maintenance company, both attend the monthly Breakthrough meetings.

"Our business is doubling each year," says Bill Pegnato. "I owe a lot of what we're doing to Breakthrough Partners. Every time I go to one of these meetings, I come away with something that makes me money."

Ivan Rosenberg and Barry Pogorel, cofounders of the CEO Group, take a different approach to serving business owners. Both veteran consultants, they coach members to draw on their inner resources to solve their problems rather than providing people with straight business advice.

"Normally, consultants work on changing behavior," says Pogorel. "The problem is it takes a long time to change habitual behavior."

Instead, Pogorel and Rosenberg encourage group members to make decisions based on the future—by determining where they want their company to be, rather than basing strategic decisions on past experiences.

"If you are stuck in a vicious cycle, you are probably operating in the present as viewed from the past," says Pogorel.

Rosenberg says one member complained that sales were down and no one at her electrical-grounding-systems business was feeling motivated to sell. She also kept a tight rein on her employees, rather than giving them room to experiment and grow.

"She came to us out of desperation," says Rosenberg. "It turned out that the message she was sending to her employees was 'I'm the best and you'll always screw up.' She realized that night that she was the one holding sales back."

Betty Robertson, founder and CEO of Lyncole Industries in Torrance, was that CEO. After only one meeting, she realized that her negative, controlling behavior was demoralizing her staff. Since that revelation, sales have picked up and actually increased 60 percent in one quarter.

"Once I started putting out the positive vibes, the business started coming back to us," says Robertson, who is also the company's chief engineer.

TIP

Entrepreneurial Self-Help Groups

The Executive Committee, 5469 Kearney Villa Road, Suite 101, San Diego, CA 92123–1159. Phone: (800) 274–2367. Annual membership fee: $8,400.

The CEO Group, c/o Crossroads Group, 4020 Colonial Avenue, Los Angeles, CA 90066. Phone: (310) 390–8703. West Los Angeles group, $100 (with one consultant); San Fernando Valley (with two consultants), $175 per meeting, plus meal costs.

Breakthrough Partners, c/o Valley Economic Development Center, 14540 Victory Boulevard, Suite 200, Van Nuys, CA 91411–1618. Phone: (818) 989–4377. Cost: $300 per month.

The Alternative Board, for information contact: Lynette Fishman, (212) 369–5764.

The Oregon Experience

When four Oregon business owners set their egos aside and asked a group of fellow business owners for ideas, everyone went home with a wealth of practical, real-world solutions.

About ninety small-business owners participated in an innovative workshop cosponsored by Lane Community College's Business Development Center and the *Eugene Register-Guard* newspaper. Jane Scheidecker, director of the Center, and workshop coordinator Peg Allison invited a diverse group of business owners to share their concerns with their peers.

Those seeking help included a bookstore owner losing sales to a new chain superstore, a bike manufacturer needing capital to grow, a business owner struggling to manage his business from a distance, and a gourmet-grocery-store owner debating whether to open a second location. A veteran flower shop owner, an accountant, a home builder, a marketing consultant, and the founder of a new drive-through espresso bar were among those business owners giving advice.

Karen Swank, owner of Marketplace Books in the Fifth Street Public Market, said she was still reeling from a 15 percent drop in sales in November and December 1993. Her trouble began soon after a Barnes and Noble superstore moved into Eugene. Although her sales picked up in January and February, Swank said she was concerned about the Christmas season—traditionally her strongest.

"We have to have an excellent Christmas in order to recoup the losses suffered last year or we will simply be out of business," said Swank, who had to let go three of her eight employees and curtail new book purchases.

Local business owners had these suggestions for her:

1. Heavily promote Marketplace's popular "frequent buyer" discount program, which offers discounts for repeat customers.
2. Establish a gift registry, similar to a wedding registry, so

people can list the types of books they'd like to receive from friends and relatives.

3. Promote the fact that her employees are experienced and knowledgeable about books, unlike the inexperienced college students working at the superstore.

4. Launch a "loyalty" campaign asking customers to support a locally owned small business.

The group listened as Dan Vrijmoet, co-owner of Co-Motion Cycles, described his need for capital to grow the tandem-bicycle company. Several business owners asked if he and his partners had a written business plan.

"No, not really," admitted Vrijmoet as the crowd groaned.

One veteran business owner said that, without a written business plan and detailed financial projections, Co-Motion's chances of obtaining bank financing or a private investor were slim or none.

But before Co-Motion spent a lot of money expanding its manufacturing operation, one participant suggested that Vrijmoet contract with outside workers to increase bicycle production. For example, Co-Motion might send a certain number of bikes out to a contract shop for assembly or painting.

David Butler, founder of CDI Vaults Inc., presented the most perplexing problem. Between 1988 and 1992, he managed the company, which stores commercial records in a former bomb shelter. But, because he couldn't afford to pay himself a big enough salary, he took a full-time job with another company located about an hour away from Eugene. Although his four employees were doing well, the business hadn't grown, since Butler was primarily responsible for sales and marketing.

The group had some excellent suggestions for him:

1. Buy a car phone and use his commuting time to call customers and keep in closer touch with his employees.

2. Hire a retired banker, insurance broker, or lawyer to work part-time as a sales representative for the company. Butler

was encouraged to hire someone who is well respected in the community and knows which companies need to store legal and business records.

Annie Fulkerson, co-owner of Oasis Fine Foods, was praised for making sure she had support for a second grocery store before moving ahead. Fulkerson tested the waters by sending a survey to 17,000 residents of the area she was considering for the new location. About 1,400 surveys came back, with most respondents urging Oasis to open a store in their neighborhood.

"Going from one store to two is a real big step," said Fulkerson, who owns the popular natural-foods store with her husband, Doug Brown. Oasis, which she described as a cross between Trader Joe's gourmet specialty store and a Mrs. Gooch's health-food and produce market, has grown 20 percent a year since opening in 1987. They want to open a second store for two reasons: the original store is outgrowing its 10,000-square-foot building; and several experienced middle managers, frustrated by a lack of professional advancement, would like Oasis to expand so they could manage and develop the new store.

Apart from raising the $1 million-plus needed to build and open the second store, Fulkerson said she was concerned about maintaining Oasis's reputation for service and quality.

She was also worried that the hours required to open a second location will keep her away from her two children. Now she leaves the store in time to meet them when they get home from school. "We've worked really hard and finally got to the point where we have a life," she said.

Still, based on the positive response to the customer survey, which cost about $5,000, Fulkerson said she's almost sure they'll open the second Oasis store in 1995.

TIP
Where to Get Help

Small-business owners seeking help can contact the Small Business Administration. SBA's free SCORE counseling program matches retired business owners with entrepreneurs. The SBA can also help you locate the nearest Small Business Development Center, which provides low-cost counseling and workshops.

Lane Community College's Business Development Center offers a variety of programs for Eugene and Springfield area business owners. The center is located at 1059 Willamette Street, Eugene, OR 97401–3171. Phone: (503) 726–2255.

Getting Organized

As a professional organizer, Sandra Seevers of EveryLastDetail Co. of Redondo Beach, California, says she does more than go into offices and put things in order. She sets up systems to eliminate disorganization because disorganization hinders productivity and costs businesses time and money.

"Organization is not about neatness," says Seevers. She recounts how some clients can appear to be organized, and yet, upon closer examination, they're not working efficiently.

"I know how to pick papers up, toss them away or store them. But that's not the problem. The problem is knowing about the client, how they work, what their work style is like," she says.

If you are not convinced that getting your business organized is worth your time and money, consider these benefits:

- You'll keep what you need daily at your fingertips.
- You won't have to call people back. Frequently people end up playing phone tag because they can't find something they need to conclude their business.

- You can set up meetings easily because you have a calendar you can work with.
- You can operate efficiently even when your assistant is out for the day or on vacation. A peer can take over because everything is set up.
- You can delegate responsibly.
- You feel like you're in control.
- You don't have to see the same mess on your desk every single day. You can start fresh.
- Time can be spent doing rather than looking for misplaced things.

Remember, the stress and frustration that result from disorganization cost small businesses money because it means extra time, says Seevers.

But organizing files isn't enough. Good communication is key to the smooth functioning of an office.

"The boss needs to tell the assistant what he or she wants," says Seevers. Most assistants want to do their best, but if the boss doesn't tell them what he wants, confusion and frustration ensue.

"If you aren't happy with the way something's being done, tell the assistant how you want it," Seevers advises. This may seem like common sense. But she says bosses don't routinely do this.

Managers, especially busy entrepreneurs, are often uncomfortable dealing with organizational problems because they usually don't have solutions. Or perhaps it's because of a reluctance to hurt someone's feelings. Sometimes, says Seevers, they simply don't know what they want. Or they expect their assistants to understand intuitively.

The first step is to state your business mission. Some will know. "But some just look at me funny," says Seevers.

Armed with a notebook, Seevers peppers managers with questions: What's not working? What frustrates you? What would you like to see changed? She solicits ideas on how the assistants can work smarter or in a more supportive manner. Their answers usually help her develop a solution to the office problem.

Most often, they'll come up with one overriding aggravation. Seevers usually focuses on that problem first. As part of the process of finding a solution, she often asks the manager to draw up a job description for the assistant. This will include a rundown on what needs to happen every day.

The act of writing a job description usually forces the manager to zero in on key issues. "All of a sudden he or she is clear about what they want," says Seevers.

Remember, company goals change. Managers need to constantly update their assistants on their expectations because they shift from week to week or year to year.

In her work, Seevers sometimes functions as a mediator. As a dispassionate observer, she can often spot the ways people are working that are causing misunderstandings and disputes.

Seevers cited the example of a client, a large Los Angeles stockbrokerage firm. She was called in by two managers who were having a hard time working with their assistant. They weren't working as a team.

The situation was a classic failure to communicate. The way the assistant told it, the bosses bombarded her all day with verbal orders, without adequate explanation of how and when they wanted the jobs done. They expected her to know instinctively. The executives would also leave the office and she wouldn't know where they were.

The managers had the habit of tossing materials they wanted to refer to—newspaper clippings, business cards, etc.—into a large box. Originally, these materials were alphabetized, but as the contents mushroomed, they became a disorganized heap. The assistant found it impossible to find anything. Neither the managers nor the assistant were checking back to make sure jobs got done.

First, Seevers found that all three kept separate calendars, in addition to the master calendar from which they were all supposed to work. But the master calendar was small—less than nine-point font—so it was hard to read, particularly if there were multiple entries.

Seevers suggested trying out new computer software that included a large calendar with big boxes for each day of the month. The assistant could print out the calendar daily. It could be easily updated. Each person would keep a personal calendar, but this would be the one they would work from as a team. Now there's a place where all appointments, commitments, and deadlines are recorded.

So far, this change has made a world of difference, according to Seevers. The three are finding it a big help and they're on the road to more open communication.

"They all said they felt much better because it was the first time they ever talked about it," says Seevers. The three have concluded that their problems aren't major.

"That was the only issue here. All that stuff, all that aggravation, hostility, kept mounting because of something like that," says Seevers.

Seevers's next challenge is to get the bosses to eliminate the box. Rather than facing the task of making order out of the chaos of the box, she has suggested that the managers start over again. From here on, they'll put new material into coherent order. The older material can wait. Seevers will return to help them reorganize files at a later date.

The computer revolution of the past decade has created a whole generation of executives and assistants who don't know how to manage paper. Many younger business people tell her, "No one's ever taught me how to deal with paper." They don't know how to create files, organized either alphabetically or by subjects.

So, now that you are motivated, how do you get started?

Facing a big, disorganized mess of an office can seem like an overwhelming task. Seevers recommends breaking the task into small jobs to lessen the sting. When she's on site, she keeps her clients focused on one small aspect of the overall job.

"Break it down into real tiny small jobs and focus on one job and don't think about anything else," says Seevers.

Don't stop. Seevers recommends setting aside fifteen or thirty minutes, for example. Don't allow yourself to be interrupted. "It's surprising how much you can get done in fifteen minutes when you're focused," says Seevers.

Dealing with a particularly wretched task, Seevers advises setting aside a fixed amount of time at the end of the day. Get yourself a timer and set it for the time you want to dedicate to the task. Then do it! That fixed amount of time should be clocked. Do this every day.

"When people call an organizer it's usually because they've been procrastinating. Procrastinators get so stressed out they can't stand it anymore."

Seevers doesn't buy into the notion that you can't set a deadline for a disorganized person. "If you tell someone there's a deadline, then you're holding them accountable," she says. If you are hiring someone to help you, ask them if they are organized or detail oriented.

When people get organized, beautiful things happen, according to Seevers. "People start to get motivated. It takes the anxiety away. They usually feel a sense of relief." People need to experience the joys of being organized before they fully realize that it's going to make a difference in their lives.

"That's when they say this organizing thing is more than just putting files in a folder," says Seevers.

Some executives even say that once they get organized, they find they have room for additional clients.

"I can't give them the twenty-fifth hour of the day. We can't manage time. What we can manage is how we do things. And if we do things in an organized way, we have more time in the day."

A professional organizer, like Seevers, charges from $40 to $100 an hour. For help here, call the National Association of Professional Organizers, a trade group based in Tucson, Arizona. At present, professional organizers aren't listed in phone directories under the headline "Organizers." Instead, organizers are under the headings "Business Consultants" or "Business Services."

Here's how a professional organizer straightened up the lives and offices of two small business owners.

"Deep down everyone wants to get organized, but it rarely happens," says Lisa Kanarek, a Dallas-based professional organizer and author of *Organizing Your Home Office for Success*, published by Plume.

Kanarek, who has been organizing homes and businesses for years, helped straighten out the lives of massage therapists Randall Winter and Marci Novak.

"Lisa was very nonjudgmental and she never called us pigs," laughs Novak, who says getting organized has been a "life-changing experience."

Kanarek helped organize the two home offices where Winter and Novak handle paperwork and administrative tasks related to their practices. The duo see clients in adjacent offices in a medical building.

"You can sort of get by with a messy office until you have your own business," says Winter. "But then the paperwork becomes like a virus that keeps growing."

One of the first things Kanarek did was to encourage Winter and Novak to move unnecessary furniture out of their offices. Then she helped establish areas in their office for personal space and business space.

"Randall and Marci have very different working styles," says Kanarek. "He's orderly and she's a pack rat."

Kanarek suggests choosing a time-management system that fits their style, rather than whatever date book is the rage this year. "I used to have stacks of bills on the desk," said Winter. "Now, I write in my Daytimer when it's time to pay the bills."

Kanarek, who began her organizing career by cleaning out clients' closets and cabinets, now commands fees of up to $1,200 a day for her organizational expertise.

"There isn't one way to get organized," Kanarek says. "I offer different solutions to fit the way someone is already working."

Getting organized not only helps reduce your personal stress, it can also encourage people to do business with your company. Why? Because a messy office sends a negative message to potential clients and customers.

"I once met with a home-based typesetter, but when I saw her children's toys everywhere, I didn't hire her," Kanarek says.

Kanarek offers these tips to get you started:

1. Sort your paperwork into four stacks: to do, to file, to read, to sort. Although many professional organizers encourage clients to deal with a piece of paper only once, Kanarek says that approach is not realistic.

Instead, she suggests doing something with each piece of paper to "move it forward" by giving it to someone else, paying the bill, or filing it.

2. Decide whether to file papers alphabetically, by category, or numerically. She recommends storing magazines and catalogs in deep, plastic stacking bins.

3. Take advantage of empty wall space. Build shelves to get your piles of stuff off the floor.

"Most people feel very overwhelmed at first, but you need to break down each project piece by piece," Kanarek says.

How Organized Are You?

Use this quiz to test your organizing skills.

1. The stacks of magazines in your office are:
    a. Over one year old
    b. Six months old
    c. One month old

2. When handling projects:
    a. You jump from project to project without completing anything

b. You have trouble deciding which project to work on first

c. You work on one project at a time until completion or until you can stop at a point that will make it easy for you to begin again

3. You keep:
   a. Only the items you use regularly
   b. Something because you "may need it someday"
   c. Unnecessary papers and possessions

4. When you get someone's business card you:
   a. Throw it in a drawer
   b. Put it in a card file or enter the information in your computer
   c. Lose it before you get back to your office

5. When bills arrive you:
   a. Put them in a specific place with your other bills
   b. Put them aside and forget about them
   c. Throw them in a pile somewhere

Answers

Question 1, c = 10 points

Store your magazines in one place when they arrive. Tear out articles you will read later and keep them in a file folder labeled "To Read." Take that folder with you when you leave your office.

Question 2, c = 10 points

Focus on one project at a time. When you need to move on to another project, stop the first one at a point where it will be easy to pick up again and start working.

Question 3, a = 10 points

Don't hold onto something because you "may need it someday." When you need it, you may not find it.

Question 4, b = 10 points

File business cards in a card file and keep the file near your phone. If you enter the information in your computer or daily planner, toss the card.

Question 5, a = 10 points

Designate one place for incoming bills. Keep them in a file labeled "Bills to Pay," or in a stacking tray labeled "Bills," until you're ready to pay them.

Rate Your Organizing Skills

If your score is:

- 50 points, don't change a thing.
- 40 points, your level of organizing is adequate, but could be improved.
- 30 points or less, take the time to get organized. Start by blocking out one or two hours to organize your office and don't take any calls during that time.

Managing Your Business for the Future: High-tech Solutions

Barbara Rodstein, a plumbing-fixture manufacturer in Los Angeles, publicly admitted at a major conference sponsored by IBM that she doesn't even have an adding machine on her desk and doesn't know how to use a personal computer. But you can be sure many other people at her company, Harden Industries, are totally computer literate.

It's okay to be computer phobic. Just don't let your personal anxieties keep your company from using technology to boost sales and productivity. With computer and fax prices in a free fall—plummeting about 10 percent a year—there is no excuse for not having the very best technology available for your employees. Computer chips are doubling in power every eighteen months, yet the prices are remaining stable. The price of a basic fax machine has fallen 75 percent in the past five years, and by the year 2003, about 52 million Americans will be using cellular phones, according to a study released by the Personal Communications Industry Association.

If you're not using personal computers, your competition is: In 1993, 16.3 million PCs were sold in America, and the number is due to increase to 17.4 million in 1997, according to BIS Strategic Decisions, an information technology research group in Norwell, Massachusetts.

With modems and computer communications software operating faster and cheaper, companies can slash telephone bills and move more data more quickly from place to place.

The wonderful thing about today's technology is that it truly levels the playing field. You could be working in a converted garage with your cat on your lap and chickens free-ranging around your yard and still win a six-figure consulting contract from American Express. (My company did.)

Technology frees you to be better organized, more aggressive in your marketing, and able to meet tighter deadlines. It cuts the time you spend writing letters, sending invoices, and drafting proposals. It can help you create a data base enabling you to communicate with customers frequently and without spending a lot of money.

Although I don't review software or equipment, this section will give you a quick overview of what's out there to help your business. Right now, there are 15 million cellular-phone users and millions of pagers. There is no excuse not to stay in close touch with your employees and customers anymore.

The telephone is your first and most important business tool, so take advantage of all it has to offer. Telephone companies are falling all over themselves to provide small-business owners with new services and options. In most areas you can order custom ringing, which allows you to know whether a business or personal call is coming through. The phone can be programmed to ring once if a customer is calling and twice for personal calls, for example.

Standby lines let you pay only for the time you use the extra line for a fax machine or overflow call line. I don't think call-waiting is appropriate for a business line because it's annoying and unprofessional, but call-forwarding is great if you want people to be able to reach you after hours at your home. Voice mail is a business essential. In fact, most business people I know get upset if a person asks to take your message. Most business people actually prefer leaving a detailed, personal message on voice mail. High-end voice-mail systems can tell incoming callers about your products or services while they wait to be transferred and take orders twenty-four hours a day. AT&T is taking voice processing a step further with its Conversant Interactive Voice Response System, which understands up to 2,000 phrases or words.

Some voice-mail and messaging systems, like the ones offered by Voice-Tel companies across the United States, are designed for businesses that need to stay in close touch with groups of salespeople, such as real-estate brokers and marketing reps. These cost-effective message services provide personal mailboxes for everyone, and although messages are not delivered immediately in some cases, the messages can be rebroadcast to endless numbers of users.

With cable companies and telephone companies fiercely competing to provide services, some analysts expect prices to fall and service to vastly improve.

One of the most attractive telephone options for a small business is an 800 number. There are about 300 companies that distribute 800 numbers, with AT&T being the biggest. You don't own an 800 number, you subscribe to it.

But don't make a decision based on price alone. You want to be sure that if you have trouble with this lifeline to your business, the service provider will fix it and fix it fast.

If you want to come up with your own vanity number, do it, but first be sure it's available. There's a national data base of 800 numbers, and any provider can check the availability. Most phone companies offer low installation charges, and often waive installation fees during sales promotions.

Before you sign up for a number, think about how it can boost your sales. They work well to handle consumer questions. For instance, Zia Cosmetics in San Francisco uses its 800 line to field thousands of calls a month from people with questions about the company's line of natural products as well as competing products.

If your line generates too many calls, contract with a reputable telemarketing center to help. You can also refer calls to a center when your business is closed or during a major sales promotion. Nebraska and Utah are home to several major telemarketing centers, although there are centers in virtually every major American city.

Be sure to visit the center, solicit bids for your project, and meet the team assigned to your account. Our company used a Los Angeles company with very mixed results. While some agents were terrific, others were incompetent and made customers angry. Telemarketing centers charge a fee for their services as well as a per-call charge ranging from about fifty cents to $1.50. Be sure to read the fine print in your contract and make sure it has a bailout clause if things aren't going well.

Jim McCann, president of 1-800-FLOWERS, appeared at several IBM "Pathways to Growth: The CEO Experience" conferences in 1994 to share his experiences with technology. He admitted that his company, despite hundreds of agents in several telemarketing centers, was unable to serve all the people who wanted flowers delivered for Mother's Day in 1994. If you are launching a major sales promotion, be careful about having the ability to handle the peaks and valleys of call volume, as well as after-hours calls.

If you are involved in telemarketing, look into the new communications technology that can not only route calls to the next available operator but pull up the customer's file before the call is answered. This way, the agent can greet the caller by name and be looking at the file at the same time.

Think, too, about buying a wireless telephone system for your office to make it easier for you and your employees to move around your store or warehouse. The new systems have the same features as hard-wired business telephone systems.

If you want to stay ahead of your competition, consider using a personal digital assistant. The pen-and-screen models resemble a child's Etch-A-Sketch, and several models actually learn to read your handwriting. Many PDAs feature electronic mail, paging, fax, and telephone services.

The videophone is also getting cheaper and more accessible for small companies. There are several models that connect to regular phone jacks and allow anyone to take advantage of the technology.

In the future, communications visionaries predict we will have two-way videophones, tiny phones that slip into a pocket or purse, and computers that understand voice commands.

To reduce your technology phobias, there are all kinds of books and magazines out there to get you started: *Home Office Computing*, *Mobile Office*, and *Portable Computing* are excellent and widely available.

One of my favorite computer books is *The Little PC Book* by Larry Magid, a fellow *Los Angeles Times* syndicated columnist. It's a lively, informative book for computer phobics, published by Peachpit Press, $17.95, (800) 283-9444.

After gathering some general information, hire a computer consultant who specializes in working with small-business owners. Sit down and carefully explain what you do and how your business works. Then let the consultant make some suggestions. Clearly outline the tasks you must accomplish and then let the experts figure out the right software program and machines to do the job.

Figure out, too, who in your company need computers on their desks, in their briefcases, or at home. If you buy several pieces of equipment at once, it not only saves time and money, but you can network or link them together for greater efficiency.

Put together a crisis-management plan for your computers and telephone systems. Think how the Los Angeles earthquake disrupted business for months.

It's a good idea to contract with a cellular telephone company to provide emergency backup services when the regular phone service goes down. I resisted getting a cellular phone for years, but after the 1994 earthquake hit Los Angeles, it was the only way to communicate with my out-of-state clients and relatives.

HIGH-TECH TIPS

Each year, the computing power available for a given price has roughly doubled, according to Nathan Myhrvold, who heads Microsoft Corp.'s advanced technology division.

Speaking to an industry group a few months ago, he made these interesting predictions:

"Smart cards" with computer memory and communications devices will eventually replace credit cards and even your house and car keys.

Expect lower telephone bills as telephone and cable TV companies compete to offer more services. But he said consumers will have to share in the $100 billion cost of upgrading the nation's cable system to a high-capacity digital network.

Getting On-line

No matter what kind of business you're in, technology can increase your profits. AT&T is launching an experimental network for businesses that will allow businesses to exchange information with branch offices, customers, and suppliers.

Think of how helpful it would be if you could do what the major automakers do: Allow your vendors and suppliers to access your computerized inventory records so it's their responsibility to send more parts when the supplies are running low.

Don't forget to tap into all the on-line services available. The industry generated $500 million in revenues in 1993, with 25 percent more subscribers signing up every year.

About 15 million people are connected in one way or another via computer link-ups, including the Internet. But if you are tempted to sign on and make a lot of money, forget it. The Internet, originally developed to link academics, is fighting commercial efforts to use the net for advertising products and services. Jayne Levin, editor and publisher of *The Internet Letter*, told *Home Office Computing* magazine that business owners have to be careful not to raise the ire of net users by blatantly pushing their products and services.

Don't send advertising pitches over the network. If you do, expect them to get zapped by angry purists. But you can sign on to special-interest bulletin boards to reach certain target markets. Internet users often subscribe to "mailing lists," or discussion groups. You can obtain a directory of mailing lists from consultants, or if you have an E-mail address you can order one.

One good source of information for new users is Daniel Dern's *The Internet Guide for New Users*, published by McGraw-Hill. Dern, an editor at *Internet World* magazine, says to get as much information as possible before signing on.

Innovative Management Styles

Owning your own business means you get to do things your way. Entrepreneurs start their own businesses to take control of their lives, not to make a lot of money. When you set the rules and write the policy manual, you can manage the business any way you choose.

I've met many entrepreneurs who manage their businesses in unusual ways. In this section, you'll meet the founders of an innovative Georgia-based household-products firm. To keep things fresh and egos in check, they take turns serving as president every few years.

You'll meet the president of an educational-products company in Kansas who stepped out of the day-to-day management of his company after recruiting a much more experienced manager from a local bank.

You'll meet Kathy Taggares, whom I affectionately call the "pizza queen." This former potato saleswoman turned a nearly defunct salad-dressing factory into a $30-million-a-year pizza- and salad-dressing-manufacturing powerhouse. In 1994, the Small

Business Administration named Kathy "California Small Business Person of the Year."

Although there are hundreds, perhaps thousands, of management books aimed specifically at entrepreneurs, I've never met a successful entrepreneur who follows anyone else's plan. Entrepreneurs, by nature, are mavericks. They quit their jobs because they didn't fit in with a corporate culture or didn't take direction well.

Successful entrepreneurs are quirky and eccentric, like The Body Shop founder, Anita Roddick, who opened her first natural soap shop in England in 1976. The tiny shop was sandwiched between two funeral parlors. She and her husband, Gordon, mixed up batches of soap in their kitchen and hand-wrote the labels. Nearly twenty years later, The Body Shop has stores in forty-five countries.

Roddick, who quotes radical political activist Petra Kelly and dresses like a flower child, says the company does much better when she stays out of the office and on the road looking for new products.

When I first heard her speak, she totally shocked a group of corporate sponsors at a major Washington, D.C., fund-raising dinner with her salty language, scathing criticism of the cosmetics industry, and slides of a naked medicine man who was proving his masculinity and strength by holding up a ten-pound bag of bricks with his erect penis.

Listening to Roddick's ribald remarks, I thought how true entrepreneurial success totally frees you from the constraints of doing business the old way. When it's your money and your company, you don't have to listen to anyone—except your employees.

The management cliché of the 1980s and early 1990s was "empowerment." Sales clerks behind retail counters were supposed to feel honored and empowered when allowed to solve a simple customer complaint without asking a supervisor. Big deal.

I've learned that true empowerment comes when you, the owner or manager, feel confident enough to let go of all the power, to surround yourself with competent people and get out of their way.

When given the time, tools, and technology to do their jobs well, employees quickly see that their contributions, however small, are critical to the success of the business. Only then do they feel truly empowered.

One common trait I've found among innovative managers is a true appreciation of their colleagues. They openly thank employees for their efforts and continually praise them for their efforts. When you share your dream with people, they'll become caught in its web. If you can't afford to offer big salaries or generous benefits, the least you can do to attract and keep good workers is provide sincere appreciation, flexibility, and a relaxed working environment.

No section on management would be complete without some thoughts on letting go of the power. Letting others take over some of your responsibilities frees you to concentrate on the big picture. If you are too busy doing the work to keep track of your goals, your business will falter. If your business is going to flourish, you have to be the leader first, and the worker bee second.

When we moved into our office in my renovated garage, I placed my desk in front of the one big picture window so I could see down the driveway and across the street to the hills. I joke that I have to see the big picture, when actually the main advantage is seeing the delivery people heading down the driveway. From my central vantage point, I can see who's coming to the door while steering the ship at the same time.

It's very tough to let go of power and authority, especially when you are accustomed to doing everything yourself. It's tough to decide what you should be doing and delegate the rest of your responsibilities to others. But truly successful entrepreneurs keep their eye on the road and steer with a light touch.

One of my favorite entrepreneurs, Geoff Rich, founder and president of Radio Today Entertainment in New York City, admits he has a tough time delegating tasks to his staff. Yet his company, which syndicates my Succeeding in Small Business® national radio report, is growing too fast for him to personally manage every detail of every project.

Although we really enjoy working together on my syndication, I insisted that he designate someone else on his staff to handle the day-to-day details. He resisted and still jumps into the fray when emergencies crop up, but he tries to let go of the project—most of the time. And, do you know what? The person we deal with, Tom Shovan, does a good job. This means Geoff, the man who can't let go, is hiring the right kind of people to help manage his fast-growing company.

No matter how small your business may be now, you'll eventually need help. As long as you hire people whose strengths complement your weaknesses, you'll succeed in finding your own strategies for success.

Meet the Pizza Queen

"I like being on the edge . . . where I'm sleep deprived, frustrated, exhausted, I'm in debt, whatever, that's what I like," says Kathy Taggares, one of my favorite entrepreneurs.

Taggares, named California Small Business Person of the Year by the Small Business Administration in 1994, first appeared in my column in 1989.

A former potato saleswoman, she bought an ailing salad-dressing factory and turned it into a food-manufacturing powerhouse. Wherever she goes, people stare at her wild curly hair, giant hoop earrings, and jewelry-laden wrists. She wears micromini skirts and spike heels, but she is no airhead. She is a savvy businesswoman who sold her condo, stocks, and jewelry and cashed in her insurance policies to come up with the down payment on the struggling factory in the late 1980s.

When she bought Bob's Kitchens, a struggling subsidiary of the giant Marriott Corp., it was worth about $6 million. She acquired it for $200,000 in cash. Since then, the company, renamed K.T.'s Kitchens, has grown dramatically to about $30 million in annual revenues, up from $20 million in 1992. In 1992, she had 200 workers. By 1994 a block-long plant in Glendale, California, employed nearly 900.

Pizza sales doubled in 1994, and her biggest problem was keeping up with the orders. Even three round-the-clock shifts can't make enough pizza for her major clients, Marie Callender, Price-Costco, scores of school districts and amusement parks.

Since her story appeared in *Succeeding in Small Business*, her company was victimized by a fast-talking con artist in a highly publicized pizza-vending-machine scam.

Still, Taggares retains her zest for a business she clearly loves. At times, she literally lives in the factory, sleeping on the couch. She and her operations chief, Joan Paris, often adopt a battlefield mentality, hunkering down to withstand the pressures of unchecked growth.

While pizza sales are skyrocketing, the company's salad-dressing sales are relatively flat. K.T.'s makes Bob's salad dressing. Bob's was once a popular hamburger chain, but slowly they are disappearing. Taggares tried to tap into the consumer trend toward healthier foods by introducing fat-free variations and new flavors. But so far, nothing's worked. "First of all, we're not big enough to put the big marketing dollars behind the brand. That takes millions of dollars," says Taggares.

Taggares finally concluded that she must accept that K.T.'s salad-dressing business is a mature label. "It's one of those product lines that they say if you can't get any more bang for your buck you should just sit back and milk it, so to speak. It's always been a real cash cow, a real high-margin business. Now we just let it go and take the money it generates and put it into other areas."

She's always looking for companies with well-established brands and products that can fit into K.T.'s original factory and a new annex located a few blocks away.

In 1993, K.T.'s started a new business, K.T.'s International, as a joint venture with a Florida-based company, Vendtron. The companies developed a line of vending machines that keeps food frozen and dispenses it hot. K.T.'s planned to supply the food that went in these machines.

Instead of instant millions, what followed, however, was every entrepreneur's nightmare: After developing the equipment, pans, and foods for this new venture, the partners had a tough time convincing traditional vending-machine operators to take them seriously. With millions of dollars sunk into this venture, they couldn't get the new machines to market.

A businessman, who appeared legitimate, approached Taggares and others at a large international vending-machine trade show in Washington, D.C. The man, who called himself Marvin Wolf, said he would like to sell their machines and had a huge marketing network behind him.

But Taggares was cautious: She insisted on checking him out. Wolf gave Taggares a long list of former associates and customers. She investigated. He had glowing references. So K.T.'s International signed a contract with him.

But what Taggares didn't know was that the references were actually professional "singers," people on his payroll whose job it was to answer the phone all day and make up a story.

"He totally scammed us," says Taggares. "We lost an enormous amount of money. It put us behind the eight ball. We were totally naive ... we didn't have a clue as to what was going on."

It turned out that Wolf sold a few machines to independent entrepreneurs, passed along a few dollars, and pocketed the rest.

Worried that she could be implicated if he was, in fact, dishonest, Taggares called the Florida state attorney general's office, Better Business Bureaus around the country, and the FBI. But none of these organizations responded.

"They said, 'Oh, you girls (Taggares's partner was also a woman) have sour grapes over a bad business deal,'" says Taggares.

In late 1993, the news media broke the Marvin Wolf vending-machine-scam story. *New York* magazine carried a piece on the swindle; ABC-TV's newsmagazine *20/20*, NBC's *Today* show, and several tabloid shows also covered the story.

"It couldn't have been a worse week in my life," says Taggares, recalling the week several TV reports aired, some showing her pizza boxes in the background.

The con man cost her $250,000 in legal fees, plus slandering her company's good name. K.T.'s also had bought $500,000-plus in pizza inventory (pans, etc.) that it can't use. Vendtron got stuck for millions, according to Taggares.

Wolf was accused of stealing $10 million and is still at large.

Kathy Taggares manages to win big in a business dominated by major food-industry players. She competes against giants by offering a high-quality product and responding quickly to customer requests.

Hers may be one of the few companies in the United States to sell a hand-stretched crust, which makes the pizzas appear more like they were made by a pizzeria.

Taggares's pizza is packed under various brand names, such as K.T.'s and Wolfgang Puck California Pizza. It also supplies house brands for big supermarket chains, such as Albertsons and Lucky markets and manufactures pizza for schools, military establishments, amusement parks, and other food-service outlets.

Taggares hopes to open another plant on the East Coast soon to service that part of the country, since shipping the pizzas is very costly. She's already looked at potential sites in Kentucky, Ohio, and the Carolinas.

In the early days, Taggares worked eighteen hours a day in the Glendale factory. Because she didn't speak Spanish, she'd communicate with workers with a mixture of pidgin Spanish and sign language. She still hasn't learned Spanish, but she's turned over some of those day-to-day factory operations to others. She also relies heavily on her manager, Joan Paris. Paris and Taggares have worked as a team for years and complement each other's skills.

"As we've grown, I've stepped back," Taggares says. "Now we have layers of management so I'm not in the factory anymore." But when a crisis hits, she moves back in.

"There's a little bit of life outside business," she laughs.

"I figure this is the calm before the storm. In all my business careers, I've worked these intense periods of time, then there'll be a slight calm, then I get kind of antsy and bored."

Stepping Aside for the Good of Your Company

Sometimes the best thing you can do for your business is get out of the way or take on a new role and let someone else make the big decisions. Successful entrepreneurs force themselves to set their egos aside for the good of the company.

Harvey Dean, founder of Synergistic Systems, knew that he didn't have the skills to manage his fast-growing educational-products company. That's when he began searching for someone he could trust to run the company.

In 1994, he decided he was worn out from the day-to-day responsibilities and wanted to concentrate on dreaming up new products. That's when he recruited a new president, Terry Towner, a veteran banking executive. Bringing in Towner freed Dean to devise new teaching modules and train the teachers who flock to the company's Pittsburgh, Kansas, headquarters. (So many visitors asked where the Yellow Brick Road was that Dean and his staff created a yellow concrete path around the company headquarters.)

It may seem funny for a guy who got kicked out of high school to be the visionary behind a successful educational-products company, but Harvey Dean is not your typical educator.

"Kids of today are so different from kids of just twelve years ago," says Dean. "Yet we sit them down and bore them."

Dean's company designs and manufactures $100,000 classroom modules that rely on computers and videos to give middle-school students a new way to learn about science and technology. Although Dean is the company's primary visionary, he refused to take all the credit. "I took five months and went around the United States looking at innovative programs," says Dean.

"I gleaned an idea here and there because I wanted to develop a new way for kids to learn."

Dean admits business has never been his strong suit.

Although he started the business in 1975, "I didn't know how to read a financial statement until 1981," says Dean, who has set up several related businesses. "After I got so far in debt, I knew I had to make this one successful because if the bank called in the loan I couldn't pay it."

Dean is a pioneer in the transformation of the nation's industrial-arts programs. In 1985, educators decided to drop the old name and call their subject "technology education."

Dean's modules feature a full laboratory designed for two students. "The students sit at each station for seven days studying applied physics or biotechnology," he explains. "Then, they change partners and go on to new station."

The system is not only fun, it works.

"Research tells us that 30 percent of students learn best kinesthetically with a hands-on approach, versus sitting in rows listening to a teacher."

Teachers have the biggest adjustment. They "must be trained by us not to be the sage on the stage."

The stations feature a switch that signals the teacher when the students need help.

Meanwhile, Dean loves his new role in the company and has no regrets about stepping out of the president's office.

"I realized that as the company was getting larger, there were just certain things I didn't do well," he says. "I needed to find someone with knowledge and experience."

The result: "Terry, the president, is very happy and I'm tickled to death."

Changing Hats

While Harvey Dean relinquished his job as president for the good of his company, Wayne Biasetti and marketing whiz Jim Biggs, the owners of Enforcer Products in Cartersville, Georgia, take turns serving as president every few years. This egoless approach to the top job keeps things interesting at the fast-growing household-products company.

Enforcer, based in a tiny town outside Atlanta, more than doubled in size and sales in the early 1990s, growing to 200 employees and sales approaching $100 million.

The company, which makes and sells about 100 insecticides and household-cleaning and maintenance products, has stuck by the offbeat management structure it set up from the beginning. By rotating the presidency and not emphasizing titles, they take an ego-free approach to managing the business.

Founder, chief financial officer, and partner Ed Brush keeps an eye on the money and computer operations, although he also plays a major role in developing the company's marketing strategy.

Tossing the title of president around has a great leveling effect on the owners and the staff.

"If you are having a bad day, chances are your partners are not, so the company can still enjoy having an owner who's positive and productive," says Biasetti, who founded the company in 1977.

Although Biasetti has an MBA, he realized that in order to be successful he needed partners with particular strengths to balance his weaknesses.

"Typically, a marketing man is not that great with money and a money man is not that great with marketing—and a manufacturing man is a whole other animal," says Biasetti, who is primarily responsible for manufacturing operations.

Biasetti says he and his entrepreneurial partners still enjoy working together despite the challenges posed by skyrocketing sales. To cope with the growth, they divided employees into eight teams focused on different product areas. They also freed their six regional sales managers from daily selling responsibilities to better manage the 100-plus sales reps around the United States.

Enforcer often beats its much larger corporate competition by being able to bring products to market fast. It also encourages sales people, vendors, raw-material suppliers, and customers to come up with new product ideas.

In fact, a household ant barrier sprinkled around the perimeter of the home was the brainchild of a new salesman who had been trying to sell the idea to his former company for years. His new bosses at Enforcer liked the idea so much they took only about forty-five days to develop and put the product on the market.

"You can't believe the passion he has for this product," says Jim Biggs, president and marketing chief. "Just about every product we have comes from the sales people."

For instance, when the sales reps told Biggs that potpourri scent was gaining popularity among consumers, Enforcer raced to create a line of flower-scented products. The company also packaged them in lavender-colored boxes rather than its traditional bright red packages.

"We can probably bring out a retail product faster than anyone else around," says Brush, chief financial officer. "We have no ego problems. Once we get behind something, we can move forward very quickly."

Thumbing Your Nose at the Big Guys

At the peak of her success in the mid-1980s, knitwear designer Brenda French had 300 employees and sales of about $10 million a year. Her sleek, flattering French Rags knits were featured in the windows of upscale stores like Bonwit Teller and she was flown first class to New York City to appear at trunk shows.

But behind the scenes, the company she founded in a back bedroom in 1978 was suffering. Department-store buyers with their "big pencils" dictated the styles and how much they would buy each season. When they bought her clothes, they ignored French's pleas to display her rayon knitwear on shelves. They hung the clothes on hangers, causing them to droop and stretch out, so it was no surprise when customers complained. On top of it all, the major retailers paid their bills so slowly French's growing company was continually starved for cash.

"At one point, I needed $500,000 a month just to break even," French recalls.

In 1990, when she was walking an emotional and financial tightrope, her factor, which provided cash advances on written orders, pulled the plug, refusing to continue financing the company. "I had no money and a payroll due," French says. "I paid the payroll out of my savings and went to my trusted advisers. They said 'Bail out.'"

But French, a true entrepreneur, was not a quitter. She took time off and went hiking in the Andes. When she returned to Los Angeles, she decided to restructure the business by selling directly to customers and sidestepping major department stores, which were filing for bankruptcy protection all over the country anyway.

"American women are totally disserved by major retailers," says Marjorie Deane, chairman and publisher of the *Tobe's Report*, one of the fashion industry's most respected trade publications.

Deane, who hired French to work as a reporter years ago, says department stores are run by bankers who don't understand that shoppers want real value and service for their money.

"Whoever gets out there and services the customer will benefit. The customer is smart," says Deane. "She'll track down someone like Brenda because she knows what she wants to look like and what she wants to spend."

Starting over with a few loyal employees and a small outlet store on Sepulveda Boulevard in West Los Angeles was not easy. But French's customers found her even when department-store clerks told them she had gone out of business.

Today, she sells directly to customers through sales agents around the country. French Rags representatives host trunk shows in customers' homes, making sure their knit pants, sweaters, vests, and skirts will fit perfectly. Everything is knit to order and color coordinated so women can add to their existing collections.

"My clothes are for the executive working woman and the executive working wife," says French, who once taught home economics in her native England. "Women who buy my clothes are busy saving the world and their families. They don't have time for clothes that are itchy or digging into them."

First Lady Hillary Rodham Clinton is one of French's customers. Mrs. Clinton appeared on several magazine covers, including *People* and *Parade*, wearing French Rags ensembles.

French, whose salty sense of humor helps her weather the tough times, says her streamlined approach to the volatile fashion business is paying off. Sales exceeded $5 million in 1994, up from $1 million posted five years before. Today, French Rags employs fifty-five people, including a dozen hand-knitters who produce the solid-color pieces on tabletop knitting machines. Large, computerized, German-made knitting machines produce the intricately patterned pieces under the close supervision of Miles Rasic, French's partner.

If your business is faltering, French says, it's important to get away for a few days to sort things out. When she went hiking in the mountains, she focused on what was good about her business: customer loyalty, high-quality clothing, creative designs. Then she eliminated the negatives: department-store buyers and financially ailing department stores.

Today, French says cash flow is not a problem because customers pay a 50 percent deposit when they order the knitwear, which cost between $500 and $600 for a three-piece outfit. If a store really wants to buy French Rags, "they buy at my prices and pay C.O.D.," French says.

When everything was crashing around her, French thought about chucking it all. But, having knitted her first dress at age eight, she couldn't think of anything else to do.

"I'm good at it," she laughs. "I can't imagine doing anything else. You know, when I look back, I realize the factor did me a favor by dumping me."

French Rags, 2226 S. Sepulveda Boulevard, Los Angeles, CA 90064. Phone: (310) 479–5648.

Coping with Fast Growth

While you may fret and feel anxious when the phone stops ringing, experts say an exploding business is often more of a problem. Too many customers can send a small business spinning out of control, as the managers race to keep up with the need for more cash and supplies.

Too much business was the happy problem facing the founders of Cool Zone Products and Promotions in Los Angeles. Sizzling summer weather boosts demand for Cool Zone's unique evaporative water misting cooling system designed to drop the temperature along the sidelines at sporting events and outdoor parties. The company also sells personal misters, which founder Michael Jones predicts will soon be as popular as "sipper" bottles.

Jones, a former skiing coach, and his partners, Chris Miehl, Mark Hensley, Jeff Leit, Keith Webb, and Anna Harper, rent their cooling systems to sports teams and corporate sponsors for games and events. The cost to rent a system varies, and the Cool Zone often donates a portion of the revenues to the team.

Corporate sponsors not only cool off the teams, but display their logos on the Team Mister cooling-fan stands. Jones first saw the mister bottle at a beauty-salon trade show in Chicago a few years ago. Relying on a tiny pump, the bottle vaporizes liquids into an ultrafine mist. Intrigued by the possibilities, he eventually developed a system of sideline cooling using water and fans.

When the Buffalo Bills learned they were going to face the Miami Dolphins at a National Football League championship game, they called Cool Zone for help. The big misters cooled down racegoers attending races at Phoenix International Raceway. "Handy Misters" even headed to Denver for the pope's visit in August 1993.

So how does the Cool Zone stay above water with their own growth? As hard as it may be to believe, the company somehow manages with its staff of six.

The Cool Zone also scored big with the 1994 Soccer World Cup. The company erected their systems across the country in eight out of nine cities where games were played.

The secret seems to be in the great commitment and spirit shared by the company partners.

"This is our baby. We want to make it grow, make it big," says

Chris Miehl, chief financial officer and vice president for human resources.

While Cool Zone is still technically a small business, its success has rocketed the company to national recognition. With the World Cup and the Superbowl under its belt, Cool Zone was busy at Woodstock and the U.S. Tennis Open.

"We each wear about twenty-five different hats, and, to borrow from the Beatles, we're working eight days a week," Miehl says.

The six partners continue to garner a lot of publicity with their product. As Miehl puts it, "We stretch ourselves and work nationwide." And how do they cope with the reality that they are a small business doing big business? "You want to be proactive, but instead you're reactive because it's often 'management by crisis,'" Miehl says. "You choke to death instead of starve to death."

Although success has taken its toll, the Cool Zone team has no regrets. Jones's passion for Cool Zone cost him his girlfriend. Miehl seconds that: "None of us have relationships." Partner Jeff Leit says they've all maxed out their credit cards and borrowed from friends and family to fuel the company's growth. Despite the personal sacrifices, Jones says:

"If you don't want it bad enough, someone else will take it."

Cool Zone, 3660 Wilshire Boulevard, #224, Los Angeles, CA 90010. Phone: (213) 480–6717.

Ward Wieman, founder and president of Management Overload of Santa Monica, California, is one of the smartest management consultants I know. His practical, no-nonsense approach has helped scores of small- and large-business owners succeed.

Wieman, an engineer by training, spent more than six years as an executive with Texas Instruments, where he held various management positions. His last job was senior vice president and head of corporate planning. He became a business consultant in 1975 and formed Management Overload in 1983.

Wieman advises many small businesses experiencing rapid growth. In some cases, Wieman's clients are competing in industries that are supposedly in the tank. By virtue of special technical prowess or marketing skill, these companies are prospering.

One of Wieman's clients, KW Summit, a Huntington Beach, California, manufacturer of high-precision metal parts for the aerospace industry, more than doubled its business in 1993, despite widespread cutbacks in aerospace.

KW took a hard look at bleak prospects in the defense industry and had the gumption to convert the business to serve the automotive industry.

With Wieman's help, KW president Ken Woodruff reoriented the business to manufacture equipment for automotive and other industries. The changeover didn't require expensive retooling; instead, it involved remarketing its products to another set of customers. Best of all, KW found higher profit margins in the automotive business—more than four times higher than defense.

For companies struggling to survive in the economic slowdown, coping with fast growth may seem like an enviable problem. But growing too swiftly can be terribly damaging to a small company, according to Wieman.

Companies that grow at breakneck speed usually do so on the strengths of their founders' skills, says Wieman. Typically, the principals possess special qualities, such as marketing genius or extraordinary technical sophistication. These special qualities set them apart from competitors.

However, as the business grows, the founder may not have sufficient management skill to ride the wave of fast growth. "Time and time again I see the same things," says Wieman. "They run out of hours in the day." And when this happens, the company is "in deep, deep trouble."

First, mistakes start to happen. "They're moving too fast, they're operating blind, because they don't have the information to make sound decisions. They've outrun their management systems, so to speak.

"They don't have enough hours in the day to think things out, to make sound decisions and to do things right. So they're making snap judgments, and some of these are going to be wrong.

"These people are operating tired. They're at their wits' end in many cases," he says.

Mistakes mount. For example, when proper materials aren't available, the company may substitute with inferior materials. Now, they have a quality problem. Some missteps are strategic. A company principal may pursue a new direction, developing the wrong product or serving the wrong customer. "They either haven't taken time or don't have the time to develop more effective systems to get things out the door," says Wieman.

Another problem: When they run out of money to fund their growth, stress begins to take its toll, says Wieman.

The founders' personal lives and/or health often go down the drain. They're typically working six or seven days a week. They're not relaxing with friends or family members. This can mean disaster for them and their businesses.

In one of Wieman's cases, his client was recovering from his fourth heart attack. His wife called Wieman in. The guy was unable to delegate. He'd fire everyone Wieman brought in to help him. He even fired his own son. "Some people just can't let go of their baby," says Wieman. A few months later, the client died.

But not all situations have to end so tragically. Wieman has a list of warning signs that may mean a business is growing too rapidly.

Wieman's warning signs:

- You hear people say, "I'm working harder and harder." or "I'm always behind. I can't seem to catch up."
- More and more mistakes are happening at work.
- Customers are angry because the business is missing due dates.
- The business can't afford any growth. The company has run out of money.

If you are suffering from any of these signs, get help now. (See tip, page 130.)

After dealing with both male and female business owners, Wieman says women small-business owners are most receptive to help. Seventy percent of his clients are female, and it's not just because Wieman loves women. "It's easier for a woman to say, 'I don't know everything, could you tell me how to do this?" In contrast, men frequently take a stoic approach, feeling they're supposed to handle whatever confronts them on their own.

Wieman says midwesterners aren't as apt to seek outside counsel as business owners from other regions of the United States. He theorizes that midwesterners have a long tradition of self-reliance.

If you want to save your business, set your ego aside and get help immediately. "You need to bring in seasoned professionals in the problem areas," says Wieman. "In 99 percent of the cases I see, they need management help."

"You may be a marketing genius and be wonderful with people, but you're not necessarily a good manager," Wieman says. "That's fine when you're running a five-person company, but not when you're managing a twenty-five-person company."

Entrepreneurs must learn management skills, says Wieman. You can buy it or learn it. He recommends "a little of both."

Work-crazed entrepreneurs should find mentors. Find a group of business people in similar but noncompetitive businesses to share your problems with.

Because most problems are people related, Wieman reminds you to hire wisely. "Call your potential customers, and if you are seeking a sales person, ask, 'Who do you respect and trust?' rather than hire your brother-in-law."

To avoid total burnout, train your employees and learn to delegate. "Most entrepreneurs feel that to get a job done right they have to do it themselves," he says. "It's very difficult to let somebody come in and do it differently."

Look for employees with skills complementary to your own. If you're a technical person, hire a marketing or management maven, for example.

If you need more space to cope with growth, carefully evaluate your business needs before moving to a bigger space. When Wieman is called in because a company has run out of space he often finds the company doesn't need more square footage but more efficient operations.

"If you've grown rapidly, I can bet you don't need more space, but new systems," says Wieman.

Management Overload: (310) 828–5590.

TIPS

If your business is growing too fast, you need help or you'll risk going out of business.

1. Consider hiring a seasoned executive on a temporary or part-time basis.

2. Be choosy about taking on new clients or projects. Unless you know you can do a good job, refer the business to someone else.

3. Get rid of your bad customers. You don't have to deal with customers who don't pay on time or give you a headache.

4. Ask customers for deposits to cover at least 50 percent of your production costs. This will boost cash flow and weed out casual customers.

5. Reduce your advertising and keep a low profile until you are ready to handle more business.

6. Find a mentor and get as much advice as possible before you make any more mistakes.

Secrets of Success

Few successful entrepreneurs work side by side with the president of the United States, but Erskine Bowles, who was chief of the Small Business Administration and then became White House deputy chief of staff, is such a person. I first met Erskine during Small Business Week in 1993, when he was the first business owner to head up the troubled agency.

Erskine believed in Bill Clinton enough to leave behind his family and his successful investment-banking firm to move from Charlotte, North Carolina, to Washington, D.C.

Less than eighteen months later, Clinton tapped him for a top White House post. Erskine and I became friends when we traveled around the country together, conducting a series of town hall meetings in the summer of 1993. His wit, humor, and stamina kept our spirits high as we faced anger, tears, boredom, and endless complaints from unhappy small-business owners.

Because I admire his management style, I asked him to contribute some thoughts to this section. He offered this excerpt from a commencement speech he wrote and presented to the graduating class of the University of North Carolina business school in 1994.

"The first is *Don't overpromise*. I see this all the time—people making promises they'll get an assignment done on Tuesday only to finish it early Wednesday morning.

"My advice is simple—do the opposite—be that person who underpromises, and for God's sake, never overpromise.

"Second, *Do the little things right*. Always be that person who makes sure that the little things—the simple things—get done and done right.

"Pay attention to details. You'll find that if you do the little things right, the big things often seem to take care of themselves.

"Third, *Always do quality*. You've heard it a zillion times and I guess it can't hurt to hear it once more, but it's true—there is absolutely no substitute for quality. If you're going to do it, do it right, do it perfect, no defects. It is absolutely possible to run a 'zero defect' operation. Just treat each assignment, or produce each product, as though you will lose the business unless it's perfect.

"Fourth, *You simply can't say 'thanks' too much*. Recognize the people who help you and thank them profusely. I've never met a person who minded being praised or thanked, even when they didn't deserve it.

"Gain the reputation for appreciating the work of others—and I'm not just talking about those above you or those at your level—but of equal importance, those who work for you. You'll find a simple 'thank you' to that clerk or that typist will carry you a long way.

"Fifth, *Find a niche and own it*. Always look for voids in the marketplace. That's where the real opportunities are.

"Sixth, *Surround yourself with really good people and then, by God, listen to them*. No one person has a corner on good ideas.

"My seventh commandment: *Encourage creativity*. Encourage people to look for better ways to get the job done. I believe this principle goes hand in glove with surrounding yourself with good people. If you are going to be successful, you can't ever believe that you have found the answer, that the way you are doing it now is as good as it can be done.

"Eighth, *Work hard*. There is no substitute for hard work. I have always found that it's that last 10 percent to 20 percent that you put into a project that separates real success from mediocrity.

"Ninth, *Take time to add to the woodpile*. I have always found that it is the busiest people who somehow or another find the time to make the biggest difference in their community. Whether you're to the right of Jesse Helms or to the left of Gore Vidal, it doesn't matter. You can find the time to try in your own way to make this world a better place.

"My last commandment is *Save time for your family*. There is nothing in my life that has been more important to me than my wife and three kids. I don't think anyone really knows what love is until you have a family. Spend time with your spouse, spend time with your kids, build up those memories.

1. Don't overpromise.
2. Do the little things right.
3. Always do quality.
4. You can't say thanks too much.
5. Find a niche and own it.
6. Surround yourself with really good people and listen to them.
7. Encourage creativity.
8. Work hard.

9. Add to the woodpile.
10. Spend time with your family.

"I have found these simple lessons to be very useful throughout my career and I believe that they have helped me to realize what success I have had."

Money

> *"People say the worst thing in starting a company is to be un-
> dercapitalized. Well, that's not true. The worst thing is listen-
> ing to the wrong people and not going with your gut feelings
> when you make your final decisions—then losing your enthu-
> siasm."*
>
> —Gregory Braendel, former CEO,
> Thrislington Cubicles

If you want to make lots of money the easy way, don't start your
own business. Keep your corporate job and feed your pension
plan.

People who dream of making big money assume the fastest
way to do it is by owning their own business. Wrong. Ask any successful business owner how many years they went without a salary
and they'll tell you: many.

Successful entrepreneurs eventually do make money, but they
make money because they work hard. They are passionate, persistent, and careful planners. Every successful business owner I've interviewed says the money came long after they had worked
eighty-hour weeks and had just about reached their mental and
physical limits. Often, just as they were about to give up, the first
wave of money hit.

That's what happened to me.

My bleakest night as an entrepreneur was spent alone in a

cheap, cockroach-infested New York City hotel room. I called home for some solace after a long tiring day of meetings. Instead of cozy chitchat, my husband, Joe, told me in a very stern voice that if I didn't start making as much money as he did, he was closing down The Applegate Group. He was understandably tired of paying all the household and business expenses. He was worn out from supporting me as I rode the entrepreneurial roller coaster. He totally believed in my dream of creating a national multimedia communications company, but the reality was too expensive.

I felt as if the wind had been knocked out of me. He gave me six months to dramatically boost my income or find a job.

Find a job?

A job!!!!

I could never work for anyone else again. I couldn't bear it. I cried and then I got very, very angry.

The next morning I accepted an offer to write a new small-business-solutions column for *Working Woman* magazine—and serve as a contributing editor. It was steady pay and provided an opportunity to work with a new editorial team.

I flew home a few days later and assured Joe that more money was on its way.

Since then, I've learned a few important lessons about money.

First, everything you plan to do will cost about twice as much as you projected and take three times as long to accomplish. This means you should always borrow more money than you think you need and set some aside for emergencies.

Next, if at all possible, never negotiate for yourself. The one deal I negotiated myself ended up costing me $15,000 I didn't have and endless amounts of aggravation.

Now, Brooke Halpin, my public-relations consultant, negotiates my speaking contracts. My business and legal adviser, Jerry Gottlieb, negotiates all my radio and television contracts, and my literary agent, Dominick Abel, sells my books.

Even when I was in the consulting business, I would leave the room and let my former partner, John Osborne, discuss fees and terms with our clients.

It's too tough to battle over money and then expect to establish a positive working relationship with the same people.

Some other thoughts on negotiating:

Before you begin, evaluate the deal and be very clear about what you want and what you can live without. Know your limits and what you are willing to give up to get the deal done. If you aren't clear about your personal bottom line from the beginning, the negotiation process will get bogged down and confused.

I've learned from experience to trust my gut instincts when negotiations begin. One consulting project that we felt uncomfortable about from the start turned out to be a professional, emotional, and financial nightmare. The high-priced attorney we hired to represent us said that he had never dealt with "ruder, more intractable people."

He urged us to walk away from the deal—actually he begged John and me to *run* away from it. But we were stubborn and inexperienced and kept slogging away. When it was over and we lost on virtually every point, we were depressed and drained. Of course, the project was a disaster.

From that point on, I've absolutely trusted my instincts. If I don't feel good about the people I will have to work with, I don't care how much money they want to pay me—I'm not interested. Life is too short to be dealing with negative energy and resistance. Money can never make up for a lack of joy in a project.

Collecting Money

Entrepreneurs are obsessed with money. Raising it, making it, spending it, losing it. Instead of worrying about money, let's focus on better managing the money you have or quickly collecting the money people owe you. Cutting overhead expenses is another way to stretch the dollars, whether you are just starting your business or are a veteran manager.

In this section, we'll focus on collecting money, cutting expenses, and alternatives to spending cash for the things your business needs.

Collecting money from people is tough. But collection experts say it's not impossible to keep the cash flowing if you follow a few simple suggestions.

The irony is that most small-business owners create their own collection problems by not being clear about how and when they expect to be paid. If you don't tell customers or clients that payment is due upon receipt or in fifteen days, most people will assume they can pay in thirty days—or more.

"We all need to be more effective in communicating about money," says Leonard Sklar, author of *The Check Is NOT in the Mail.*

Sklar and other collection experts say too many small-business owners wait too long to contact potential deadbeats. The secret to successful collecting is to call as soon as the payment is a day or two late.

"Within thirty days, you can collect a huge chunk of the money owed," Sklar says. "At six months, the chances are much less."

Another option is to ask your clients or customers to pay a portion of the bill up front, before you begin the work or ship the product. This is becoming a much more common practice among small-business owners and service providers.

"The problem is many business owners are desperate for business and too many are fearful they'll lose the client if they set strict terms," says Bonnie Barnett, a Glendale, California, collections consultant.

Barnett says many small-business owners also have trouble asking for money because they consider many of their customers friends. This is exactly why you should have a standard credit-rating procedure and use it for everyone, whether or not you know them personally.

Barnett, who once owned a collection agency, says the collection industry, especially in California, is in a state of flux and basically unregulated by state officials. But you are still protected against collection-agency abuses by some state and federal laws.

What if you just can't get people to pay up?

If numerous letters and phone calls to debtors prove fruitless, it may be time to turn the accounts over to an experienced agency. But don't be surprised if the agencies you call respond cooly. Many collection agencies prefer to work with very big, high-volume clients like hospitals, department stores, and banks. Some, however, set up special divisions to handle small-business accounts and will be eager to help you.

TIPS

In addition to providing bookkeeping and financial-management services, Chellie Campbell teaches a popular Financial Stress Reduction Workshop. For information, write to Campbell at 860 Via de la Paz, Suite B5, Pacific Palisades, CA 90272.

Leonard Sklar's book, *The Check Is NOT in the Mail*, is filled with practical tips and strategies for granting credit and collecting money. The book is available for $22.00 (plus California sales tax) from Baroque Publishing, 744 Jacaranda Circle, Hillsborough, CA 94010. Phone: (415) 348-7071.

Collection agencies work on a contingency basis, usually keeping about 35 percent of what they collect as payment for their services.

Barnett and others offer these tips for finding the right agency for you:

1. Ask for a client list and call other clients for references.
2. Visit the company offices to check out the operation first-hand.

3. Meet with someone other than the outside sales person. If possible, meet with the owner or manager.

4. Don't base your decision primarily on price because paying an agency a higher percentage to work harder on your behalf may actually bring in more cash.

"The sooner you start collecting, the more you'll collect," advises Chuck Piola, executive vice president of NCO Financial Systems Inc. in Blue Bell, Pennsylvania. "In tough times, when people have only so much disposable income, the company that asks them first and is persistent is the one they will pay."

NCO, a national collection agency, is currently collecting receivables for a variety of small businesses, including office-supply companies, appliance stores, auto garages, hardware stores, law practices, and dry cleaners.

Many people have a difficult time asking for money because no one teaches us how to talk about it, according to Chellie Campbell, who owns a bookkeeping service in Pacific Palisades, California.

Campbell advises business owners to discuss financial arrangements up front and in great detail before closing any deal.

"Say, 'This is the price and these are the terms,' then ask, 'Do you have a problem with this?' "

TIPS ON GRANTING CREDIT

Eric Shaw has a motto: If you give good credit, collections will follow.

Shaw, president of New York Credit Inc. in Marina del Rey, California, helps big and small businesses manage their credit and collections problems. Collections problems stem directly from granting credit to the wrong customers. Unfortunately, many small-business owners, eager for business, extend credit without fully checking out prospective customers. Shaw points out that extending credit puts you squarely in the role of a banker. This means that, like a banker, you should carefully check credit references before extending one dollar of credit.

Here are some of Shaw's tips:

1. In addition to a signed credit application, require customers to sign a release form that permits their bank to provide you with necessary financial information.
2. Ask for at least three trade references and call the companies listed for verification.
3. Ask customers to provide you with copies of their last three monthly bank statements.
4. Study the statements to answer these questions:
    a. How much cash is going in and out of the business each month?
    b. Are there any overdraft charges on the statement?
    c. Does the person write any big checks close to the amount they want in credit from your firm?

Next, ask for a full financial statement, including a profit-and-loss report and both year-to-date and year-end reports. If the company appears shaky, ask the owner to sign a personal guarantee for the amount of the credit. Last, but not least, request copies of the owner's personal tax returns.

Debt-Collection Tips

If you've granted credit carefully and someone still doesn't pay, Les Kirschbaum, president of Mid-Continent Agencies, Inc., a leading national collections firm based in Rolling Meadows, Illinois, has these tips for drafting appropriate collection letters.

Be thorough and concise. "You can be tactful without burying your message in sentence after sentence of platitudes. After all, the message you want to convey is pretty simple—you want to be paid—immediately," notes Kirschbaum. "The simpler the message, the stronger point you make."

Consider the relationship. When writing to a valued customer, your letter shouldn't be too strong or demanding. Depending on your experience with the customer, you may want to phrase your message in such a way as to leave him an "out" or allow a grace period in which the bill must be paid.

On the other hand, if the delinquent account is a poor customer, you may choose to leave no stone unturned in your collection letter. "However, hostility is usually met with hostility. If the customer thinks you're being unnecessarily nasty, he will probably feel justified in not paying you," Kirschbaum cautions.

Tell the customer what he owes. Don't make the customer dig through old invoices to figure out how much he owes—spell it out.

State your demands. Never assume that the customer will know you are requesting a payment. Ask for the money and tell him where and how to send it to you—today. Enclose a postage-paid reply envelope. Or, if you desire just a response, clearly spell out a telephone number or address and the action you want the customer to take.

Make your letter easy to understand. Requesting payment may not be enough of a motivator. Suggest that the debtor may damage his credit rating by not paying.

Notify the customer of your next course of action. Detail what your next action will be and when.

Check your spelling. Always have someone proofread your letters for clarity as well as grammar and spelling.

Kirschbaum also offers a list of ten basic blunders in accounts receivable:

1. Waiting until after a shipment is sent to mail the invoice
2. Not developing a sound credit procedure that is clearly understood by customers
3. Not using a detailed credit application

4. Failing to develop a credit file and continuously monitoring your customers
5. Not establishing an individual line of credit for each new customer
6. Not developing credit procedures that alleviate potential problems
7. Failing to monitor slow-paying accounts
8. Not notifying customers of your terms
9. Not focusing on in-house collection efforts between thirty-one and sixty days
10. Failing to follow up on a timely basis

Cutting Costs

Are you so busy running your business you barely have time to sit down and pay the bills? Although you're sure you could save money if you reviewed every invoice and shopped around, who has the time?

People like Douglas Arbuckle do. Arbuckle, founder of Cost Containment Solutions in Louisville, Kentucky, helps small-business owners figure out how to save money on office supplies, printing, overnight delivery services, and telephone bills. Arbuckle is among a growing number of expense-reduction analysts and consultants popping up around the country. While Arbuckle and his partner, Tom La Baugh, are independent consultants, some analysts buy franchises to serve business owners, while others are accountants who analyze costs as an extra service to clients.

The concept is simple: An objective outsider painstakingly reviews your expenses to see where money can be saved. While some analysts charge a fee for the work, Arbuckle works on a contingency basis; for every dollar he saves during a twelve-month period, he collects 50 percent. He reviews your bills on a quarterly basis, and if he can't save you any money, he collects nothing. But, after two years in business, his clients say he's saved them thousands and thousands of dollars.

"Most companies think they do a pretty good job purchasing," says John Clark, president and founder of Midland Communication Packaging Co. in Louisville. "But, in a small business, you are so busy serving your customers, you tend to get lackadaisical about what you're buying."

Clark, whose forty employees make customized, vinyl-covered, three-ring binders, says Arbuckle's recommendations saved his company about $20,000. "To our little company, that's a lot of money."

Arbuckle met with Clark's employees to gather information before he launched his attack on expenses. "I can take an area and analyze it to death," says Arbuckle, who formerly monitored manufacturing and production costs as an executive for several major corporations.

"He made us more aware of costs," says Ken Nicolas, managing partner of McCauley Nicolas & Co., an accounting firm with forty-five employees and offices in New Albany, Indiana, and Louisville. "Now, we think about getting bids before we make a purchase."

Nicolas says that, in addition to finding better vendors for office supplies, printing, and overnight delivery services, Arbuckle renegotiated the terms of the maintenance agreements on his firm's copying machines.

"We were able to save money without anyone noticing and without any hardships," says Ron Weisberg, executive vice president and one of the owners of Prudential Parks & Weisberg, a Louisville real-estate company. "I was a little shocked that he was able to do so much better than we had done," Weisberg says.

While the services provided by Arbuckle and other expense-reduction experts sound great, Barry Schimel, a Rockville, Maryland, CPA and author of *100 Ways to Prosper in Today's Economy*, cautions business owners about believing that cutting costs is the only way to boost profits.

"You can't cost-cut your way to prosperity," warns Schimel, who counsels small-business owners around the country. "To improve profits, you also need more sales and adequate margins."

COST-CUTTING TIPS

If you hire an outside consultant to help reduce expenses, make sure you can remain with your vendors and suppliers if you choose to. Some cost-cutters pool their clients' orders to deal with specific vendors and may insist you use the companies they contract with.

If you want to launch your own cost-cutting program, here's how:

1.   Set aside a Saturday or Sunday to go through at least three months' worth of checks and invoices for office expenses.

2.   List all your monthly expenses, including office supplies, cleaning supplies, overnight delivery service, telephone bills, printing and photocopying expenses. Focus on a few areas to shop around for better prices.

3.   If you are too busy to do it, assign a responsible employee to comparison shop and give him or her time to do it right.

4.   Check the prices in office-supply catalogs versus your local office-supply superstore or independent stationery store. It takes time, but it's worth it.

5.   After you collect new bids and prices, go back to your existing vendors and suppliers and ask them to meet or beat their competitors' prices. Many will do it because they don't want to lose your business.

6.   Whenever possible, buy supplies in bulk at a discount.

7.   Join with other small-business owners to form a purchasing cooperative. You'll be able to negotiate better prices by buying in larger quantities direct from the manufacturers.

Schimel's *100 Ways to Prosper in Today's Economy* is available from Acropolis Books, 13950 Park Center Road, Herndon, VA 22071. Phone: (800) 451-7771.

Schimel's popular book features 100 ways to cut costs, including locking the office supply cabinet, subletting unused office space, canceling insurance on idle vehicles and equipment, and photocopying on both sides of the paper.

Cutting Costs: Leasing Office Space

With so many American skylines featuring see-through office buildings, you'd think getting a great deal on commercial space would be easy. But many small-business owners are not taking advantage of the bargains out there because they don't understand how the complex leasing process works.

"The funny thing about leasing is that most people don't realize you can structure things any way you want—nothing is set in stone," says Andrew Johnson, author of *Tough Times—Tough Tactics*, a how-to guide aimed at helping small-business owners "even the sides" in a lease transaction.

Even if you are working with an experienced real-estate broker, Johnson says you should be well informed and know what to expect.

Renting commercial space is much trickier than renting an apartment. A commercial lease is a complicated and binding legal agreement that should not be taken lightly.

Before you begin looking, figure out what area of town is best for your business.

1. How accessible do you want to be from the airport, train station, freeway, subway, or bus stop?
2. Is the area safe for employees and visitors?
3. Are there restaurants, service businesses, and shops nearby?
4. How long is the commute for most employees?
5. How much traffic will you encounter during rush hour?

Next, compute how much space you'll need. According to Johnson, a good rule of thumb is 150 to 200 square feet per employee, plus 15 percent for traffic flow. He recommends renting storage space in the building for files and supplies, rather than storing it in expensive office space.

Rita Bennett, founder of Bennett & Associates in downtown Chicago, was one entrepreneur who followed the advice in Johnson's book. Bennett, who has lived abroad for years, began her multicultural training and relocation business at home in the early 1990s.

"My husband's law firm provided almost no support when we moved," she says. "I learned the hard way what it's like to go abroad with no support."

Bennett's firm helps Americans prepare for every aspect of life in a foreign land, ranging from how to shop for groceries to how to set up an office.

"About 80 percent of our business relates to helping companies transfer personnel abroad," Bennett says. "Families like to move when school is out, and companies have tax reasons to move people by January 1," she says.

With business booming, she and her staff quickly outgrew her home. In 1992, they moved into a shared office suite and began looking for permanent quarters. Because they serve mostly *Fortune* 500 clients, the small firm has to maintain a professional image. They needed spacious conference rooms as well as individual offices for employees and the eighty part-time trainers and associates who fly in for training sessions.

A few weeks after signing a letter of intent to lease a "perfect space," Bennett gave notice to her landlord. At the last minute, Bennett's deal fell apart.

"The greatest frustration is the amount of time it's taken to find places, being led to the brink and then having deals fall through," says Bennett.

Meanwhile, she and her relocation team have marked up page after page in Johnson's book.

"Wendy, my office manager, read it cover to cover and it's really been helpful," Bennett says.

LEASING TIPS

Here are more of Johnson's tips:

Compile a list of building managers to survey over the phone. Ask if they have the amount of space you're looking for and what rental rate is being quoted. Ask what kinds of concessions are being made to new tenants. Many landlords offer one month of free rent for every year of the lease term.

Once you narrow your search, begin making site visits. Bring a notebook to record all the details. As you approach the building, check out the neighboring buildings to see if the area is well maintained. Does the building have "curb appeal"?

Park in the parking structure, if there is one, to see if the parking area is well lit and well marked. Check out the lobby to see if it's clean and attractive. How do the elevators work? Do they take forever to reach the lobby? Is there a directory of tenants?

Once you get to the floor, visit the bathrooms and note the neighboring tenants. Find the emergency exits and check for fire escapes and fire sprinklers.

If you are planning to make an offer, be prepared to present the landlord with detailed financial information.

And, remember, before you sign a lease, always have a real-estate attorney review the fine print.

If you are looking for retail space, Johnson reports on a trend: Many small-business owners can negotiate a lower base rate by offering their landlord a percentage of sales.

"If you've got a newer product or you are not quite sure what your cash flow will be, try to get a lower base rent and offer a percentage of gross sales, maybe 5 percent to 6 percent," says Johnson. Be prepared to open your books to your landlord and set a limit on the percentage to protect yourself.

Tough Times—Tough Tactics sells for $39.95, plus applicable California sales tax. The fifty-nine-page book features a glossary of real-estate terms and sample lease agreements. To order, call

(800) 270-4848, or send a check or money order to: Johnson Commercial Brokerage, 4121 Camino Real, Suite 100, Los Angeles, CA 90065.

How to Woo a Banker

Small-business owners across America are still frustrated. Despite expansive, heart-warming "we love small business" advertising campaigns launched by banks across the country, many entrepreneurs complain they still can't qualify for traditional financing.

The truth is, most bankers prefer to lend to stable, profitable businesses and generally want to see at least two sources of repayment. And, while entrepreneurs are happy to take calculated risks, bankers are taught to avoid taking financial risks at all costs.

"Many bankers have been taught to look at a business with a high level of skepticism," says Rudolph Estrada, president and chief executive officer of the Summit Group in South Pasadena, California.

Martin Liebman, executive vice president of Marine Midland Bank, and regional president for Marine's New York City metropolitan area, says another problem is that many small-business owners don't "speak the language of accounting or finance."

"Many small-business owners are not sure what they want and are not sure what to ask for," says Liebman, who's been a banker for thirty years. "Before you go in to ask for a business loan, be very clear in your mind what you need the money for and how much you need," he advises.

He suggests bringing your accountant with you to an initial meeting with a loan officer. And be fully prepared to discuss how you will repay the loan, especially if business slows down or you are somehow pushed out of the picture by illness or other calamity.

Bankers want to know what will happen to your business if you become incapacitated. They want to know if someone else on your management team is qualified to step in and run your business.

Before applying for a loan, try to get some insights from a friend or relative in the banking industry. Or, better yet, meet with a retired banker who is willing to play devil's advocate and discuss your loan application.

To combat a banker's skepticism, be prepared to answer questions beyond the ones on the loan application. Bankers want to know how you plan to repay the loan, and usually require more than one source of repayment.

Before approaching your local banker, remember that most commercial loans, except for mortgages, are basically short-term, lasting two to five years. If you'll need the money longer than that, you should probably seek alternatives, including equity investors with patience.

Whenever possible, deal with someone who sits on or has the respect of the bank's loan committee.

"All too often, banks rely on order takers to deal with prospective borrowers and clients," says Estrada, who serves on the White House Commission on Small Business. "Unfortunately, these individuals are ill equipped to deal with sophisticated business matters and/or lack the experience to develop a strong case to secure approval for your request."

Estrada, whose management-consulting firm helps banks manage their small-business lending programs, suggests dealing with smaller banks whose decision makers are placed closer to the front lines.

However, in many cases, a big bank offers more financial clout and can provide personal service if you make contact with the right person.

While the bank is busy checking your credit references and ability to pay, be sure to spend some time checking out the bank's liquidity and solvency.

"Make every attempt to determine the financial and managerial integrity of their business," Estrada advises.

Once you find a strong bank and a banker you can trust, bring that banker into your business and consider him or her a respected adviser. "A banker has a tendency to promote your needs to his supervisors when he feels he has been consulted and made to feel that his input is valuable," he says.

Warner Heineman, a veteran business banker who serves as senior adviser to First Business Bank in Century City, makes this surprising statement:

"Numbers mean nothing. Character is absolutely number one for me. I want to deal with capable, honest people."

Like many seasoned business bankers, Heineman said he relies on gut instinct when it comes to determining whether or not to make a loan.

"I haven't really had a loan go bad in all my years," he says. "Although I have had a loan go slow."

BANKING TIPS

1.   Before you apply for a loan, establish a strong relationship with your bank. Move all your accounts—business and personal—into the branch and introduce yourself to the manager or commercial loan officer.

2.   Make sure your company's financial statements are in order before you apply for a loan. Ask your accountant for help on this.

3.   Bankers want to know two basic things: what you plan to use the money for and how you intend to pay it back.

4.   If possible, apply for a little more money than you need because it's better to have some money in reserve than to wish you had applied for more.

5.   To present a full picture of your company, include product samples, promotional literature, customer testimonials, and press clippings with your loan application.

6.   If you want to save money on your bank fees and services, *Banking Smarter* by Dennis Suchocki and Andrew Smith is a great resource. The workbook sells for $39.95, plus $5 for shipping/handling. Write to P.O. Box 5108, Scottsdale, AZ 85261. Phone: (602) 423-8384.

SBA Guaranteed Loans

1. The U.S. Small Business Administration generally *does not* make loans, but they do *guarantee* loans submitted and made by financial institutions, generally banks. The SBA *does not* have a "grant" program for starting a small business.

   a. The SBA guarantees loans of up to $500,000. There is no theoretical minimum, although most lenders are reluctant to process commercial loans of less than $25,000.

   b. Prospective borrowers *will be required* to provide their own money. This contribution will normally be 30 percent to 50 percent of the total capitalization of the business.

   c. An existing business will be required to provide financial statements showing the business is a profit-making concern, does not have delinquent tax, and will have a debt-to-worth ratio of approximately 3:1 after the loan is made.

   d. The SBA charges the lender a 2 percent guaranty fee on the guaranteed portion of the loan. SBA policy allows the lender to charge this guaranty fee to the borrower.

2. SBA guaranteed loan program "interest rates" are based on the prime rate as advertised in the *Wall Street Journal* according to the following schedule:

   a. Loans of less than seven years: prime rate plus 2.25 percent.

   b. Loans of seven years or more: prime rate plus 2.75 percent.

3. SBA guaranteed loan maturity (length of loan) is based upon the following schedule:

   a. Working-capital loans: five to seven years.

   b. Fixed-asset loans: seven to ten years.

   c. Real estate and building: up to a maximum of twenty-five years

4. The most important part of your discussion with the lender is to be prepared with data to answer the lender's questions. A *Business Plan* that includes the items below will be most helpful to you in presenting your proposal.

    a. Projected profit and loss statement

    b. Cash flow projections

    c. Market analysis

    d. Marketing strategy

    e. Description of the business

    f. Product or service advantage

    g. Management ability—résumés of the key staff should be included

    h. Financial information (personal and business)

    i. Cash requirements

5. Business proposals that are ineligible for the SBA guaranteed loan program are:

    a. Partial purchase of a business

    b. Lending institutions

    c. Real estate held for speculation, investment or rental

    d. Religious organizations and their affiliates

For further assistance, please contact the National Business Association (NBA) at (800) 456-0440 or your local SBA office. The SBA is the federal agency responsible for helping entrepreneurs succeed.

The SBA's GreenLine Program

In response to hundreds of business owners telling him that they just couldn't get revolving credit lines, former SBA administrator Erskine Bowles helped create the GreenLine Revolving Line of Credit program. The program, launched nationally in July 1994, provides an SBA guarantee on up to 75 percent of a revolving credit line issued by a bank.

"It is one of our most important credit initiatives of the year," says Bowles. "We are aiming at financing the materials and labor needed to build a product and finance the sale of that product until the cash is collected."

A qualifying company can use their GreenLine for a maximum of five years. Interest rates are negotiable between the bank and the borrower, but interest cannot be more than 2.25 percentage points over the prime rate.

Alternatives to Bank Financing

Small-business owners are tired of bankers telling them that things are getting better and more funds will be available soon. The private sector, tired of waiting for Congress to act, is creating a secondary market for small-business loans as a way to attract more capital.

In the early 1990s, Chrysler Corporation's finance subsidiary issued $350 million in securities backed by a pool of small business loans secured by real estate. In March 1993, The Money Store issued $76 million in securities backed by the unguaranteed portion of some Small Business Administration loans. And in April 1993, Santa Monica–based Fremont General Corp. sold $200 million worth of securities backed by a pool of small and medium-size business loans.

There are also smaller players in the market. The Target Income Fund, distributed by Finance 500 Inc., based in Tustin, California, has packaged and sold more than $12 million worth of short-term small-business credit lines and loans, according to president Lance Hicks. The fund, which is registered with the Securities and Exchange Commission, has a diversified portfolio containing short-term loans and credit lines issued to small businesses. Hicks said many of the businesses are thriving, but for one reason or another had trouble obtaining traditional bank financing.

Borrowers range from makers of plastic, clothing, computer

software, and hospital equipment to several small employment agencies and freight companies.

"The fund is essentially run like a bank," explains Hicks. Business owners submit applications for funds to be used for a revolving credit line or short-term loan. The loans, which generally carry an interest rate of 4 percent to 5 percent over the prime rate, are heavily collateralized by accounts receivables and corporate assets.

"The ongoing challenge is to match the money we have available with the best companies," says Hicks.

The job of finding the right companies to lend money to falls primarily to Reid Rutherford, chairman and chief executive officer of Palo Alto–based EXXE Data Corp. The company designs software and systems to help banks and other financial institutions pool and sell small-business loans.

"The last market left for the banking industry is the small-business market," says Rutherford. The problem? "Banks do have money to lend now, but the reality is that they don't want to put it out in small amounts," Rutherford says.

TIP

The Minneapolis-based Community Reinvestment Fund has created its own unique secondary market by packaging and reselling about $8.4 million worth of economic-development loans, housing-rehabilitation loans, and affordable-housing loans. "We pool the loans and use them as collateral for a bond issue," explains John O'Brien, vice president. "Then we sell the bonds to banks, insurance companies, and pension funds."

The unrated bonds can be sold only to institutional investors, but so far interest in the bonds has been strong. The fund has purchased loans from state and local government entities in Michigan, Iowa, Minnesota, Wisconsin, California, Florida, Illinois, Washington, Oregon, and Colorado. For information, contact the Community Reinvestment Fund, 2400 Foshay Tower, 821 Marquette Avenue, Minneapolis, MN 55402.

Rutherford says he's optimistic that the secondary market for small-business loans is about to take off, and his thirty-five-employee firm is prepared to provide the tools to help financial institutions make it happen.

For information on applying for a Target Income Fund loan or credit line, write to EXXE Data Corp., 1170 E. Meadow Drive, Palo Alto, CA 94303-4234, or call Finance 500 Inc. at (714) 730-9087.

Bartering to Save Cash

More and more small-business owners, looking to stretch every dollar, are turning to barter as an alternative to paying cash for things they need. The nation's 520 or so barter exchanges offer thousands of members everything from tires to hotel rooms and billboards.

In 1992, barter transactions in the United States and Canada totaled $6.45 billion, up from $5.9 billion in 1991, according to the International Reciprocal Trade Association in Great Falls, Virginia.

Gary Berger, owner of the Bronx Zoo Florist in downtown Chicago, began bartering about ten years ago, swapping cars, clothes, cigarettes, and toothpaste to overseas buyers. Today, he barters wholesale flowers and floral services for hotel rooms, advertising space, photocopying machines, and tires. In 1993, he bartered about $30,000 worth of goods.

"I use barter for things I can use in my business because I can't pay my rent with barter dollars," says Berger, who has about eight employees.

He says many novices make the mistake of trading valuable inventory or services for luxuries and personal items rather than using barter to boost their businesses.

"It's wrong to take your inventory off the wall and convert it into a trip to Las Vegas if you haven't paid your rent," Berger says.

Here's an example of an exchange Berger worked out through the Chicago Barter Corporation: Berger provided elegant flower arrangements to a financially troubled hotel in exchange for several rooms. Then he swapped the hotel accommodations to a trucking company whose trucks carry billboards advertising Bronx Zoo flowers.

"On Valentine's Day, we parked one of their trucks outside our store on State Street to promote a special on roses," Berger says.

Doug Dagenais, vice president of Chicago Barter, says the barter industry has matured in recent years.

"Barter is becoming a normal financial tool rather than some strange philosophy," says Dagenais, whose barter network includes more than 2,500 clients in Chicago and surrounding areas. "I think our whole industry has gained more credibility."

In recent years, IRS rulings have clarified the tax implications of bartering. In general, barter dollars are treated the same as regular dollars for tax purposes.

Most barter networks charge a fee to join and collect a commission on every transaction. Chicago Barter charges a 10 percent to 12 percent cash commission on each transaction; the commission is usually split equally between buyers and sellers. Clients willing to pay a one-time retainer fee of $500 can take advantage of the 5 percent commission. Those willing to pay a 6 percent commission on trades can join for free.

In addition to the commissions and fees, clients pay about $30 a month to maintain an active account, says Dagenais, who accepts about $1,000 a month in barter credits as part of his salary.

According to Dagenais, many small-business owners use barter to repay debts. For instance, a landscaper who belonged to the barter exchange owed a hardware store money for equipment and repairs.

"The landscaper could have given the hardware-store owner lawn services, but the owner didn't want that," says Dagenais. "So the landscaper provided lawn services to our network. He paid the trade credits he received to the hardware-store owner."

Bob Meyer, publisher of *Barter News*, says the secret of successful bartering is to "acquire something that replaces a cash purchase."

Want to learn more about bartering?

Barter News covers the domestic and international barter industry for its 30,000 subscribers. An annual subscription is $40. Write to: P.O. Box 3024, Mission Viejo, CA 92690.

For information on how barter can help your business, or to locate a barter exchange near you, send a thirty-two-cent stamped, self-addressed envelope with your request to the International Reciprocal Trade Association, 6305 Hawaii Court, Alexandria, VA 22312. Phone: (703) 237-1828.

Bronx Zoo Florist: (312) 664-0098.

Microloans

Remember the old cliché "small is beautiful"?

Well, small is beautiful for thousands of entrepreneurs who have borrowed millions of dollars in small amounts from America's 200-plus microloan programs. Microloans, usually $25,000 or less, differ from traditional loans because they are mostly offered to low-income borrowers and usually require little or no collateral.

Foundations, banks, and the U.S. government, through the Small Business Administration, support microlending as a way to give struggling entrepreneurs a significant boost. The SBA, which relies on about 100 community lenders to disburse funds, set aside nearly $50 million for microloans in 1994. In 1993 and 1994, about $5 million reached 517 small-business owners, with the average loan amounting to $9,719.

"We are helping to provide people with unprecedented access to the financial tools they need to market their creativity and skills and get a real opportunity to achieve economic self-determination," said former SBA administrator Erskine Bowles.

Microloan programs especially benefit women and minorities, who have traditionally had the toughest time convincing bankers to give them credit. Most programs are designed to serve low-income people earning $15,000 a year or less. Some programs, like the MICRO program of Tucson, Arizona, lend only to existing businesses. The MICRO program, believed to be the nation's largest, with thousands of loans averaging $1,700, also emphasizes job creation.

The Coalition for Women's Economic Development (CWED) in Los Angeles has issued several hundred microloans since 1989, with a 98 percent repayment rate. CWED's loan program, like many others, is based on a peer-support model developed by the Grameen Bank in Bangladesh. Borrowers must join a lending circle made up of five or six women who meet regularly to discuss both business and personal issues relating to money.

Glenda Harris and Deborah Payne, of Chicago, were reluctant to apply because they were sure the low-interest loans offered through the Women's Self-Employment Project were just too good to be true. "I carried a paper about the program in my briefcase for years," says Harris, a jewelry designer who borrowed $1,500 from the Full Circle Fund program. Harris used most of the money to buy an ample supply of the colorful beads, old coins, and amulets she uses to create one-of-a-kind ethnic jewelry. Once she built up her inventory, she displayed her wares at weekend street fairs. In a good month, she earns $1,000.

"Sometimes, I'm overwhelmed because my jewelry is selling so well," says Harris, who also earns up to $100 an hour for teaching jewelry-making classes.

Dress and hat designer Deborah Payne used her $900 loan to buy an industrial sewing machine and an ironing table for her basement workshop. That was all she needed to expand her production of custom-made clothing.

"I'm doing so well, I was able to quit my part-time job working in a lunch program at a school," says Payne, who made a $39.45 loan payment every two weeks. Things are going so well, Payne dreams of opening a retail store someday.

Although many microloan recipients have poor credit and are often unemployed, late payments and defaults are rare. In fact, the repayment rate is about 95 percent for most microloan programs, including Chicago's Full Circle Fund.

"Peer support works the best," says Connie Evans, executive di-

rector of the Women's Self-Employment Project (WSEP) in downtown Chicago. "Women begin to redefine community and break
out of their isolation. The kind of changes these women make are
incredible."

First Chicago Bank and AT&T have contributed thousands of
dollars to the Chicago's Women's Business Development Center
to support its microloan program, according to center director
Hedy Ratner.

In the past years, Ratner says, the Center's financial programs
have lent local women more than $2 million to fuel their business
growth.

Across the country, Utah's Microenterprise Loan Fund, based
in Salt Lake City, helps applicants who were rejected by a bank.
To qualify, they submit a detailed business plan and promise to attend a monthly support meeting where loan payments are collected.

Sam Guevara, owner of the Art House graphic design firm,
chaired a monthly Business Assistance Program meeting.

"Everyone has been right on time with their payments and
made it to every meeting," says Guevara.

What kinds of businesses received help?

MICROLOAN TIPS

For more information about microloans, contact your local
Small Business Development Center or SBA office.

Women in Chicago, write to WSEP at 166 West Washington Street, Suite 730, Chicago, IL 60602.

(See Resource List for more information.)

Baker Aaron Colunga borrowed $8,000 for equipment and pay-
roll expenses to improve the bakery he operates at a Reams grocery
store. Marjorie Ball used her $5,000 loan to expand Cottage Craft
Mercantile, which produces and distributes craft patterns.

What kind of businesses didn't get funding?

"We rejected someone who wanted to buy used equipment and resell it to Mexico," says Guevara. "The problem was, he spoke no Spanish and had no clients or contacts in Mexico."

Free Money

AT&T Capital Corporation and the American Institute of CPAs are offering $50,000 in grants to small businesses that combine a socially responsible mission with a sound business plan. Entrepreneurs in Houston and Philadelphia were eligible to compete for the first grants in 1994.

For an application and information on the Partners for Growth grant program, call (800) 235-4288.

Other grants available for business owners include the *Working Women* Magazine Start-Up Grant, which offers $50,000 to the entrepreneur with the most intriguing and solid business plan. Dun & Bradstreet and the National Federation of Independent Business also sponsor a national "Best of America" grant program with substantial cash awards.

Contact the companies for details.

Finding a Corporate Sugar Daddy

Brothers Sam and Derek Burris had been working in their parents' Ace Hardware store in Los Angeles since they were in first grade. So when a sales representative for Benjamin Moore, the paint company, asked the brothers if they would like to own their own paint store, they thought it was too good to be true.

It wasn't.

The Burris brothers are among 200-plus minority entrepreneurs who've contributed some cash and a lot of sweat equity toward owning their own Benjamin Moore outlet. Moore's "temporary co-ownership" program provides the initial funding needed to open a neighborhood paint store—usually around $200,000. As soon as the business becomes profitable, the entrepreneurs begin buying back the stock until they own the business outright. The program has given small-business owners a head start in Atlanta, Chicago, Newark, and San Francisco, among other cities.

"This is not an altruistic move on our part, this is good business for Benjamin Moore," says Billy Sutton, western division vice president for the company, which has fifty stores in Southern California and about 5,000 nationwide.

Although Moore's program has been around since the 1960s, it is attracting attention because access to capital continues to be the number-one challenge for small-business owners—especially minorities. While dozens of corporations, like IBM, joined Rebuild LA, a business coalition formed after the 1992 Los Angeles riots, few major companies offer direct financial assistance to entrepreneurs.

Sutton says Derek and Sam Burris were "terrific candidates" for the paint company's financing program.

Benjamin Moore, based in Montvale, New Jersey, seeks out people with an interest in revitalizing their communities as well as owning their own business.

"Opening their own business in their neighborhood meant the world to them," Sutton says. "I don't know of any better symbol of recovery than a paint store."

"We live in this area and we grew up here," says Sam Burris, who played football with the Dallas Cowboys before injuring his knee. He was selling insurance when he joined forces with his brother to open the store in 1993.

The brothers found a vacant brick building and contributed a few thousand dollars of their own to buy stock in the store. Moore provided funds for the improvements and stocked the store with products. The Paint Station, located at 529 E. Manchester Blvd. in Inglewood, employs six full-time and two part-time workers, including the brothers.

"We love it," says Burris. "We'd rather exert ourselves working for ourselves."

So far, sales have exceeded Benjamin Moore's projections,

Burris says. At this rate, he and Derek will own the store outright by 1996. (Moore does not share in any of the profits or appreciation of the stock.)

John Bryant, founder and chairman of Operation Hope, a nonprofit organization dedicated to economic empowerment for minorities in Southern California, says Moore's program "sounds like heaven."

"We minority entrepreneurs have the energy, drive, passion, and commitment, but we don't have the capital," says Bryant, a former investment banker who now devotes his time and energy to helping minority entrepreneurs obtain financing. Bryant says Moore's program makes sense because the "minority entrepreneurs understand the market and community because they grew up there."

Bryant, who sits on Rebuild LA's board, has been working with Joan Wilson, government-affairs manager for the Southland Corporation in Southern California to encourage more minorities to buy 7-Eleven franchises.

"We would like to have more minorities buy franchises, but our biggest problem is getting people financed," says Wilson. Franchise fees vary, but it takes about $75,000 to buy a 7-Eleven franchise. Wilson says for years she's been encouraging the U.S. Small Business Administration to provide loan guarantees to 7-Eleven franchisees, but the agency has opposed it.

"The problem is we supply everything," says Wilson. "The franchisees don't own the building or the property so they don't have any collateral to put up for the loan."

SBA spokesman Mike Stamler says lack of collateral is the problem, not financing a franchise. "Franchises receive about five to six percent of our loan guarantees," says Stamler. "There is no rule against franchises, but we do have rules that require the owner to have an equity stake in the business."

TIPS

For information on Benjamin Moore's temporary co-ownership program, write to Benjamin Moore Co-Ownership Program, 3325 South Garfield Avenue, Los Angeles, CA 90040, or write to Benjamin Moore & Co., Montvale, NJ 07645.

Southern California entrepreneurs interested in buying a 7-Eleven franchise can contact the Southland Corp., Franchise Dept., 120 S. State College Boulevard, Brea, CA 92622.

Going Public: Life in a Fishbowl

Just about every successful entrepreneur dreams of selling stock to the public to fuel his or her company's growth.

But in reality, going public is not as glamorous or rewarding as many small-business owners think, according to chief executives attending Cruttenden & Co.'s Southern California Growth Stock Conference held every year in Newport Beach, California.

For two intense days, forty-eight small companies touted their products, shared their dreams, and opened their books to potential investors and money managers. The companies ranged from a Washington State computer-sound-card maker to an Irvine, California, company mining South Seas coral for use in bone grafts.

The secret to a successful public offering hinges on investor confidence in your company's products, but more importantly, your management team, according to Steve DeLuca, Cruttenden's director of research.

"Investors like to invest in people with experience," says DeLuca. He points to the enormous success of Callaway Golf Co., whose founder, Ely Callaway, had already started a successful winery.

Of the thousands of small companies that attempt to sell stock, only a tiny percentage succeed. In 1993, for example, Cruttenden, an investment-banking firm that focuses on West Coast companies, received about 1,000 business plans. Of those, it chose about half a dozen companies to take public.

"Sometimes, going public isn't the right move," DeLuca says. "While everyone wants to go public, staying private has its benefits."

The biggest benefit of staying private is not having to open your books and your management decisions to scrutiny by investors and the Securities and Exchange Commission. The SEC requires public companies to file frequent and detailed reports on every aspect of the business.

In 1993, Interpore International, based in Irvine, California, raised about $12 million through an initial public offering, or IPO. Interpore's management decided to go public after spending five rounds of venture-capital financing to fuel its growth.

The company, which has approval from the U.S. Food and Drug Administration to transform coral into bonelike material used by orthopedic surgeons to repair broken bones, needs about $1 million to conduct clinical trials on each product. The company produces both blocks and granules for surgical use.

"The coral provides a matrix and scaffold for the human bone to grow into," says David Mercer, president and chief executive officer.

Mercer says the market for Interpore's products is growing because each year America's 14,000 orthopedic surgeons perform about 800,000 bone grafts. The company may also benefit from recent concerns about the safety of using bones from cadavers. Another alternative, using portions of the patient's own bones for grafts, usually requires at least two surgeries and often results in medical complications, he says.

After spending an enormous amount of time and money to complete the public offering, Interpore's top managers say they have a tough time spending the company's newfound cash.

"Until we went public, our emphasis was on cash flow," says James Jungwirth, Interpore's former chief financial officer. "We lived and died by cash flow and whether or not we would be able to make the payroll."

Since going public, their emphasis is on pleasing the shareholders and showing a profit. The company, which posted sales of about $14 million in 1993, has seen its stock price increase to $9 a share, up from the initial price of $7. Interpore trades on NASDAQ. (Its trading symbol is BONZ.)

Jungwirth admits the IPO process was grueling. "You have to be prepared to answer a lot of pointed questions and not get defensive," he says. "The process will also take a lot longer than you think."

Lambert Thom, a money manager for John Hancock Capital Growth in San Francisco, says he looks to invest in companies with "real products, real revenues, and real cash flow."

"We like to know how the company addresses its competition," says Thom, whose firm has about $100 million invested in smaller companies.

Thom's investor group likes to take a long-term position in stable but fast-growing companies. Thom was particularly interested in Quidel Corporation, a San Diego maker of fertility and allergy tests. Thom's fund invested about $6 million in Quidel.

Did Thom find out about Quidel at past investment conferences? No.

"I met a doctor on an airplane who mentioned the company," he says.

TIPS ON GOING PUBLIC

Here are some things to consider before trying to take your company public:

1. Do you have a well-written, comprehensive business plan?
2. Do you have a competent management team with an experienced chief financial officer?
3. Do you have money for legal fees, underwriting, and traveling across the country to meet with potential investors?

4. Do you have a solid, growing company with proven products?
5. Do you need money to grow the company or to pay off early investors?
6. Are you willing to give up your privacy and work in a fishbowl?
7. Is there a growing market for your products or services?
8. Are you patient and persistent?

Attracting Private Investors

Andrew Ha had a big problem. His BeeperKid child-safety device won a gold medal from a prestigious design society as one of the best-designed new products of 1992.

The problem was BeeperKid, a pager-size device designed to beep when a toddler moves more than fifteen feet away from his parents, didn't work. "It was unreliable, inconsistent, and featured the wrong technology," says Ha, president of A+H International Products, based in Long Beach, California. Ha, who had already invested about $1 million in the prototype, needed a solution fast.

Ha saved his company and solved his problem by teaming up with Quarterdeck Investment Partners, a fledgling boutique investment firm with offices in Los Angeles and Washington, D.C. Quarterdeck, which focuses on defense conversion projects, not only invested about $1 million in Ha's firm, but found a major defense contractor with just the right technology to fix BeeperKid. The product finally hit the market in upscale catalogues in 1994.

Ha's guardian angel is Jon Kutler, a former managing director of Wasserstein Perella & Co., a prestigious investment-banking firm. After a difference of opinion prompted Kutler to leave Wasserstein in 1993, he founded Quarterdeck. Capitalizing on his skills as head of Wasserstein's Southern California defense and aerospace practice, Kutler was convinced he could help large and small defense companies find commercial markets for their products.

But Kutler, a former Navy officer with a Harvard M.B.A., says defense contractors should not rely on the government to help them. Instead, he believes they should turn to private investors for new capital. "Billions of dollars on Wall Street are chasing initial public offerings and the hottest buyouts," says Kutler. "We think that money could be channeled into defense conversion."

Kutler's argument makes sense, especially since there is not enough federal money to help every defense-related company. In fact, in 1993 alone, the federal Technology Reinvestment Project, a five-agency group, distributed $470 million in grants to U.S. military contractors for commercial-product development. The problem is the defense contractors submitted 2,844 proposals with a total price tag of $8.5 billion.

Kutler says savvy defense companies should restructure themselves to attract private capital rather than wait around for government aid. "Look at consumer markets that make sense, then go back and find the technology," advises Kutler.

Another obstacle to private investors is that many people assume defense technologies are off limits or classified as top secret. "In many cases, the raw technology is not classified," says Kutler, who relied on a nonclassified technology to make BeeperKid work.

In Quarterdeck's first year, Kutler invested in three companies, including A+H Products and Seescan, a Gainesville, Florida, company that uses antisubmarine-warfare technology to build devices that see underwater. The devices have several commercial applications, including searching for buried treasure and for toxic materials dumped into the ocean.

Beyond looking to help small U.S. companies, Kutler is exploring investment projects in Estonia, Hungary, and France.

Meanwhile, Andrew Ha is working on new uses for his BeeperKid technology. Theme parks might rent the beepers to families with toddlers. Families concerned about the safety and whereabouts of elderly relatives may be another market for the product. Ha says the beepers could also be embedded in cellular telephones or portable computers and beep forgetful owners who leave them behind.

What inspired Ha to develop BeeperKid, which will probably retail for about $100?

"I came across the idea while playing golf," says Ha. "I left a putter on the course and thought, wouldn't it be great if there was something on my club that reminded me to pick it up?"

TIPS

Jon Kutler has these tips for small-business owners interested in taking advantage of defense-related technologies:

- Don't just look for a technology. First, find a market for a product.
- Stay lean and mean. Trim expenses and run your company efficiently.
- Don't try to go it alone. Find a strategic partner who can provide technology or capital.

Quarterdeck Investment Partners can be reached at 10100 Santa Monica Boulevard, Suite 945, Los Angeles, CA 90067. A+H International Products is at One World Trade Center, Suite 800, Long Beach, CA 90831.

Selling Out and Staying On

Selling your business for several million dollars and then staying on to run it sounds too good to be true. But that's exactly what brothers Walter and Howard Lim did with their Aerosol Services Co. based in City of Industry, California.

The contract packaging company, with sales of about $50 million a year, has been the Lims' major asset since its founding nearly thirty years ago.

In 1991, Walter Lim's estate-planning attorney encouraged him to consider selling a portion of the business to free up cash for his retirement.

"My attorney kept telling me I had to make my estate more liquid," says Lim.

Although Aerosol Services, which fills and packages hair gels, hair sprays, shampoos, and other consumer products, was solidly profitable, it was not a sexy, fast-growing, high-technology business that attracts many investors. The Lims' challenge was finding a buyer who not only wanted a stable, long-term investment, but was willing to let the Lim brothers remain in charge.

"We were looking for a very special type of investor," says Lim. "We wanted people we felt comfortable with."

Lim, who is president and chief executive officer, also wanted to protect the jobs of his 250 employees. He also needed to protect his brother Howard's job. Howard is chief financial officer and general manager.

Realizing they needed professional help to sell the business, the Lims met with several middle-market investment-banking firms. In 1993, they retained Lloyd Greif, a veteran investment banker whose mission was to find just the right buyer.

Greif, president of Greif & Co. in downtown Los Angeles, says that although Aerosol Services was a solid company, it had several strikes against it; it had two owners over fifty who wanted to keep their jobs, sales had been relatively flat between 1989 and 1992, and the business itself was fairly mundane.

Before Greif brought in a single potential buyer, he spent hours with the Lims, determining exactly what they wanted in terms of dollars and future employment. He worked with the company's accountants at Coopers & Lybrand to make sure the books and records were in order.

Based on his extensive interviews, he encouraged the Lims to emphasize their research-and-development capabilities rather than their filling and packaging services. They also decided to add a new line of equipment designed to handle nonaerosol products like shampoos.

"We wanted potential buyers to know that the company could develop different formulas and effectively become a research-and-development arm for their customers," says Greif. "We very much focused on this proprietary capability."

Armed with his clients' wish list, Greif began contacting potential investors. There were more than a dozen serious lookers, but the field soon narrowed to a group of private investors from Newport Beach, California. In 1994, the Gordon+Morris Group created the Aerosol Services Holding Corporation to purchase a majority interest in the company.

Walter Lim declined to reveal the exact sales price, but says it was a cash deal. Greif says the Lims own about 40 percent of the newly restructured company. The brothers also have open-ended employment contracts that enable them to stay on as long as they want to.

Since the sale closed in early 1994, Lim says his only contact with his new owners has been a quarterly board meeting. Beyond that, he says nothing else has changed.

Lim advises entrepreneurs interested in selling their businesses to have their financial records audited for at least three years before the sale. He also recommends carefully documenting your operating procedures and making sure there are no legal or regulatory problems that may surface to jeopardize the deal.

SELLING OUT TIPS

"A lot of people who want to sell their companies don't understand how much work is involved," says Walter Lim. He has this advice if you are preparing to sell your business:

1.   Retain an experienced investment banker or broker who specializes in small or midsize companies.
2.   Hire someone you feel extremely comfortable with, someone you can confide in and trust.
3.   Be prepared to spend a lot of time providing detailed information to your investment banker. Then be prepared to share it with any serious potential buyers.
4.   Be clear about exactly what you want out of the deal before you start negotiating.
5.   Include your accountant and attorney on your advisory team to handle the tax and legal matters.
6.   Be open and honest with your employees when it comes time to announce your plans to sell.

Greif adds these suggestions:

1.   Work with an investment banker who understands entrepreneurs and can provide a high level of service.
2.   Allow your investment banker to act as a buffer between you and your prospective buyer. This prevents your emotions from jeopardizing the deal.
3.   Carefully check out any company before you retain it. Ask for references. Choose a firm that is familiar with your industry.
4.   Determine who in the firm will be representing you and your company.
5.   Be clear about financial arrangements before you sign any contracts.

There are many books about selling small businesses. For a basic overview, try *Buying and Selling a Small Business*, by Michael Coltman, $8.95, Self-Counsel Press, 1704 N. State Street, Bellingham, WA 98225.

For a more sophisticated approach, including detailed listings of equipment appraisers and aquisition funds, try *Cashing Out: How to Value and Sell the Privately Held Company*, by A. David Silver, $39.95, Enterprise-Dearborn, 520 N. Dearborn Street, Chicago, IL 60610-4354.

Dealing with Venture Capitalists

Most entrepreneurs believe venture capitalists expect them to trade their decision-making power and a big chunk of equity in exchange for the cash.

Although venture capitalists do expect generous returns on their investments, they want to be your strategic partner, not your boss, according to four experienced venture capitalists appearing at a recent Los Angeles Venture Association breakfast meeting.

"You should view us as your business partner," said Frank Do, a principal of Chemical Venture Partners in Los Angeles. Every year, Do's firm invests about $250 million in growing companies, managing a $2.5 billion investment portfolio for Chemical Bank in New York.

Last year, venture capitalists invested about $3 billion in U.S. businesses, a fraction of the $15 billion or so invested by private investors. Still, small-business owners flood venture-capital firms with hundreds of business plans every day.

"We receive about 1,000 plans a year," said Thomas Gephart, chairman of the Ventana Growth Fund in Irvine. Of those, a handful of companies receive funding from Ventana.

What kinds of companies are attracting venture capital in the 1990s? Telecommunications, business-to-business services, medical products, and companies involved in cleaning up the environment are hot, the venture capitalists said. Biotechnology and software companies are having a tough time. Biotech companies are having trouble coming up with marketable drugs, and software prices are plummeting.

When asked for an example of a good deal, Do shared this success story:

A few years ago, Chemical Venture Partners bankrolled a doctor whose company provided X-ray services to nursing homes. The company flourished, acquired other small players in the market, and was eventually sold with the help of an investment banker. While Chemical earned about $7 million on its investment of a few million dollars, the doctor received $9 million when the company sold. By agreeing to stay on and work for the new owners, the doctor received an additional $9 million after three years.

Robert Hoff, general partner of Crosspoint Venture Partners in Irvine, said his firm had recently backed a team of people who ran the vehicle-financing department at a bank.

"They did an incredible job building a $1 billion portfolio when they were working for others," said Hoff. "We thought it was likely they would do even better when they began working for themselves."

With Crosspoint's help, the new firm quickly built up a $75 million credit line for financing vehicle purchases.

Have you ever wondered where venture capitalists get their money?

Much of it comes from public and private pension funds. Every five years, for example, Crosspoint raises $60 million to $65 million from pension funds.

Crosspoint then invests between $1 million and $5 million in about twenty growing companies.

Unlike banks, which charge a fixed amount of interest on loans, venture capitalists expect to earn about ten times their initial investment after five years. Most venture capitalists also seek to own about 20 percent of the firms they invest in.

So how do you get a venture capitalist to consider investing in your company?

First, you have to find the right firm to approach. Most people rely on the *Pratt's Guide to Venture Capital Sources.* The directory, published annually, lists about 800 venture-capital firms around the world, providing names, addresses, phone numbers, and industry preferences, among other details.

"The key is finding the right match," says Yong Lim, *Pratt's* editor. "Many entrepreneurs make the mistake of going to the biggest companies when a smaller one might be better."

Although the companies listed in *Pratt's* aren't individually screened, Lim tries to make sure the companies are legitimate venture capital firms.

TIPS

Attracting Venture Capital

Here are some tips from successful venture capitalists:

1.   Include a six-to-ten-page summary with your business plan. Include a brief overview of what your company does, your management team, your competition, and prospects for growth.

2.   Venture capitalists want to know who is running the business and who the brains behind the products or services are.

3.   If you have a great idea but no experience, team up with a veteran manager before you seek venture capital.

4.   Find a firm that already invests in your industry.

5.   Be prepared to show you've invested your own money in your company first.

6.   Prepare detailed, audited financial reports. These are more important than pie-in-the-sky projections.

7.   Ask your attorney or accountant to introduce you to a venture capitalist.

8.   Remember, venture capitalists look for experienced management teams first, great products and ideas second.

Pratt's costs $225, plus $5 shipping and handling. It's available by writing to Venture Economics, 40 West 57th Street, New York, NY 10102-0968. Or call (212) 765-5311.

For information on joining the Los Angeles Venture Association, write to LAVA, 1341 Ocean Avenue, Suite 129, Santa Monica, CA 90401.

Joining a Franchise

When business is slow, small-business owners often feel vulnerable and lonely. But, instead of giving up, many are signing up with major franchisers who provide additional training as well as moral and marketing support.

"Businesses join a franchise to take advantage of the marketing support and the economies of scale," says Meg Whittemore, franchise editor of *Nation's Business* magazine and coauthor of *Financing Your Franchise* (McGraw-Hill).

Whittemore said print shops, hardware stores, automotive repair shops, hotels, and travel agencies are among the small businesses most likely to convert to a franchise.

"Conversion is often a way to preserve the small-town retail base and that would have disappeared without a bigger framework," she says.

Kim Whitfield, of Fort Walton Beach, Florida, joined a bigger travel company because she was looking for marketing support, additional training, and information.

"When I was independent, it was hard to call the agency down the road for help," Whitfield says. Because most airlines, hotels, and cruise ships pay travel-agency commissions based on volume, Whitfield says she knew she could make more money right away by converting to a franchise.

Whitfield contacted 10 travel-agency franchisers before settling on Travel Agents International Inc., based in St. Petersburg, Florida. The company has about 360 locations nationwide. She chose TAI because the company charges franchisees a monthly fee rather than a percentage of sales, which could be as high as 10 percent for the other travel franchises she considered.

Since converting to TAI, Whitfield says her business has nearly doubled. She posted more than $1 million in sales in 1993 and expected more in 1994. Whitfield is one of sixteen independent travel agencies that joined TAI in recent months, according to Roger Block, president. Block, a former banking executive who seriously considered putting travel agencies in his bank branches before federal banking rules changed, said TAI agents can earn up to 50 percent more on commissions than small, independent agents.

"Most mom-and-pop agencies don't have the professional marketing materials that we do," Block says. "Because we all operate under the same name, we contribute to a marketing fund and can produce glossy, four-color brochures."

In addition to marketing materials, TAI provides ongoing sales training and close to 100 educational seminars a year for its agents. "Sixty percent of people who go into a travel agency are ready to purchase something, but only 15 percent of the sales are closed," says Block. He says TAI trainers work with agents to dramatically improve their closing rates.

Block says he likes to sign up successful agencies doing between $2 million and $10 million in annual sales. If an independent agency fits the bill, it can join TAI for an initial $2,900 fee. The first year, the agency pays a $500-a-month royalty fee, which increases to $750 after that. The agency must also make some physical improvements, such as buying wooden, not metal, desks and buying new TAI signs. TAI agents are also required to wear navy-blue blazers with the company logo.

"You have to look prosperous and successful for people to trust you with their money," Block says.

Andy Trincia, spokesman for the International Franchise Association in Washington, D.C., says that although his trade association does not keep track of the number of conversions, conversions have become more common in recent years.

"It's a great way for people with successful businesses to increase their chances of longevity," says Trincia. "Franchise companies are going to pursue the successful independents."

Increased buying power and cooperative advertising campaigns attract many business owners to franchises, according to Don Boroian, chief executive officer of Francorp, a franchise consulting firm in Olympia Fields, Illinois.

"We are seeing an increase in conversion franchising principally because the economy has taken a big toll on small independent businesses that cannot compete with the Kmarts and Wal-Marts in retailing," says Boroian.

TIPS

Converting Your Business to a Franchise

1. Meet with other franchise owners in your area and ask them how responsive the franchiser is to their needs.
2. Shop around. Review the franchise offerings from several companies to compare the benefits and disadvantages.
3. Make sure you are mentally prepared to give up full control over your business.
4. Check with state and federal agencies regulating franchising to make sure the company you choose is reputable.

Retirement Planning Strategies*

All entrepreneurs face the challenge of balancing the financial needs of their money-guzzling businesses with their personal needs to plan for comfortable retirements.

When you work for a big company, forced saving is easy. The company usually provides employees with company-sponsored 401(k) plans or an established profit-sharing program. Small-

*Portions of this appeared in the September 1994 issue of *Working Woman*. Reprinted with permission.

business owners, on the other hand, must take time away from their businesses to research their options and set up their own retirement programs.

The conflict is this: Any small business, whether it's profitable or not, demands constant infusions of cash, competing for the very same dollars you know you should be saving for your retirement.

"If the choice is funding a pension plan or the next investment, the entrepreneur will fund the investment to save the company," says Loraine Tsvaris, a senior vice president at U.S. Trust in Manhattan.

Tsvaris and other investment advisers warn that too many entrepreneurs face the risk of not being able to retire in style because the bulk of their assets belong to the business.

The way to secure your personal future is to make sure your business has other sources of capital, including bank financing and a substantial business credit line. Establishing a strong banking relationship early in your entrepreneurial cycle is essential, according to bankers.

"Part of the reason why businesses suck so much money from their owners is because they are self-funding—doing everything with their own money," says Judith Phillips, vice president of Harris Trust & Savings Bank in downtown Chicago.

The problem is especially acute for women business owners, who have a tougher time getting traditional bank financing. "If these women had external financing and good counsel, this wouldn't be the case."

Despite recent financial inroads, many women business owners contend they have a tougher time than their male colleagues when it comes to obtaining bank loans.

Phillips recommends that a business owner develop a close relationship with a bank early in the company's history. Most banks require a business to be at least three years old and profitable before they'll make a loan, but these requirements are easing.

You might even begin by applying for a "microloan," a loan of under $25,000, and repay it quickly to establish a solid credit history. (See Microloans, page 157.)

In addition to helping you finance the growth of your business, most major banks have trust departments that can provide you with retirement planning information and accounts. You may spend a few thousand dollars formulating a detailed retirement plan, but it will be money well spent.

"Now is the time to plan your finances and figure out where you want to be in twenty years," advises Phillips. "It's not too soon to be thinking about retirement because twenty years goes by so quickly."

Phillips suggests hiring an experienced and well-recommended fee-based financial planner. It's best to work with someone who makes his or her money by giving solid advice rather than from the commissions generated by selling investment vehicles.

Entrepreneurs between the ages of forty and fifty should also look into their parents' financial situation and be sure the family is well aware of any estate-planning or tax issues related to their parents' financial health.

Although it may seem premature, by the time you turn thirty you should be setting some money aside every month and every year, even if the amount fluctuates. Starting early makes financial sense too.

There's a staggering difference in outcome based on compounding interest rates, according to Jonathan Lewis, a financial planner for Smith Barney Shearson in Sherman Oaks, California.

"If someone contributes $2,000 to an individual retirement account every year for seven years, between the ages of twenty-eight and thirty-four, the account would have the same value as if they began contributing at age thirty-five and kept going for thirty years," says Lewis.

Lewis says his greatest challenge is encouraging busy entrepreneurs to stop long enough to set up a retirement plan. A good first step is to figure out how much money you'll need for a comfortable retirement and then work backward to figure out ways to reach that financial goal.

Bob Carlson, publisher of *Retirement Watch* newsletter, says one way is to estimate how much you'll need to get through your first year of retirement, then subtract your guaranteed payments, including your pension and Social Security. While many people think their expenses will drop during their retirement years, Carlson cautions that just the opposite may be true. You might travel more or devote yourself to expensive hobbies.

How much time you devote to planning for your retirement depends on where you are in the entrepreneurial cycle and how close you are to needing the money.

At fifty-two, Phyllis Apelbaum became acutely aware of her mortality, especially after surviving a bout with breast cancer a year ago. But for partners Julia Dunlop and Patty Schreiber, both in their mid-thirties, retirement seems very far away.

Apelbaum, president and owner of Arrow Messenger Service in Chicago, started Arrow in 1973 with a $3,500 inheritance from her father. Twenty-odd years later, she runs a bustling full-service messenger company with 170 employees and sales in excess of $5 million.

The company, which also provides trained temporary help for mailrooms and photocopying departments, has grown by about 15 percent a year.

"Throughout the earlier years, all I could do was just get by," says Apelbaum, who is a single mother. Her first major investment was a condominium in downtown Chicago in 1981.

"It was a year before I allowed myself to buy a piece of furniture," she admits. "Between the mortgage and the condo assessment, I thought, What if something happened to Arrow? What would I do?"

A few years later, as the company grew and prospered, she bought a summer house near Lake Geneva in Wisconsin for herself and her son, Mark, who later joined her to serve as vice president of operations for Arrow.

Although Apelbaum initially plowed every spare dollar back into the business to fuel its rapid growth, she was determined to set aside a few thousand dollars each year. "I always saved in small ways," she says. "I used to buy savings stamps and turn them into savings bonds. Saving was natural for me."

As the business flourished through the 1980s, she began buying "old-lady blue-chip stocks" for her Individual Retirement Account. She was conservative in her choices.

"I don't run for the newspaper when the Dow goes up or down," says Apelbaum. In addition to her stocks and real-estate portfolio, which includes Arrow's building on Walton Street, Apelbaum has several insurance policies. Her recovery from breast cancer last year pushed her to evaluate her insurance coverage.

"I want to be sure I have enough insurance to cover the inheritance taxes," says Apelbaum, who purchased additional annuities in 1994.

Apelbaum both safeguarded her retirement and decorated her home by investing in art, specifically paintings by Carmel, California, artist Raymond Page.

"I enjoy the paintings, but I know if things get tough, I could sell them."

A few years ago, Apelbaum made an uncharacteristically risky move with some of her retirement funds. She invested more than $50,000 in a start-up company committed to developing a female condom that was approved by the FDA in 1994. The Reality brand finally reached drugstores in the fall of 1994. She invested in Wisconsin Pharmacal, which makes the Reality condom, because she believes in its president, Dr. Mary Ann Leeper.

"It's the only stock I look at in the newspaper," she admits. "This product could be my ship coming in. I've felt very good about it for a long time."

Apelbaum has this advice for entrepreneurs trying to divide money between their business and their retirement fund:

"When you are starting out, you are putting all your hopes, dreams, and what little bit of money you have on the line," she says. "When you get healthier, begin to balance the needs of your life with the needs of your business."

While Phyllis Apelbaum is about ten years away from tapping her retirement fund, Julia Dunlop and Patty Olver Schreiber, the thirtysomething owners of the graphic arts firm Olver Dunlop Associates, have about thirty years to go. Their seven-year-old design firm, which recently moved into expanded loft space in Chicago's artsy River North area, employs six, including the partners. Revenues in 1994 were around $500,000.

The partners launched the business with their own funds. Three years later, solid cash flow and a good reputation helped them to secure a revolving commercial credit line, which meant they could rely on the bank rather than their own paychecks to fund their growth. It also freed them to contribute to retirement funds and even to think about providing retirement benefits for employees.

Schreiber, who is thirty-five and recently remarried, began 1994 with the goal of putting about $3,000 a month into various retirement funds with her husband. "He also has a 401(k) plan at work." Their strategy is simple: They follow a strict household budget and pay into savings every month, mostly investing in mutual funds. They use only one credit card and try to pay off the balance monthly.

Dunlop, thirty-six, is a bit ahead of Schreiber, retirement planning-wise. Her dual-income household has been saving about $4,000 a year since 1983. Her husband, a former banker who now owns an equipment-leasing business, set up IRAs invested in high-growth stock funds. Setting money aside is a priority for their family, Dunlop says. "We have a low-key lifestyle," says Dunlop. "We have no new furniture and we don't take huge vacations."

The partners hope to set up a retirement plan for their young employees. "Most of our employees are between twenty-three and twenty-seven years old," says Dunlop.

"We know what we do now can make a huge difference in ten years," adds Schreiber.

Bambi Holzer, a vice president and retirement-planning consultant for PaineWebber in Los Angeles, says, "About 75 percent of my business comes through accountants who insist that their entrepreneurial clients see me."

The biggest problem: "Americans are not savers—we're spenders," Holzer says.

But self-employed entrepreneurs have many attractive retirement options to choose from, according to Jim Berliner, a principal in Westmount Asset Management, based in Century City, California.

"There are very few hurdles to setting up IRAs, Simplified Employee Pension, or Keogh plans," says Berliner, whose firm manages about $60 million for many entrepreneurs and self-employed professionals. "These have very low cost and few legal reporting requirements, yet you have the ability to put away as much money as people working for big, big companies."

TIPS

Bob Carlson's newsletter is an excellent source of information for anyone preparing for retirement. Carlson is an attorney, CPA, and insurance consultant. Subscriptions to his newsletter are $99 a year. For information, write to: Kaliedescope Publishing Ltd., 1420 Spring Hill Road, Suite 490, McLean, VA 22107. Or call (703) 821-0571; (800) 820-0422.

12 Steps to a Worry-Free Retirement, by Daniel Kehrer (Kiplinger Books, $14.95) is a great resource. Kehrer, editor of *Independent Business* magazine, has written a practical, readable book featuring a step-by-step financial plan to help you figure out just how much money you'll need to invest now to meet your personal retirement goals. It's available in bookstores or by calling (800) 544-0155.

Fear of Finance: The Women's Money Workbook for Achieving Financial Self-Confidence, by Ann B. Diamond, is a bit simplistic, but another good source of retirement-planning information. Her workbook is based on financial-planning seminars that she conducts for women. The HarperCollins book sells for $12.50.

Berliner, like other financial planners, says there is no magic number for how much entrepreneurs should set aside each year.

"Put aside as much as you can afford," he suggests. "Make the sac-rifice if you can."

And remember, the money you put into tax-exempt invest-ments now will actually reduce your tax liabilities because you'll pay taxes later when you retire.

A final word of advice from Berliner: Don't wait any longer to begin planning for your retirement. "The cost of procrastination is high."

MORE SAVINGS TIPS FOR ENTREPRENEURS

1. Even if you don't pay yourself a salary, write a check to your savings plan every month when you sit down to pay your bills. It doesn't matter if it's only $50, the money will add up quickly.

2. If you do nothing else, set up an Individual Retirement Account and sock away $2,000 a year. It will reduce your taxes and build your nest egg.

3. If you need office equipment or furniture, consider buying it used and put the difference between the new and used price into your retirement savings account.

4. Launch a cost-reduction plan around your business (start by reading *Save Your Business a Bundle*, by Daniel Kehrer [Simon & Schuster]). Put all the money you save into your re-tirement fund.

5. Find a good fee-based financial planner to help you create a retirement plan to fit your needs. One size does not fit all when it comes to retirement plans.

6. Accept that if you are lucky, you will get old and need money to live on after you are tired of working so hard!

Legal and Insurance Issues

When it comes to legal matters, entrepreneurs should have one goal in mind: to spend as little time and money as possible with lawyers. However, lawyers are essential when you are negotiating a business deal, signing a commercial lease, or protecting your trademarks or patents.

How do you find an ethical, experienced lawyer when you need one? The secret is not waiting until you are facing a legal emergency. Ask friends and colleagues for referrals, and whenever possible, look for someone who understands your business or industry. Your state or local bar association can also make referrals. If you are going to need patent or trademark protection, don't scrimp on finding good legal advice. This is a very complicated area of law, and you will end up placing your company's key assets in jeopardy if you make a mistake. (One note: I obtained trademark protection for Succeeding in Small Business® on my own, but it took many hours to accomplish.)

I was smart enough to seek good counsel when I was given the opportunity to sign a syndication deal with the Los Angeles Syndicate. I quickly learned that most business attorneys didn't have a clue about syndication matters. I was referred to several entertainment law firms, because they were skilled in contract negotiations. But when several firms asked for a $3,500 to $5,000 retainer, I knew their services were way beyond my reach. Thanks to my best adviser, my uncle Steve Coan, I was introduced to someone who saw the potential of what I was doing and was willing to work on a percentage basis.

We laugh about the tiny checks I sent Jerry Gottlieb during the first few years of our working relationship. Some months, I didn't send enough money for him to buy paper for his photocopying machine. Now, they are a bit more substantial and I owe a tremendous amount of my business success to his savvy negotiating skills.

Once, I hired the managing partner of a major law firm to negotiate a deal with a very big client. It cost about $20,000 in legal fees and the project was a disaster, through no fault of the attorney. The lesson learned: My attorney told me he didn't like the way the deal was coming together and advised us to walk away. I didn't and paid the price.

If you are in a fast-growing, sexy business, you may be able to find an attorney willing to represent you in exchange for equity in your company. This happens a lot in the high-tech field, but most attorneys are not willing to take that kind of financial risk.

For many basic legal questions, contact the Nolo Press at (510) 549-1976. They publish a series of excellent self-help legal books for small-business owners.

A Great Alternative to Litigation

Across the country, more and more small-business owners and managers are turning to mediators and arbitrators to solve prickly problems without going to court.

Mediation helped office manager Peggy Jester collect delinquent medical bills. Frustrated by the lack of results when she turned past-due accounts over to a traditional collection agency,

Jester, who manages a Louisville medical office, says she was surprised at how much money mediator Mark Stein brings in. He also charges her half what the collection agency does and maintains good relations with patients.

"Mark sends out a nice letter asking why people haven't paid their bills and wondering if they want to discuss anything with the doctor," says Jester. "His approach is very effective and very few patients are offended."

Stein, president of Mediation First, with offices in Louisville and Atlanta, is one of thousands of mediators helping small-business owners resolve all sorts of disputes from breach-of-contract to sexual-harassment claims.

"Mediation is not a substitution for sound legal advice, but it is a substitute for litigation," says Stein, who has been a mediator for about fourteen years.

Mediators act as neutral third parties, bringing people face-to-face to settle their disputes. Mediation is not only a quick and direct way to solve problems, it is extremely cost effective and seeks to repair relationships rather than to destroy them.

"Mediation works to solve disputes without the wasteful expense of lawsuits, lawyers, legal maneuvers, posturing and the like," says Joseph Hellman, a family-law specialist in New York City. "By eliminating lawyers' posturing, mediation creates a forum for people to speak directly to each other."

Hellman, who mediated a dispute between three sisters sorting out the future of their family's retail business, serves as a mediator for a pilot program set up by the U.S. District Court in New York City.

"If the mediator's got the right kind of imagination, almost any problem can be solved," Hellman says.

Stein, of Mediation First, says many companies are turning to mediators to settle sexual-harassment claims. He serves as the neutral party, bringing the people face-to-face to work out their differences. Most of the time, a solution can be reached in one session.

"In most cases I've dealt with, the woman simply wants the harassment to stop," Stein says. "She doesn't want to lose her job or to see the man lose his job."

Stein has helped business owners settle harassment cases and saved them the time and expense of going to court. He also mediated a nasty dispute between a utility company supervisor and his coworkers by bringing them all together for a frank discussion.

"We met and representatives of the department came up with an agreement with their new supervisor," Stein says.

The Los Angeles County Bar Association's Dispute Resolution Services Inc. is a pioneer in the mediation field. The program began in 1978 as a Neighborhood Justice Center in Venice. About 1,500 volunteer mediators settle disputes in six offices in Santa Monica, Long Beach, Pasadena, East Los Angeles, Hermosa Beach, and Los Angeles. For information on the program, call (213) 896-6526.

Between July 1, 1992 and June 30, 1993, DRS mediators handled about 650 business-related cases, out of 6,000 total, according to executive director Lauren Burton.

"We have a wide variety of trained mediators," says Burton. "Some are lawyers and social workers, but we also have psychologists, realtors, engineers, and newspaper reporters."

People pay $20 to initiate a mediation. If the dispute is business-related, it costs $150 for the first session; subsequent sessions cost $100. In some cases, the fees can be waived.

Burton, who served on a federal commission exploring the future of the American judicial system, says that by the year 2020 the primary methods of solving disputes will be mediation and arbitration.

"Courts will be reserved for the most serious of cases," she says.

While just about any sort of conflict can be resolved through mediation or arbitration, if you want to establish any sort of legal precedent, you'll need to go to court.

While mediators act as neutral third parties and help the parties reach their own solutions, arbitrators listen to evidence and make decisions the parties agree to abide by.

"The single biggest advantage of using private arbitrators is to have the matter decided by someone who has expertise in the particular industry or profession you're in," says Rocco Scanza, regional vice president of the American Arbitration Association in Los Angeles. "The idea is to get someone within your business or industry who understands the customs and practices."

The association has thirty-six offices around the United States. Scanza says most arbitrations take less than four months to complete and can cost thousands of dollars less than litigation.

Nationally, arbitrators resolve about 60,000 cases a year, with 3,500 to 5,000 cases handled in Los Angeles, Scanza says.

In most cases, if you agree to arbitrate a dispute, you cannot appeal the decision.

TIPS

Mediation and arbitration work best when:

1. Both parties agree to participate voluntarily in the process.
2. The parties agree on a neutral third party and agree to split the cost of his or her services.
3. Both sides are seeking a speedy and cost-effective resolution of a conflict.
4. Both sides agree to abide by the decisions reached.
5. Both sides want to maintain a business relationship after the dispute is resolved.

American Arbitration Association, 140 W. 51st Street, New York, NY 10020. Phone: (212) 484-4000.

Mark Stein, Mediation First, 101 Crescent Avenue, Louisville, KY 40206. Phone: (502) 897-3020.

The Importance of Patents

In 1986, Jeff Haines, president and chief executive officer of Royce Medical Products in Westlake Village, California, decided the best way to grow his company was to launch a new line of innovative orthopedic products. Haines poured money into developing new products and obtaining patents for them.

"It's a strategy that's been so effective it's made us a leader in our little part of the medical-products industry," says Haines, whose company holds more than twenty domestic patents. "In fact, 75 percent of our total sales come from the new products we've patented since 1986."

Unfortunately, many small-business owners are reluctant to protect their products because they think obtaining a patent is too expensive or time-consuming. But the U.S. Patent and Trademark Office is not an impenetrable fortress. In fact, the government lends a hand to entrepreneurs by offering reduced filing fees for individual inventors and small businesses. And even with outside legal help, it can cost as little as $2,000 to patent a simple product or technology.

Although it usually takes between eighteen and thirty-six months to obtain a patent, it's worth the wait: A U.S. patent offers protection for seventeen years.

"Patents are useful as a sword to keep other people away from your market," says Steven Sereboff, a patent attorney with Spensley, Horn, Jubas and Lubitz in Century City, California.

Sereboff, who specializes in computer-related patents, says patents can be moneymakers, even if you don't intend to manufacture the products yourself. Once you obtain a patent, you can license others to make and sell the product.

A good tip: Work with a patent attorney who is familiar with your industry. Most people don't realize that patent attorneys are required to have an undergraduate degree in engineering or one of the physical sciences. In addition to passing a bar exam, they have to pass a comprehensive exam given by the U.S. Patent and Trademark Office.

Christopher Darrow, who represents Royce Medical, was a mechanical engineer who got laid off from his aerospace job in the early 1970s.

"The patent system is good for competition in general because it forces competitors to come up with something new," says Darrow, a partner with Poms, Smith, Lande & Rose in Century City who has helped individual inventors and multinational corporations win patents.

Once you obtain a patent, it's essential to protect it from infringement. Patent infringement suits, which are filed in federal court, can be costly. However, Darrow says about 90 percent of all infringement cases are settled prior to trial.

In many cases, infringers end up buying licenses to manufacture the product. This not only strengthens your patent, but brings in additional revenues.

In addition to protecting Royce Medical's splints, braces, and other products, Darrow has helped other inventors patent an earthquake-resistant dome and cardboard sunshades for automobiles.

Because the system is designed to stimulate competition, the new and different versions of successful products are often much better than the original.

Darrow and other patent attorneys say small businesses should incorporate their patent program into their overall business plan and set aside money to cover the expenses.

You can write to the U.S. Patent and Trademark Office for application information: Commissioner of Patents and Trademarks, Washington, DC 20231.

One Inventor's Tale

"People say that inventions are like the movie industry. Lots of movies fail, but people keep making them because the one picture that makes it big makes up for the others that don't."—Scott Penza, inventor

Many entrepreneurs dream of bringing a new product to the market and making millions, but few even get through the patent process. Here's one entrepreneur who did.

Scott Penza worked so hard getting a patent for his favorite creation that, when he finally did get the patent, he says his initial reaction was more relief than joy. "It was more like a very long pregnancy. All I felt initially was relief," Penza says.

Creating practical gadgets with clever names like Lamp-Shades is the mission of Penza's company, West Los Angeles–based The Penzart Collection. His other invention, for example, is Crib Notes, a device that plays nursery rhymes when it senses a baby crying.

Penza's baby is called Lamp-Shades, a pair of Ray-Ban sunglasses perched on the top end of a gooseneck reading lamp. The reading lamp is also an eye-catching conversation piece. It sounds simple, but Penza says it took more than three years to perfect because he had to find just the right technology and design to create his vision of a pair of sunglasses that would feature glowing frames while still functioning as a reading lamp.

Penza is emphatic about what his invention is and what it isn't. "It's not a lamp with a pair of sunglasses on it. It's a pair of sunglasses that are a lamp," he says.

Rather than using neon, he discovered he could make the frames glow with electroluminescence, a technology that has been around for more than fifty years but until recently has been used in relatively few applications—like jet-aircraft instrument panels, personal pagers, and designer wristwatches.

Penza expected to go to market in late 1994 with his invention, which received a patent in February 1994. He won't say how much he spent to develop Lamp-Shades and get the patent, but he says anyone who applies for a patent should expect to spend "a minimum of $5,000 just to get the initial paperwork going and to get the initial design work done."

One of the biggest obstacles Penza faced was from designers and manufacturers who said his invention couldn't be built. "We were told 'No, no, no, you can't do it,'" he says. He estimates he talked to sixty designers and manufacturers. Some said the lamp couldn't be built or wasn't practical. Part of the problem was that he wanted to interest a designer or a manufacturer in fronting some of the development costs in return for a share of the profits.

Penza finally got his patent—number 5,283,725—dated February 1, 1994, with the help of a law firm specializing in patents. He describes it as "a beautiful document with the gold seal of the Patent Office." He strongly recommends that anyone thinking of applying for a patent hire a legal firm that specializes in patent law.

"You can try to do it on your own, but there are issues that arise that really require an expert," he advises.

When to hire the firm, however, is debatable.

Many inventors wait until they have a prototype and finished drawings before they approach a patent-law firm on the theory that they'll spend less money for lawyers that way. That thinking is sound, he says, but he hired his law firm when all he had was "a cocktail napkin sketch and a couple of rough mockups that I had done."

The disadvantage to his approach was that it cost a little more in legal fees, but the advantage was that it allowed the law firm to work with him in addressing patent issues throughout the course of his developing the lamp.

"There are two schools of thought here. One is that you're going to spend a lot of money if you don't already have the product built before you hire the law firm. That's true, but if you go ahead and walk into a law firm, you might save yourself a lot of trouble if you find out during the process that what you're trying to patent has already been patented," Penza says. "It would be a horrible waste of time to spend three or four years working on something and then find out that it has already been patented."

Penza says that whether a product qualifies for a patent depends on the answer to one question: "Is it unique?" He says his lawyers proved that Lamp-Shades is unique because this was the first time a pair of sunglasses illuminated in this way. As early as 1908, someone invented reading glasses that had a light bulb in the nosepiece, Penza says, but that invention required the wearer of the glasses to lug around about forty pounds of batteries and a six-foot cable.

Among the lessons Penza says he learned in developing and patenting Lamp-Shades:

- Don't give up your day job. Penza has a full-time job in the advertising business, and his six partners also have full-time jobs.
- Don't put all of your money and time and resources into one product unless that's the only product you have. Devote at least a third of your time to one or two other products.

Penza says the one remaining question about Lamp-Shades is "Will people buy it?" "The market will answer that," he says.

Contact Scott Penza, president, The PenzArt Collection Ltd, 1511 Sawtelle Boulevard, Suite 288, Los Angeles, CA 90025. Phone: (310) 364-4313.

Nolo Press created a software version of David Pressman's excellent book, *Patent It Yourself*. Contact Nolo Press, 950 Parker Street, Berkeley, CA 94710. Phone: (510) 549-1976. Nolo has several other great books on how to obtain trademarks and patents on new products.

Licensing Tips

Sometimes you can save the time and trouble of inventing something by licensing the rights to make or distribute someone else's invention. Rudy Cervantes, for instance, was one of the first people to convince Walt Disney Studios and Charles Schulz (*Peanuts* creator) to allow him to put Mickey Mouse and Snoopy on novelty neck ties.

Sports teams, colleges, television shows, hit plays, rock stars, video heroes like the "Mighty Morphin Power Rangers" all grant entrepreneurs the right to use their images on an endless variety of merchandise.

The secret to licensing success is predicting a trend and getting to the originator before anyone else does. You also need capital to produce the products, a distribution system, and an attorney who is experienced in licensing and obtaining legal rights to trademarked and patented material.

Some people, like Skip Pierce, took advantage of working for a major company and having access to popular characters—in his case, Mickey Mouse and Donald Duck.

Pierce, president of Sounds Fun, Inc. used licensing to put a new twist on character wristwatches. Picture Mickey Mouse or Donald Duck telling you the time as their mouths move in sync with the actual character voices. Pierce is the man who invented the technology behind the synchronized mouthpiece. And while he was at it, he went ahead and perfected the voice chip as well.

Pierce has been a progressive engineer for more than twenty years. During this time, he also nurtured a healthy working relationship with Walt Disney Imagineering, where he spearheaded the development of the audio and video systems that ultimately ended up at the Epcot Center and Tokyo Disneyland.

Pierce spent five years with Disney, and another eight years consulting for them.

That thirteen-year time investment in Disney ultimately played a pivotal role in their licensing Pierce's wristwatch technology.

But what probably helped Pierce most was that he had himself a truly original product. No one else had ever been able to give a voice and matching lip movements to a character wristwatch.

Pierce says his Disney license allows him to manufacture and sell his product line of character timepieces nationwide, and in many international markets, as well.

"This was a new category that had never been seen before. None of Disney's other licensees had ever done this," Pierce says.

What kind of advice would Pierce give to a burgeoning inventor?

"Come up with a product that's so exciting they can't help but give you a license," Pierce laughed.

Limited Liability Companies:
An Important New Entity

by Mary Hanson, Esq.

Business owners and their advisers should consider a new form of business entity when structuring their businesses.

This new type of entity is called a limited liability company (LLC). It provides the best characteristics of S-corporations (a popular form of small-business ownership) without their limitations. It also offers a combination of benefits that no other legal entity can provide.

Nearly every state has adopted laws authorizing LLCs.

The key attraction of the LLC is that it combines the corporate flow-through tax characteristics of partnerships and corporations with the limited personal liability provided by corporations.

In partnerships and limited partnerships, general partners are

Reprinted by permission of Mary Hanson. Mary Hanson is a business attorney in Torrance, California. She works with owner-operated businesses and publishes a newsletter on topics of interest to business owners. Subscriptions to the newsletter are available by calling (310) 543-1355.

exposed to personal liability from the operation of the business. In contrast, the LLC provides protection from personal liability to all shareholders or equity owners (called "members" in an LLC), whether they take part in management or not.

The LLC can be very useful in particular for joint ventures between companies (or companies and individuals) and for entities that would otherwise be (or would have liked to be) corporations.

Tax Treatment

The IRS considers an LLC to be a form of partnership rather than a corporation. In recent years the IRS issued rulings on the treatment of LLCs formed in compliance with their respective state laws. Those rulings, which allowed the partnership (flow-through) treatment, gave the LLC movement an additional boost. States like Nevada and Wyoming make the LLC "bulletproof."

This means the LLC is assured of the desired partnership treatment for federal tax purposes. Other states, such as Delaware and Illinois, allow greater flexibility for the parties and their attorneys to create an LLC with various characteristics. Of course, the flexibility allows the possibility of missing the requirements and being treated as a corporation.

Drawbacks

There are drawbacks to using the LLC. One drawback is that banks, businesses, and other institutions may be unfamiliar with LLCs and reluctant to do business with them.

Another concern is that an LLC should wait for the state to authorize LLCs. Some states' LLC laws do not authorize the use of LLCs for professional practices, even though the LLC may be an appropriate and desirable entity for a law practice.

Business owners and advisers also need to check the state tax treatment of LLCs. Each state has different tax arrangements. In California, LLCs are required to pay a minimum franchise tax, as corporations are, and are also subject to a tax on gross receipts. In short, some states impose a state tax on the LLC, so that the LLC is not a 100 percent flow-through entity.

The LLC will undoubtedly be more costly to form than a corporation or even a limited partnership, since it has characteristics of both.

The flexibility allowed in determining the management responsibilities, tax matters, voting rights of the members, rights of members to participate in management, buyout provisions, rights to transfer interests, etc., means that much more time must be spent by the individuals and the attorney in the formation of an LLC than would be spent on the formation of a corporation.

Insurance Tips

Most entrepreneurs have a tough time dealing with insurance matters because they can be confusing and insurance often seems like a needless expense. But avoiding insurance is not prudent. The key is to find a good independent insurance broker who represents several carriers. This way, you explain what you need to your agent and let him or her do the legwork to find the best policies for you.

A good book to start with is *Insuring Your Business*, by Sean Mooney, Insurance Information Institute Press, 110 William Street, New York, NY 10038.

Here's a basic list of insurance issues to think about:

1. Health insurance for yourself and your employees
2. Disability insurance for yourself and your employees
3. Liability insurance for your business
4. Business-interruption insurance
5. Vehicle insurance for cars, trucks, etc.
6. Workers' compensation insurance

Finding affordable health insurance remains one of the most challenging issues for most business owners. Many companies turn to their trade or professional associations to qualify for lower-cost group rates. In many small businesses, employees whose spouses have corporate jobs are encouraged to remain covered by those group policies. Although business owners are generally compassionate and want to take care of employees, the cost of health insurance for a small business can be astronomical. That's why so many businesses do not offer health coverage, or if they do, delay it for several months after employment.

Short- and long-term disability coverage is a must for all business owners. No one likes to think about getting hurt or falling ill, but think what would happen to your business if you couldn't work for even a month. (See next section on what happened to the Sak family.)

Although disability coverage is costly, it's worth it. You can reduce the premiums if you are willing to go three months without benefits after an illness or injury. Be sure to shop around, though, and get several estimates before you settle on a policy.

Liability insurance is also essential to protect your business if someone gets hurt on your property. But preventing accidents should be your top priority. Even one slip-and-fall accident can wipe out your insurance and make it very difficult to obtain future coverage. If you have expensive equipment, be sure to insure it against theft. You can cut costs by selecting a high deductible, though.

Business-interruption insurance is also costly, but can save your business from ruin if you are displaced by a fire or other calamity. Some policies cover payroll costs, others will pay rent and other expenses until you can get back on your feet. Business-interruption policies are very complicated and specific, so make sure you really understand what the policy will and will not cover.

If your business owns vehicles, be sure to buy adequate insurance coverage for them. If your needs change and, for instance, you are not taking that old truck off your property anymore, reevaluate the coverage and reduce it. Make sure your policies cover your employees, if they are driving company cars. And, before you hand anyone the keys, run a motor vehicle check and look into his or her driving record. This is perfectly legal and is usually available free or for a nominal charge from your state department of motor vehicles.

Last, but certainly not least, is workers' compensation insurance. The requirements vary from state to state. Some states make it easy for employers to get coverage and provide it to very small businesses or difficult-to-insure businesses. Other states make it very tough and expensive.

California has some of the strictest antifraud provisions in the country and has, in recent years, actually reduced the cost of insuring workers.

This is another area where a skilled consultant can save you time and grief.

Key-Person Insurance

Remember how tough it was on everyone when your manager or top salesperson went on vacation last year? The office just wasn't the same without him or her around.

Imagine how you would feel if that key person was gone forever—either permanently disabled or, worse, dead. Apart from the emotional turmoil, can you begin to calculate the financial impact his or her loss would have on your business?

Although no one likes to think about death and disability, making sure you and your partners or key employees are adequately insured can prevent the collapse of your company. In these tough times, it's tempting to scrimp on insurance, but savvy small-business owners do everything they can to protect what they have.

Key-person insurance, as it is called, is purchased by the business to cover a specific individual. You can buy both disability and life insurance for key people. The premiums are not deductible as a business expense, but if and when the benefits are paid, the money is tax-free. Most key-person policies name the company or corporation as the beneficiary, according to insurance professionals.

Years ago, Jim Sak, owner of Rose Rentals Inc. in Florence, Alabama, realized he was relying more and more on his young sons, Eugene and Duane, to help him and his wife, Betty, manage the family business. Eugene was responsible for the retail rental operation, while Duane looked after the equipment and repair side of the business. "When my insurance agent pointed out how important my sons were to the business, I realized I'd be in dire straits if they weren't around here," says Sak, who purchased key-person disability and life-insurance policies for his sons in the early 1990s.

Within weeks after the life insurance policies were issued, Duane Sak fell seriously ill with a rare blood disease. After undergoing medical treatment, including chemotherapy, Duane recovered and returned to work. But his frightening and unexpected illness threw the family into a spin.

"We didn't collect any benefits from the policies we bought, but we realized how close we came to the edge," Jim Sak says.

Brad Hall, the Saks' independent insurance agent, says he is especially sensitive about making sure the small-business owners he serves have adequate insurance coverage. When Hall was four, his forty-nine-year-old father was killed in an automobile accident.

"We had to sell his successful plumbing and heating business for ten cents on the dollar," Hall says. "My father's death was a major reason I'm in the life insurance business."

Hall and other insurance professionals say the cost of the premiums is minor compared with the money you would spend to keep the business going if a key person dies or becomes disabled.

"Small-business owners have so much of their personal and business assets tied up in the business, they usually don't have the cash available to weather a crisis," says John Aschenbrenner, vice president of individual markets for the Principal Financial Group in Des Moines, Iowa. Aschenbrenner, whose company insured the Sak family, said small-business owners should review all their insurance coverages at least once a year.

John Davies, an executive with Massachusetts Mutual, says small-business owners without adequate insurance coverage may

face a moral dilemma if an uninsured, key employee dies or is seriously disabled, leaving his or her family without any income.

If that happened, would you be able to meet another family's
living expenses?

"People have fire insurance for their business, yet they are
much more likely to be disabled than burned down," Davies says.

Take Action

If you don't have personal disability insurance call your agent
and get some NOW. Did you know that three out of ten workers
between the ages of thirty-five and sixty-five are disabled for ninety
days or more? Nearly one in five will become disabled for five
years or more before they turn sixty-five. These unsettling statistics
are from the UNUM Life Insurance Co. of North America in Portland, Maine.

Disability costs can exceed 8 percent of payroll, and half of
these costs include direct-benefit payouts and administrative costs.
Disability can also increase your company's medical costs.

If you think no one in your company, especially you, will become disabled, think again. In 1990, American companies lost 60
million workdays from occupational injuries and illnesses, according to the UNUM disability experts.

The leading disabling illnesses are cancer, AIDS, back pain,
Epstein Barr syndrome, carpal tunnel syndrome (caused by repet-
itive stress injuries to the wrists), heart conditions, and psychiatric
and stress-related illness.

When you are looking into buying disability insurance, ask
about both long- and short-term policies. Short-term policies usually replace 40 percent to 70 percent of earnings, while long-term
policies replace about 60 percent of predisability earnings.

The longer you wait to receive benefits, the cheaper the coverage will be.

One note: If you work at home, you'll have a tougher time
obtaining coverage. Insurance companies are wary of insuring

home-based entrepreneurs because they think we'll purposely drop a filing drawer on our foot to collect benefits.

What's Your Insurance IQ?

Many people aren't quite sure what kind of insurance they need, how much they need, or how they should shop for it. What's your insurance IQ?

1. Which of the following types of hazards is not covered under the standard homeowners' policy?

    a. Fire   c. Wind

    b. Earthquake   d. Theft

2. There is little need for disability insurance because you are far more likely to die before age sixty-five than become disabled for at least ninety days. *True or false?*

3. A good rule of thumb for determining how much life insurance you need is to buy an amount equal to six times your annual income. *True or false?*

4. Even if you leave your job, you may be able to continue health-care coverage under your former employer's policy. *True or false?*

5. If your car is an older model with little value, what portion of your insurance should you consider dropping or taking the highest deductible possible?

    a. Uninsured motorist   c. Comprehensive

    b. Collision   d. Towing

6. You should always buy term insurance instead of whole-life because term buys you more coverage for each dollar spent. *True or false?*

Credit: Institute of Certified Financial Planners

7. You should have "replacement-cost" homeowner's coverage instead of "cash value" coverage, even though it is more expensive. *True or false?*

8. The liability portion of a homeowner's policy, typically between $100,000 and $300,000, is sufficient for most families. *True or false?*

9. Before buying a life or health-insurance policy, check the company's credit rating with at least three or four of the five rating services. *True or false?*

10. Most people should have credit insurance to ensure their loans will be repaid. *True or false?*

Answers

1. *b. Earthquake.* Flood coverage is not standard.
2. *False.* A thirty-five-year-old is three to four times more likely to be disabled at least ninety days than to die before age sixty-five.
3. *False.* No rule of thumb is good for everyone. You should buy an amount that meets your needs, goals, and stage of life.
4. *True.* By law, you may be able to continue coverage for another eighteen to thirty-eight months, though you'll have to pay the entire premium.
5. *b and c.*
6. *False.* No one type of insurance is right for everyone.
7. *True.* Replacement coverage (better yet, "guaranteed replacement") pays for the cost of rebuilding your home or replacing contents. Cash value only pays for what an item was worth at the time (its garage-sale price).
8. *False.* Most financial planners recommend that people consider "umbrella" liability coverage up to $1 million. It's cheap, it covers other insured assets such as a boat or

car, and might save you from losing all your assets in the event of a lawsuit.

9. *True*. Never depend on one rating service. The carrier should have a top rating from at least two or three of the rating services.

10. *False*. Most credit insurance is overpriced. Beef up your savings to handle payments or increase your basic life and disability coverage.

If you answered at least eight out of ten correctly, great. Five to seven is fair. Four or less, you'd better bone up on insurance. In any event, it pays to seek impartial insurance advice before buying.

Family

Succession

Running any small business is backbreaking. Mix in family history, sibling rivalry, jealousy, envy, and greed, and it becomes even tougher. Although family-business experts differ on why, most agree that the majority of American family businesses don't make it to the third generation. The founder's insistence on being fair to all the children usually ends up destroying the business.

"Succession planning requires a real commitment to the business and the family," says Mike Cohn, founder of the Phoenix-based Cohn Financial Group and author of *Passing the Torch* (McGraw Hill).

Cohn says, "Too many succession plans are death driven." He suggests every family have a detailed plan in place, long before they need it. Although not every family can afford to hire specialists to draft a succession plan, there are all sorts of books, college courses, and seminars available.

According to Cohn, the toughest family-owned-business problems are:

- Children who don't work outside the business before coming into it.
- Children who don't know when the company ownership will pass to them.
- Founders/parents trying to treat all their children equally.
- "Intergenerational baggage"—doing things the same way the founder or second generation did it.

Cohn introduced me to the Rosen family, a family working hard to keep the business going while stepping through a thicket of emotional and transitional problems.

Harris Rosen said he is doing everything he can to ensure that his family's Pawtucket, Rhode Island, candy business, E. Rosen & Co., passes safely to his children. He's hired a financial expert who specializes in the financial aspects of succession planning. For a while, the family met monthly with a coach who helped them sort through the emotional issues surrounding an eventual change of command.

"My dilemma is very simple," says Rosen, who is in his early sixties. "I know I should never be a millstone around my sons' necks, but I want to stick around because it's fun and I enjoy the business."

Harris, better known as "Hershey," inherited the family candy business from his father, who started it with $1,800 he borrowed from his father. Rosen has spent forty years in the business, which is best known for its Schoolhouse Candy line. The company makes jelly beans and other sweets in plants in Massachusetts and Rhode Island.

Long ago, he established rules for allowing his children to enter the business. "I required my sons to go to the graduate school of their choice, to work on the outside for three years, and to be financially independent of me before I decided whether or not they could come into the business," Rosen says.

Robert and John, now in their early thirties, met their obligations and began working their way through various departments.

They learned how to make candy, sell it, and even how to mold plastic Easter baskets.

Sensitive to how his long-time employees might feel about the heirs joining the firm, Rosen says he encouraged his employees to welcome his sons into the business.

"We have lots of outside people here who are vice presidents," Rosen says. "They knew that no one need fear for his or her job because there was only one job my sons wanted and that was mine."

TIP

Resources

The Family Firm Institute, an association of professionals who advise family businesses, publishes an annual *Directory of Consultants and Speakers*. The 1994 *Directory* lists more than seventy family-business resources, some of which may offer advice on hiring relatives. It's free from: The Family Firm Institute, 12 Harris Street, Brookline, MA 02146. Phone: (617) 738–1591; fax: (617) 738–4883.

Beyond Survival: A Guide for the Business Owner and Family, by Leon Danco, $19.95 plus $3.50 shipping, is available from The Center for Family Business, P.O. Box 24268, Cleveland, OH 44124. Phone: (216) 442–0800.

Keeping the Family Business Healthy, by John Ward, $29.95, can be obtained from: Jossey-Bass, 350 Sansome Street, San Francisco, CA 94104. Phone: (415) 433–1767.

Networking with other small family businesses can be helpful. Check local listings for a family business association in your area. One such group is: The Midwest Association of Family Business Owners in Oakbrook Terrace, Illinois. Phone: (708) 495–8900; fax: (708) 495–8901.

Rosen's daughter, Elizabeth, in her mid-thirties, is a graphic designer who has decided not to work for the company. However, she will inherit a portion of the business and attended the monthly family-counseling sessions.

Once a month, family-business consultant Kathleen Wiseman spent a day with the Rosens in a Providence hotel room. Together, they sorted through a myriad of personal and business challenges facing the family.

"The trick here is to understand and celebrate the differences and then to negotiate them," says Wiseman, founder of Working Systems in Washington, D.C.

Wiseman says the coaching process is "tough." Hershey Rosen has a strong personality and his sons are close in age.

"But this is a family with many resources," says Wiseman. "This transition is something Hershey has looked forward to and he is very willing to listen to his sons."

Keeping It in the Family

In a secret ballot, on a vote of four to three, Erich March's dream of managing his family's thriving Baltimore funeral services business died. The eldest of four children who grew up above the family's first funeral home in Baltimore, March assumed he would succeed his father, William March. Like his younger brother Victor, he went to college. While Erich studied psychology and creative writing at Johns Hopkins University, Victor chose accounting and returned to the family firm after a stint at Coopers & Lybrand.

When the family and nonfamily management team gathered in the conference room in the early 1990s, Victor's financial experience heavily influenced the vote and he won.

"The vote made me wonder," says Erich March. "Four to three is a close race." He doesn't know who cast the deciding vote. He only knows that he and two others felt he should be Marcorp Ltd.'s chief executive.

Upset over his defeat, he admits thinking about quitting the business his father and mother started in 1957, but only for "about thirty seconds."

What did he do after losing the vote that day? "I just went back to work."

March says he eventually accepted his defeat. "I love my brother and everything is for the good of the company."

Victor March remembers the vote as well. His brother was extremely disappointed.

"My dad recommended who he would like to see succeed him and it was me," says Victor. "Then we went through the process of putting up nominees."

Victor understands why his father felt his financial and accounting background was better suited to managing the flourishing funeral services company, which primarily serves Baltimore's black community.

"There are things I'm doing here that I had certainly seen in work in the real world," says Victor, who has grown the business to 130 employees and $10 million in annual revenues. "I had seen how businesses needed to diversify to be successful."

The senior March, who still drops in a few days a week to see how things are going, shares a small office with Erich.

"My oldest boy thought he should be it," admits March. "I sensed a bit of tension after the vote, but it passed."

Pitting brother against brother rarely happens in the business world, but volatile emotions and rivalry set America's family businesses apart from the mainstream. Given this often-wrenching turmoil, it's not surprising that, historically, 70 percent of family-owned small businesses do not make it to the second generation, according to Connecticut Mutual Life Insurance Company, whose agents help families draft succession plans. If a company manages to complete a successful transition, only between 10 percent and 30 percent of those companies will successfully be passed along to the third generation, according to family-business consultants.

It's time that family-business owners begin grappling with their future. According to the U.S. Small Business Administration, nearly 50 percent of all family-owned businesses in the United

States are expected to need some sort of transitional planning by the year 2000, since many businesses were started by men who served in World War II.

If you don't deal with succession planning when the founder is healthy, you may face the terrible consequences of death-driven estate planning. Without the careful transfer of ownership and a management-succession plan, a family too often ends up selling the business to pay estate taxes of more than 50 percent in some states.

Succession planning, once considered a taboo subject for family discussion, has come out of the closet. The *Family Business Advisor* newsletter offers intimate details and management counseling every month. The Family Firm Institute represents hundreds of family-business consultants and succession planners around the country.

It's no surprise so many family-business owners shy away from the topic of succession planning. Not to means they must admit they are mortal. Notice how many family business owners say "If I die" rather than "When I die." Apart from the admission of mortality, it takes substantial time and money to create a solid succession plan. Deciding who will run the company when Dad or Mom is gone drags up deep emotional issues and forces parents to make painful and often unpopular choices.

Succession planning can be expensive and time-consuming. A well-crafted estate and succession plan can cost up to $100,000 if the family business has substantial assets and many children to deal with. The best plans are created by a team of specialized advisers. The team should include an experienced professional counselor to handle the emotional and relationship issues, a savvy tax attorney to handle the legal and estate issues, and a skilled accountant to oversee the complicated and confusing state and federal tax ramifications.

Succession planning also forces a family to grapple with their very reason for being in business. Based on interviews with scores of family-business owners and family-business advisers, I've put together these suggestions:

Tip One: Admit You Are Mortal and Need a Succession Plan

"A business owner can be exposed for years and years to these issues, yet he isn't ready to act," says Ross Nager, a partner at Arthur Anderson's Center for Family Business in Houston, Texas. "Then something happens, maybe a friend dies and it becomes a trigger."

That's exactly what happened to Thomas Moser, founder of Thomas Moser Cabinetmakers in Auburn, Maine. Moser, fifty-eight, was shocked when a fifty-seven-year-old friend died unexpectedly.

"Suddenly, I'm seeing an end game coming up," says Moser, a former English professor, who began making handmade furniture to decorate the old New England homes he and his wife, Mary, renovated. Although they enjoyed remodeling kitchens and reviving the centuries-old homes, they were always at the mercy of the weather. "With free-standing furniture, you have more control," said Moser, who creates elegant, upscale furniture based on eighteenth- and nineteenth-century designs.

His friend's death forced Moser to grapple with his own unspoken fears of dying young. "I've outlived my father, who died at forty-nine, and my father-in-law, who died at fifty-six," says Moser. "I've never been security driven; perhaps that's the character of the entrepreneurial spirit. Now, I'm feeling 'intimations of mortality.'"

Since he doesn't have a substantial life-insurance policy to pay estate taxes, he wonders what would happen to his successful family business if he should die soon. The fear of sudden death is coupled with the fact that he had designated no successor among his four sons, all working in the twenty-one-year-old family business. He was also feeling restless and wanted more time off to travel and explore the rain forests.

He admits he's always managed the business by the seat of his pants, although he believes it could grow much faster with a professional manager at the helm.

His sons, all in their thirties, have different jobs. Matthew is in sales, Andrew works on the production floor, Aaron is in contract sales, and David is the company's showroom coordinator. The sleek furniture painstakingly produced by Moser's 100 employees is sold through showrooms in San Francisco, Philadelphia, Dallas, and Portland.

Sales are about $6 million a year and the Mosers plan to open new showrooms in New York City and possibly Pasadena, California.

In 1994, Moser began discussing a succession plan with his accountant and spoke with other family-business owners he knew around Maine.

"It's like talking about sex education, I don't want to but I have to," he says.

Besides grappling with which son is best suited for the top position, Moser says he is deeply concerned about the fate of his loyal employees. "We have profit sharing now," he says. "The success of this company is due in large measure to the people who work here. I have an enormous debt to them."

Moser considered creating an employee stock-ownership plan or ESOP, as it is called, as part of his ownership succession plan. With a well-crafted ESOP, the employees, as well as his sons and grandchildren, can share ownership of the company. ESOPs can reward nonfamily managers with company stock, an attractive option to the traditional transfer of ownership when parents pass along their stock directly to their children.

Family-business owners with children working in the business have to be careful about how they treat nonfamily managers and employees. Morale can plummet if nonfamily employees realize their career options are limited or their jobs are in jeopardy if a family member steps into a top-management slot. Moser and other family-business owners can benefit by creating an outside board, according to Dr. Leon Danco, considered one of the nation's pioneers in succession planning. He recommends creating a board when your business is mature enough to last through a change of leadership. Another tip: Create the board when things are peaceful, not when a major turf war has broken out.

"Family as family members have no place on a board," Danco says. Instead, invite successful business owners and industry leaders you respect to sit on your board and pay them for their time. (Meeting fees range from $1,000 to $5,000 for smaller companies.) If good people are hesitant to become legal directors of your company because they don't want to be liable for corporate problems, create an informal board of advisers as an alternative.

Tip Two: Take a Realistic View of Your Children and Relatives

Not every founder can expect to find the perfect replacement already on the payroll. If your employees cringe when your son strides into the office an hour late, that's a signal that he may not be the right choice to succeed you. As difficult as it is, you have to objectively assess your children's skill and experience. If it's lacking, don't overlook it. Send them back to college, off to a training program, or out to work for someone else.

If you have the opposite problem and no one wants your job, accept that you can't force your children to love the business the way you do. Remember, your business is what kept you away from all those Little League games and school plays.

But if your son or daughter or nephew shows a real interest in the business, encourage it. Start by assigning a small project and see how he or she works, with you and the other employees. Does he show initiative? Does she seem to enjoy her work? Does he ask you a lot of questions about the business? You can tell if someone is truly finding joy in their job, or simply showing up to collect a steady paycheck.

When Noemi Pollack began the Pollack Public Relations and Marketing Group, she was content to represent a few local clients. She had no clear vision for the Century City, California, firm, which now employs eight and has billings of about $1 million, other than to enjoy herself.

She rarely thought about the future until her youngest son, Stefan, proposed that he join the firm. He was twenty-two, fresh out of college, and she didn't take his offer seriously.

"I said, 'Write me a job description.' I really put him through the hoops to find out what he would do if he reported for work on Monday morning," Pollack says.

She was so impressed with his marketing plan, she hired him. But her young son's arrival sent the small agency into a spin.

"My number two person was extremely threatened by Stefan," recalls Pollack. "She was not to be consoled, and despite my assurances, she left eighteen months later."

Through the years, Stefan has learned to downplay his role as the boss's son. "I've really made a point of treating him like an employee here and he has resisted that," she says. To ease tensions around the office, she urged Stefan to take a course in interpersonal communications.

The Pollacks' story has a twist: While Stefan had no public-relations experience, Noemi's oldest son, Gregory, is a public-relations executive with big-agency experience. But thirty-two-year-old Gregory has never shown an interest in joining his mother's small firm.

"We've both agreed that we would not be a good team, temperamentwise," says Noemi.

She is the sole owner of the firm. Stefan has no equity in the company, but Noemi has a simple provision in her will turning over the sole proprietorship to him.

"Stefan will get the whole company, with all its wonderful ways, burdens, and debts," she laughs.

What does this proud mother like best about working with her twenty-seven-year-old son? "His loyalty, dependability, and trustworthiness."

She admits to worrying about the day when Stefan might decide to go elsewhere. "I've learned to depend on him so much," she says. "Would I be disappointed if he came to me with a great job offer? Yes, but I've told him he's free to move on."

Stefan says he plans to stay. He says he enjoys working with his mother, although once in a while they "bump heads."

"She's very headstrong," Stefan says. "She knows what she wants. I'm very headstrong and ambitious, too."

He says the toughest thing about working for his mother is having to back off at times because, at least at this point, she is very definitely the boss. "I remember that she's the president and not my mother."

Stefan Pollack relies on his mentor, Dr. Alan Carsrud, visiting associate professor of entrepreneurship at UCLA, for counsel from time to time. Carsrud teaches a popular family-business seminar at the school.

"The big issue in family business is that people don't listen," says Carsrud. Most of his students and private consulting clients lose sight of why they are in business and whether or not the business is worth passing along. "Every family-business owner must ask himself or herself, 'Is the business here to feed the family, or is the family here to feed the business?' "

In other words, are the people depending on the business to support them really the best people to be running the business?

Carsrud says one of his toughest consulting jobs involved a thirty-four-year-old son whose father dangled the family business "like a hot dog in front of his face."

"He promised the son he would take over someday, but someday never came," says Carsrud. The son finally realized his father was manipulating him and moved on to create his own success.

Tip Three: Rely on Nonfamily Mentors to Train Your Successor

Fred Ruiz, president and chief executive of Ruiz Food Products Inc. in Dinuba, California, waited about five years before taking over leadership of the family's prosperous Mexican-food-products company from his father, Louis.

In the mid-1960s, the Ruizes started their business with $400 cash, a freezer, and a stove built from junkyard scraps. They began making bean enchiladas, selling trays of the Mexican staple to mom-and-pop grocery stores in Central California's vast agricultural valley.

In the beginning, they made bean enchiladas because there were fewer restrictions from the health department and they couldn't afford to meet the kitchen standards required to fill tortillas with meat or cheese.

Ruiz, who has been honored by the U.S. Small Business Administration for his entrepreneurial efforts, began his succession plan early, at about forty, because he wanted to assure the smooth passage of the company from his father's hands to his.

"I began dealing with succession planning when I was forty," says Ruiz. "Although my father and I had started the company together, I felt the company belonged to me. I felt I had done the bulk of the work and it wasn't fair for my brothers and sisters to have it."

When sales hit $12 million, compared to about $100 million in 1994, Ruiz sat down with a team of attorneys and accountants to draft a detailed estate plan. He negotiated a buy-sell agreement with his parents, Louis and Rose.

They transferred the stock to Ruiz and his employees. In turn, the family set up a trust to provide the senior Ruizes with a comfortable lifestyle. Louis Ruiz drops in to visit the food-processing plant nearly every day, supervising the maintenance department because he still loves to tinker with the food-processing equipment.

"My dad walks around, tells me everything that's wrong, and then goes back to his house," laughs Ruiz. "He's chairman of the board, but it is real frustrating for him. Although he hasn't been involved in the day-to-day operations for ten or twelve years, he still wants to be recognized."

Ruiz owns 48 percent of the stock and the company's ESOP owns 52 percent. Unlike many family-business owners who have no clear successor, Ruiz's eldest daughter, Kim Ruiz Beck, had expressed a strong interest in succeeding him. She's proud of her long-standing devotion to the business, beginning with her first job stamping cardboard boxes when she was seven years old. When her mother couldn't go on business trips, Kim accompanied her father to trade shows and business lunches.

None of Ruiz's other children, a son and daughter in their early twenties and a ten-year-old son by his second wife, have entered into the succession-plan equation, at least not yet. And, unless they apply for jobs soon, Ruiz says it's unlikely that Kim will have any competition from her younger siblings.

"If they want to own the company, they have to work for it," says Ruiz.

Although father and daughter frequently disagree, Ruiz says he and Kim have a terrific working relationship. It wasn't always so. When she was fourteen, she quit in a huff.

"I was working at Rosita's Mexicatessen, which was really a little outlet for our products at our old Tulare plant," recalls Kim. "I was a teenager and extremely sensitive. I felt like he was being overly critical toward me."

"Although she was doing a good job, I always found something to criticize," Ruiz admits. "You know how parents are."

She stormed out that day, but eventually returned to work in the payroll department and kept working until she went off to California State University at Fresno to get a degree in marketing. Degree in hand, Ruiz began as a data processor and moved on to become a brand manager. She's a vice president, reporting to the senior vice president for sales. Ruiz believes it's best that she report to other executives, not to him.

"I have a lot of respect for Kim," says Fred Ruiz. "She doesn't abuse her position in the company by saying to people, 'I'm going to tell my dad.'"

Still, Kim says she "feels sorry for those managers who have me reporting to them. But my job is to make my boss look good." Ruiz says her internal mentors are working very hard to teach her every aspect of the family's Mexican-food-making business because they know she is being groomed to succeed her father.

But it will be years before she takes over from Fred, who not only runs the business but serves on a variety of corporate boards and frequently judges business competitions.

Executive vice president Tom Colesberry will be named president long before Kim will, and she says it's okay. "My father is so busy, he books appointments a year in advance."

Right now, in addition to her marketing responsibilities, Beck says she plans to spend more time with her young children Tyler and Travis.

"Tom and my father make a great team," says Beck. "My father is a visionary. Tom knows the numbers."

Tip Four: If Need Be, Look Outside the Family for a Successor

Jacob Voogd (pronounced "vogued"), chairman of Evergreen Holdings, Inc., in Irvine, California, always liked having a tough outside board of directors. But he wasn't so happy when the board instructed the then-sixty-four-year-old entrepreneur to appoint a successor. "I told my wife, Joanne, I'm not indispensable," says Voogd. The board was concerned about Voogd's health. His zest for good food added to his girth, and company insiders said some board members feared Voogd might drop dead of a heart attack.

Although Voogd's daughter, Carla Ray, served as company treasurer and his son-in-law, Greg, worked in the oil collections department, the board felt neither was suited to succeed Voogd at the helm of the innovative oil-recycling firm, which collects and purifies oil collected from about 6,000 sites in California. Gas stations and quick-lube operators pay Evergreen to take their dirty oil away.

Although Evergreen gained national attention when soon-to-be Vice President Al Gore Jr. visited the company's Northern California recycling facility, it was time for the company to reach beyond its very specialized recycling niche.

After interviewing several executive-search firms, Evergreen retained Korn/Ferry International, one of the nation's largest recruiters. Account executive Virginia Ellison spent hours with Voogd and his management team, not only drafting a job description, but searching for clues as to exactly the type of person Voogd and the board wanted to fill the demanding position. Typically, executive search firms charge a fee equal to 33⅓ percent of the candidate's first-year salary and bonuses. It may seem hefty, but isn't finding the perfect person to run your business worth the investment?

Ellison says Voogd was unusual in that he had very specific qualities in mind for his successor. He wanted someone who was strong in the areas he was weak. He wanted someone he could trust. And, more than anything, he wanted someone who could make the company grow.

A months-long nationwide search brought in a handful of qualified candidates, mostly from the oil industry. The ultimate winner was David Camp, a former executive with Amoco Corp. in Atlanta who holds a Ph.D. in chemical engineering. He uprooted his family and moved across the country in September 1992.

Camp has made major changes. At the request of her father and the board, Carla Ray resigned as treasurer. Camp said Voogd felt it was best to "reduce the family influence at the company."

Camp also brought with him some of Amoco's management techniques, which are resulting in increased revenues and improved morale. "I'm putting in place policies that take away some of the vagaries of a family-run company," says Camp. "There were a lot of policy issues that weren't getting resolved."

Camp sits down with his top managers for a weekly brainstorming and problem-solving session. His consensus-building approach is much different from Voogd's more traditional "I'm the boss" management style.

Voogd, meanwhile, is spending his time traveling.

"He's enjoying life and he deserves it," says Camp.

Tip Five: Create a Skilled Succession Planning Team

"Family-business owners are starting to demand more of their advisers," says John Ward, a family-business consultant and professor at Chicago's Loyola University. "All the awareness building about succession planning is waking up lawyers and accountants."

Ward says select your team carefully. Talk with other clients and ask specific questions about the personality and working style of the advisers you may hire. Remember, you will be sharing your most intimate family secrets, hopes, and dreams with these people. If you don't feel comfortable with someone, move on.

Your accountant is a good place to start. If he or she isn't skilled in estate-planning issues, ask another family-business owner for a referral. You want someone fully conversant with the changing tax laws and someone who has done this work before.

Scores of major universities, including UCLA, the Wharton School at the University of Pennsylvania, and Loyola in Chicago, have special family-business programs and the professors often provide consulting services.

If your corporate attorney is not familiar with estate planning, again, ask for a referral. These legal documents are complex and require a plethora of agreements, including buy-sell agreements, stock transfers, deeds, property transfer agreements, wills, and often charitable trusts.

While you may feel that you are too busy or that things are going too well for you to delve into succession planning, force yourself to do it. And make sure you have someplace to go, before you pass along the reins.

"Semiretirement is screwing up the business part-time," says Leon Danco, whose book, *Beyond Survival*, is a family-business classic. "The outgoing generation has to have somewhere to go. The founder needs to know, 'What do I do when I stop banging my head on the desk?' "

Danco says most family-business founders equate retirement

Portions of this section first appeared in *Money* magazine.

"somewhere between euthanasia and castration." But, he emphasizes, you cannot have succession until "you've disposed of the first generation."

SUCCESSION TIPS

1.   Don't wait for the founder to fall ill to begin planning for the future.

2.   Assemble an experienced team of advisers to craft your succession plan. Include an accountant, tax attorney, and possibly a family therapist to deal with sensitive emotional issues.

3.   Face your own mortality and make your wishes for the future known as early as possible.

4.   If you can't find a family member to succeed you, look outside the family. Cast a wide net. Hire an executive-search firm to help, if necessary.

5.   Insist that your children work outside the family business before you find jobs for them.

6.   Treat your children and your employees fairly. This will minimize resentment among your employees.

Passing Along Your Business to Your Employees

Su-Fung Zau admits she's been losing sleep ever since her bosses asked if she would like to own part of the company where she works. Zau, who has served as controller of A.B.E. Corp., for the past six years, will eventually be a co-owner of the thriving, El Monte-based used office furniture company.

"When the Rays talked to me about it, I was shocked," said Zau. "It's a very unusual situation. Most family businesses go to the children or the grandchildren."

Many times, for many reasons, family business owners find it best to turn the business over to employees or recruit experienced outsiders.

For years, owners Bob and Lois Ray have grappled with who should inherit the business they founded in 1966. They decided that one of their sons, who works in the business, should inherit a piece of the company and other assets. But the Rays said they didn't feel he has the skills needed to manage the fast-growing business. They also ruled out their other children for various reasons, including the fact that one son owns a competing used furniture business.

The Rays' attorney, Rod Burkley, said he's been urging them to craft a succession plan for the past 15 years. Finally, when Bob Ray turned seventy, he began considering A.B.E.'s future. After much discussion, the Rays decided that Zau, who has been helping Lois Ray manage the company's finances for years, and general manager, Rick Follis, were best suited to own and manage the company.

"This is my choice," said Bob Ray. "If I'm going to sell to anyone, I'd like to sell it to my employees."

"I couldn't have chosen two people who I could have any more faith and trust in," said Lois Ray, who, as treasurer, has managed the company's finances for years. "I can't believe our good luck."

The Rays, who said they did not discuss their succession plan with any of their children, said the transition will take place gradually over the next few years. To make it easy, the Rays plan to give Zau and Follis generous cash bonuses so the successors can gradually accumulate the company stock.

"We'll probably sell it (the stock) to them as fast as they can afford to pay for it," said Bob Ray. "They'll own a small percentage at first, but it gives them a hell of a start. And, it will keep them dedicated toward making money for the company."

Follis, thirty-two, said he was working for a competitor when he met Bob Ray about four years ago.

"We have a relationship like nothing I've ever had before," said Follis. "Mr. Ray is like my family. We have the absolutely best communication—we think alike, we act alike—he's just got a few years on me."

Follis admits he and Zau, who is forty-two, felt a little awkward at first when they learned they were eventually going to co-own and manage the company.

"I'm very aggressive and she's very quiet," said Follis. "I've learned how to be more respectful."

"We respect each other," said Zau, of Follis. "We all know he's very smart."

Both agreed their skills and experience complement each other. Follis said his goal is to make the company a lot of money. Zau's is to save the company money.

The young successors are already testing new ways to boost sales, which have more than doubled in the past few years. Follis pioneered the concept of selling refurbished office partitions, as well as furniture. Zau said she is encouraging the company to expand its marketing efforts into the local Asian market.

"It's like a wonderful dream," said Follis. "I've never heard of this sort of thing happening before."

Burkley, who is a Torrance, California, attorney, said he is relieved the succession plan is finally taking shape and he's busy drafting the legal documents to implement it.

"By definition, succession planning involves other people," said Burkley. "Let them know who they are and what's expected of them."

Mike Cohn, founder of the Cohn Financial Group in Phoenix, is an accountant who specializes in succession planning.

"People tend to approach succession planning as a transaction and it's not," said Cohn. "It's a process."

Cohn said a winning succession plan requires years of open communication. Once the decisions are made, the owners have to spell out who will manage the business, who will own the business, and what will happen to the employees and shareholders.

"Most succession planning is death-driven," said Cohn. "We want to orient the process to thinking about today."

Meanwhile, Lois Ray says she is ready to pack up and spend some time relaxing in Hawaii.

"Bob and I have worked hard all of our lives," said Ray. "I want to enjoy the fruits of our labor."

But, she admits getting Bob to let go of the day-to-day challenges won't be easy.

"He's like a mother that won't let go of her child."

Surviving the Owner's Death

Very few small businesses survive the death of their owners, but the ones that do usually have one thing in common: they bring in outside expertise to help the successor solve existing problems and assure employees that the company has a future.

When Jim Smerz, president of Air Comfort Corp. in Broadview, Illinois, was diagnosed with cancer in the late 1980s, competitors were sure the company would fold. But they didn't expect that his wife, Nancy, who had been helping Jim manage the company behind the scenes for years, would step in after his death and turn the ailing firm around.

She accomplished the turnaround by hiring her former CPA-turned-crisis-manager to help her lay off dozens of employees, close a money-losing branch office, negotiate a new credit line, and refocus the company on its core business—servicing commercial heating and cooling systems.

"It was like being the captain of a lifeboat," says Smerz about the pain of laying off long-time workers. "If there were too many people, I knew we'd get swamped and all go under."

In addition to the layoffs, Smerz faced another major, yet fairly common, business disaster. When the company's banker heard that Jim Smerz was terminally ill, he demanded immediate payment of the company's maxed-out $1 million credit line.

"Our banker demanded the $1 million paid in ninety days because he didn't think a woman—meaning me—could run the business," recalls Smerz.

Incensed, Smerz and turnaround consultant Randy Patterson met with several other banks until they found a bank willing to stand by the company and its new owner and president.

While firing people, finding a new bank, and slashing costs were rough, Smerz's biggest challenge was firing a long-time employee and personal friend who expected to succeed Jim Smerz as president.

"I dismissed him very soon after the funeral," Smerz says. "In fact, it was about twenty minutes after I took over."

Despite the emotional and financial toll, all the changes Smerz made have paid off. Air Comfort, which was losing about $300,000 a year on sales of $10 million in 1991, posted a $250,000 profit on sales of about $9.1 million in 1992. In 1993 and 1994, the company was profitable again.

Air Comfort, which has been in the Smerz family since 1945, has about ninety employees working in two offices in Broadview, Illinois, and Merrillville, Indiana.

Smerz, who considers herself "more like Martha Stewart than Marge Schott," says she relied on adrenaline to keep going during those terrible months after her husband died at age fifty-two. "There was no way to stop feeling terrible," says Smerz. "I got up in the morning and gritted my teeth. But the people here at the company were very supportive."

Looking back, she wishes she and her husband had fully discussed the options and prepared better for the transition.

"We never actually sat down and said, What shall we do here?" says Smerz. "It just kind of evolved because my husband thought I could do it."

Her advice to others: If you or your key manager is seriously ill or injured, tell your banker, vendors, suppliers, and customers as soon as possible to keep the rumors at bay. She also suggests writing an emergency plan detailing the new chain of command and management team. And be sure to name a successor immediately so there is no confusion among your employees and customers.

"A lot of people are just a diagnosis away from what we went through," she says.

Looking back on how far the company has come, Smerz says she regrets not making the tough changes while her husband was alive. She worries that he died feeling guilty about leaving the company in poor shape. But she also believes he would be proud of her leadership and willingness to admit she needed help to turn the company around.

Pushing your ego aside is essential if a troubled business is to survive a major crisis, says David Allen, executive vice president of Buccino & Associates in Chicago, a crisis-management consulting firm.

"A small-business owner's ego is so wrapped up in the business, most won't get any help without a third party, such as an attorney, banker, or accountant, acting as a catalyst."

Allen says troubled small-business owners often refuse to admit they need help, even when their company is facing disaster.

"Denial is a word we use a lot," says Allen, whose firm has dozens of turnaround professionals based in six offices around the country.

Going Global

There is a myth passed from entrepreneur to entrepreneur: If your business isn't doing so well at home, think globally. That's where all the money is, and millions of consumers are hungry for American goods.

The problem is, it's a myth. If your business is faltering domestically, you won't have the time, money, or resources to crack the global market. That said, there are still tremendous opportunities abroad, and small businesses are vigorously participating in the global economy. About half of American companies with revenues under $100 million exported their products in 1993, according to a survey by the New York accounting firm of BDO Seidman.

Successful entrepreneurs who expand their businesses overseas follow these steps:

- They do their homework and learn everything possible about the country they want to do business in.
- They find smart, ethical partners in those countries.
- They commit their own time and resources to make the

deals because in many countries face-to-face contact between principals is expected.

- They take advantage of every resource the U.S. Department of Commerce has to offer, as well as private and nonprofit export information services.
- They rely on various state economic-development agencies to help them forge international business relationships.

The Export Small Business Development Center in downtown Los Angeles has become a beacon for entrepreneurs in California and beyond. The center hosts seminars, classes, and offers free and low-cost counseling services at (213) 892–1111.

"We are absolutely overwhelmed with the demand and the successes," says center director Gladys Moreau.

The passage of the North American Free Trade Agreement brought in hundreds of requests for information and help.

Moreau and other export experts say the biggest problem faced by entrepreneurs is an unwillingness to spend the time and money really figuring out the best way to deal with foreign business owners.

While Europeans may look and dress like Americans, they don't think like Americans. For example, the concept of due diligence, which is fairly standard in American business dealings, is considered offensive and intrusive to Europeans.

Cultural differences can also kabosh a seemingly perfect deal. One of the best books on doing business abroad is *Communicating with Customers Around the World*, by K. C. Chan-Herur. This nifty book has specific tips and suggestions for doing business in scores of countries. In it you'll learn tips like:

Never present a business card with your left hand in Asia, Africa, or the Middle East. The left hand is considered unclean in those countries. Never wear shoes in a Japanese home or restaurant. In France, never slap an open palm over a closed fist as it's considered vulgar. And in Spain, never give your host dahlias or crysanthemums because they are the flowers presented at funerals.

To order this $12.95 book, write to AuMonde International

Publishing Co., P.O. Box 471705, San Francisco, CA 94147–1705. Phone: (415) 281–8470. California residents add sales tax. All U.S. orders require a $3 shipping charge.

If you are interested in going global, another good basic guide is *The Learning Annex Guide to Starting Your Own Import-Export Business*, edited by Karen Offitzer ($8.95, Citadel Press, Carol Publishing).

One of the best free resources is a series of colorful country guides offered by AT&T. While they include ads and information on the company's international calling services, the guides are filled with tips on business etiquette, the local economy and customs. For back issues, call (800) 922–5324.

There are too many good books and resources out there to name them all here. If you feel overwhelmed by the prospects, start a file on one particular country that interests you. Clip articles and keep a journal on the country and all the information you collect. Talk to other business people who have been there. A good next step may be to sign up for a trade mission. The Small Business Administration hosts frequent trips abroad for entrepreneurs. You have to pay all your own expenses, but the government agencies provide a guide and will often schedule meetings or bring you to a trade fair or other event.

With so many great books and resources there is no excuse for making mistakes. And no excuse not to participate in the global economy.

"One in six American manufacturing jobs is now directly or indirectly related to exports," says Joe Cobb, an international economics expert for the Heritage Foundation, a Washington, D.C., think tank.

What to Know Before You Go

Ten Tips to Communicating Effectively with Customers Around the World

- *Keys to Success:* Observe, listen, and speak, in that order. Keep an open mind and show respect.
- *Do Your Homework:* Get briefed on must-know information, e.g., current business etiquette, communication do's and don'ts, cultural and customer sensitivities, current events and relevant history.
- *When and Why Meet:* Avoid dates on or around national holidays or vacation. Reconfirm date, time, objective, agenda, and people involved in meeting.
- *Language:* Learn to say a few words in your customer's language, such as "Hello," "Thank you," "Please," and "Excuse me." Bring your own interpreter.
- *Business Cards:* Bring lots of business cards—printed in both the local language and English.
- *Introductions and Greetings:* Use customers' last names, not their first names unless invited to. If unsure, ask how they would like to be addressed. Speak, act, and dress more formally and conservatively.
- *Communication Do's:*
  - Take time to create rapport and trust. People like to do business with friends.
  - Be sensitive to eye contact level, physical distance, time, and other nonverbal clues.
  - Avoid judgmental questions.
- *Communication Don'ts:*
  - Avoid discussing politics, religion, and social conditions.

- Avoid the U.S. "OK" sign.
- Avoid copying local gestures unless you are sure about their meanings and exact movements.
- *Business Gifts*: "Safe" gifts, such as pens, books, or quality items with a small corporate logo.
- *When in Doubt*: Follow your host's or local staff's lead.

Translate Your Materials into Dollars

Avital Technologies Inc., a Buffalo Grove, Illinois, maker of auto-security systems, moved quickly to open a sales office and begin serving the huge Mexican market soon after the North American Free Trade Agreement (NAFTA) was passed by Congress.

Marketing-department staffer Janice Patterson was responsible for making sure the company's brochures, sales materials, ads, trade-show displays, and technical manuals were translated into Spanish.

"It's always a good sales tool to have information available in the native language," says Patterson. "It means you care enough to make the information available to everyone."

Even though Mexican installers and sales reps might speak English, Avital, which has about twenty-five employees and forty sales reps in the United States, felt it was necessary to translate its technical and installation manuals.

"While words like 'on and off' are in English, we translated the instructions and the color of the wires into Spanish," Patterson says.

Your success in the global marketplace depends in part on carefully translating business materials into foreign languages, according to Gladys Moreau, executive director of the Export Small Business Development Center in downtown Los Angeles.

"Putting your presentation materials into another language communicates the serious purpose of the exporter," says Moreau. "It says you are not just flying in today, but making a commitment."

Moreau's Export SBDC provides referrals to translators, as well as counseling and seminars on doing business abroad. SBDC staffers speak a dozen languages and point business owners in the right direction.

Although translations are not cheap, it helps your foreign agents or distributors to move quickly into the local market, Moreau says. She recommends hiring translators here rather than asking your foreign agents to do it.

"If you don't do it here, you are at the mercy of the person at the other end," she says.

TIPS

Business owners interested in exporting are turning to the Export Small Business Development Center for help. Last year, a survey estimated Export SBDC clients exported $150 million worth of American goods. This year, Export SBDC director Gladys Moreau expects the total to double to $300 million. The Export SBDC is located at 110 E. Ninth Street, Suite A-669, Los Angeles, CA 90079. Telephone: (213) 892–1111.

The U.S. Small Business Administration is working with the Export-Import Bank to encourage lenders to participate in a new small-business financing program for exporters. The SBA can guarantee up to 90 percent of a loan amount up to $750,000. The money can be used to make or purchase goods for export or to finance accounts receivable.

Business owners interested in federal loan guarantees for exports can contact their local SBA office, or call the SBA Office of International Trade at (202) 205–6720.

Moreau also recommends hiring your own interpreter when doing business abroad. Be sure to fully brief the interpreter, explaining what your company does and what your business goals are for that particular country.

Barbara McDaniel, cofounder of Access Language Services in

Woodland Hills, California, says the translation market is growing as more American companies expand their horizons.

"Americans are being more sensitive to language when they conduct business overseas," says McDaniel, who formerly worked as a cross-cultural consultant in Chicago. Her firm relies on a stable of 200 freelance translators. Most of the requests are for translation into Spanish, French, German, and Italian.

With America's multiethnic workforce, many businesses hire translators to translate internal documents such as safety and training manuals. Translation services are not cheap: McDaniel says one should expect to pay about $1,000 to translate twenty pages of English to another language. In many cases, translators charge by the word.

Doing Business in Mexico

Steven Rothenberg didn't wait for Congress to sign off on the North American Free Trade Agreement. His tiny Santa Clara, California, software company moved quickly to sell computer programs to the Bank of Mexico to beat his competition.

Rothenberg, whose firm develops personal computer-based credit and collections software, admits he was surprised at how relatively easy it was to close the deal with the giant Mexican bank. Because he doesn't speak Spanish and never dealt with anyone in Latin America, Rothenberg retained an international attorney skilled in international software copyright laws and fluent in Spanish.

Rothenberg hooked up with Richard Neff, a Torrance, California, attorney well versed in copyright law. Neff, who has worked in international law for fourteen years, is the author of *NAFTA: Protecting and Enforcing Intellectual Property Rights in North America*.

"We clearly lead the world in the export of software, films, sound recordings, books, and copyrighted products," Neff says.

"The United States exports more than 70 percent of the software in the world."

Neff represents Rothenberg and several other small-business owners doing business in Latin America. He says that Mexico's expanding economy is hungry for American products and services. Mexico is already America's third-largest trading partner behind Canada and Japan. Total trade between Mexico and the United States is expected to exceed $70 billion a year, and by the end of 1994 Mexico will be America's second-largest consumer market, importing more than $50 billion worth of U.S. goods.

Neff and other international consultants credit President Carlos Salinas de Gotari with moving swiftly to strike down the majority of Mexico's trade barriers.

"Eighty-five percent of the permits once required to import U.S. goods have disappeared," Neff says. And, although shipping goods to Mexico is still not as smooth as shipping to Switzerland, U.S. companies are reporting fewer problems with Mexican customs officials, and shipments have a better chance of arriving intact.

One of Neff's primary objectives is to reduce the financial strain that can come with conducting international business, allowing countries to more easily take their business abroad. One of the ways he accomplishes this is through rigorous communications with his network of lawyers that spans forty-five countries. "My data base is gold," Neff says. And Neff's efforts to cultivate positive relationships with his international colleagues provides him with a variety of perks. He gets discount rates for his services by bartering information, and his network is so large that he can quickly provide needed services to business owners like Rothenberg.

Unlike many small businesses eager to sell internationally, Rothenberg didn't set out to sell his software in Mexico. Bank of Mexico officials found Rothenberg at a credit card industry trade fair a few years ago.

"When they invited me to a meeting in Mexico City a month later, I almost didn't go," Rothenberg says. "I didn't speak Spanish and I thought it was a real long shot that they would buy software from a small company like mine."

But an American member of the bank's staff convinced Rothenberg to attend the meeting, and his continued involvement in the negotiations increased Rothenberg's level of comfort. "I learned that you need to be patient but you also have to be firm," says Rothenberg. "The bank officials wanted us to come down and install the software before the contract was signed, but I said no."

It took about seven weeks to negotiate the contract for the deal, which was worth less than $200,000. The bank paid promptly via wire transfer, and Rothenberg sent a company representative to Mexico to set up the training program for the software, which is designed to help banks keep track of debts and recover money faster.

Rothenberg says "an incredible army of people" worked on the project, including a team of electricians who were called in at the last minute because the building where the computers were being installed lacked sufficient electrical power.

Apart from having to hire two temporary workers to translate the software and training manual into Spanish, the Mexican deal didn't cost the company more than servicing a domestic client.

Here are some tips for doing business in Mexico:

1. Find a trading partner with a good reputation and the right connections inside and outside the government.
2. Don't underestimate the importance of personal relationships. Plan on spending time getting to know the people. Prepare to spend a few hours on small talk, discussing sports and family.
3. Don't expect to make a quick buck. Deals take longer to put together, and you can expect to be paid slower, usually in ninety to 120 days.
4. If you are attracted to the lower minimum wages, remember there are hidden costs, including mandatory profit sharing and generous Christmas bonuses.

5. Be prepared to draft new contracts; most U.S. contracts do not apply under Mexican law.

Doing Business in Russia

Let's meet some successful entrepreneurs who have ventured outside the country to test their mettle in the international economy.

Ask American entrepreneurs what it's like doing business in Russia and they'll tell you: It's an adventure.

But little by little, as the emerging, independent republics improve telecommunications and attempt to slash red tape, American business owners are making progress in reaching Russia's 285 million eager customers.

Organizations like the year-old Russian-American Chamber of Commerce are also working hard to encourage trade and long-term opportunities. The chamber, based in Aurora, Colorado, acts as an information clearinghouse and works with about twenty other business groups to assist business owners on both continents.

"Americans are latecomers to this marketplace," says Deborah Anne Palmieri, chamber president and author of three books on the Russian economy. "Because of the Cold War, America has had the latest economic involvement with Russia."

Since the demise of communism, Palmieri says American companies have been rushing to catch up with German, French, and Japanese companies that have been operating in Russia for decades.

"There really are a lot of opportunities for small-business owners if they can get past the fear of dealing with a culture with which they are unfamiliar and get past the language barrier," Palmieri says.

Americans must also be willing to help train a new generation of Russian workers whose parents relied on the state to provide every necessity.

One of the best ways to learn about doing business in Russia is to talk to someone who's been there. Peter Reynolds spent an unforgettable year teaching a Russian crew how to operate a river boat on the Amur River in Russia's Far Eastern Territory.

Reynolds's challenges were many; he spent four days convincing local bureaucrats to clear a shipment of towels for the *Amur Star,* the eighty-passenger ship he was responsible for. After all the aggravation, Reynolds was finally allowed to pay a tax of less than $5 and collect the towels.

One of his most memorable management tasks was explaining to his Russian crew why they needed to use underarm deodorant—which he imported from America along with soap, coffee, and condiments for the ship's passengers.

In addition to language and cultural barriers, Reynolds coped with radical currency fluctuations and telephone lines that went mysteriously dead for forty-eight hours at a time. He also lived in an apartment owned by a KGB agent who assured him it had hot and cold running water. However, he was without a drop of hot water for eighty-six days in a row.

Now he can laugh about his experience in Khabarovsk, a city of about 700,000 people with only four restaurants.

"I think the Russians are among the most wonderful, accommodating people in the world," says Reynolds. "I decided I had made as much of a contribution as I could."

George Rose, a Russian-born attorney who specializes in putting Russian-American business deals together, says there has been remarkable progress in the last few years and it is getting easier to do business over there.

"The Russian learning curve has increased substantially as they learn how to do business with Americans and Western Europeans," says Rose, a partner in the Century City–based firm of Korbatov, Rose & Rubinstein. Rose and his partners, all natives of Russia, rely on their background and experience to help both Russian and American clients.

"The infrastructure has improved," says Rose. "You can place direct calls and you can get things printed out in Word Perfect."

Exchanging currency is also easier because, he says, it "seems like every grocery store" has a money-exchange counter. There are also about 2,000 commercial banks operating in Russia. But Rose says Americans who made a quick profit importing containers of consumer goods in 1989 and 1990 are finding it tougher to make money today.

"Some of the better opportunities have been taken," says Rose, adding that Russians are more savvy and are no longer accepting one-sided deals favoring their American partners. "If they feel they are being cheated, they will simply walk away."

But entrepreneurs willing to build any kind of manufacturing operations are warmly welcomed by many Russian republics, especially the Baltic nations closer to the West. There are still tremendous opportunities to serve Russian consumers, who need everything from clothes to toothpaste to sugar.

"There is one stratosphere of Russians who are very wealthy and the country is slowly getting richer," says Rose, adding that somehow many Russians have American dollars to spend.

"Franchising is also an excellent opportunity for small-business owners," says Rose. "If you could open a Baskin Robbins ice-cream store in the Russian Far East, you could make millions."

On the down side, Rose and Palmieri say many American entrepreneurs are being scared off by the well-publicized increase in crime and corruption. Russian mobsters are demanding protection money and threatening to harm business owners who don't pay up.

Americans are often stymied by having to deal with sixteen different legal entities, instead of one U.S.S.R.

"Within Russia you have many different entities and districts, each one with its own bureaucracy," says Rose. "It's good for law firms, but not so good for businessmen."

TIPS

Here are George Rose's tips for American entrepreneurs in Russia:

1. Plan to lose money on your venture for the first three or four years.
2. Buy political-risk insurance and insurance that protects your investment from drastic fluctuations in the rate of currency exchange.
3. If you don't speak Russian, hire an experienced guide. It might be a local business person, a consultant, or an attorney.
4. Look for opportunities to try something over there that you can't do over here. For example, there are entire towns without telephone systems or one ice-cream shop.
5. Be patient. It may take fifteen faxes to get one response.
6. Realize that when a Russian says no, he or she may not mean it.
7. Before you do anything, call the U.S. Department of Commerce for help, at (202) 482–4655.

Deborah Palmieri says the Russian-American chamber spends about $12,000 a year on newsletters, data-base services, and other sources of information. In recent months, her staff has worked with companies trying to establish a Russian-American television network and has worked to find financing for a Russian company that makes hydrofoils.

She offers these additional tips:

1. Remember that you are dealing with a society in the midst of an absolutely earth-shattering transformation.
2. Be aware of the criminal underworld.
3. Collect detailed information about your industry and specific business niche, including the geographical area you want to do business in.

4. Find the right Russian business partner. Beware of in-experienced Russians who claim to have a lot of contacts but who don't.

5. Have a written "risk-minimization plan," with specific scenarios outlining how you will deal with problems.

6. Use all the support services that exist, including the Commerce Department's Business Information Service for the Newly Independent States (BISNIS). It's based in Washington, D.C.

7. Set up your own communications systems, including computer electronic mail or satellite telephone systems.

Other resources include: *The Russian Survival Guide: Business and Travel*, published by Russian Information Services in Montpelier, Vermont. In addition to providing consulting and translation services, the company also publishes guides, maps, and information. For a free copy of their catalog, *Access Russia*, call: (800) 639–4301. Or fax: (802) 223–6105.

The Russian-American Chamber of Commerce, The Marketplace—Tower II, 3025 S. Parker Road, Suite 735, Aurora, CO 80014. For information, call (303) 745–0757.

Entrepreneurial Volunteers

If you are a successful entrepreneur willing to work long hours under challenging conditions for no money, the Citizens Democracy Corps wants you.

The private, nonprofit organization, based in Washington, D.C., has sent about 350 American entrepreneurs abroad to counsel and inspire novice business people in Central and Eastern Europe and the former Soviet Union.

"We look for business people who've been successful, not MBAs or doctors," says Marty Stein, who chairs the Corps' entrepreneurial program.

Stein, chairman of EyeCare One Corp. in Milwaukee, Wisconsin, says the Corps needs volunteers who "know how to get through the swamp without getting bitten by the alligators."

CDC needs successful entrepreneurs who are willing to spend three months or so overseas. Their mission: sharing secrets of success with local business people and supporting a worldwide free-market economy. The CDC provides volunteers with air transportation, local housing, and interpreters.

"For retired people like myself, this is just a wonderful way to get democracy going over there," says Myron Bort, a veteran meat-packing executive who had been to Ukraine several times as a CDC volunteer. Bort's parents emigrated to the United States from the Ukraine in 1910.

For thirty-five years, Bort owned a successful meat-packing plant in Canfield, Ohio. At its peak, his fifty-five employees provided processed pork and beef to forty-five supermarkets. Since retiring in 1985, Bort has volunteered for twenty projects for the CDC and other organizations, making good use of his ability to read and write Eastern European languages.

"I like to make sausages," says Bort, who recently returned from a stint at a meat-packing plant about ten miles from Kiev. "I like to put my boots on and try to teach the people how to make a profit."

At its peak, the plant's 2,000 workers produced about 110 tons of sausage a day. When the Soviet Union shattered and Moscow no longer controlled sausage production, the Kiev plant lost about 90 percent of its business.

On a good day, Bort and a skeleton crew of 300 made about six tons of sausage. He says the plant's managers were looking for incentives to encourage local farmers to send their hogs to the plant.

Robert Kennedy, president of Superior Chaircraft in Belton, Texas, brought his manufacturing experience and his wife, Bettye, to the Czech city of Pilsen.

"When I read about the CDC program, it appealed to me as a worthwhile and educational opportunity," says Kennedy, whose twenty-four-year-old company makes office furniture and employs about 250 workers in Texas and Southern California.

Kennedy and his wife spent three weeks working with Pavel and Zdena Fadrny at their company called Kazado. Like thousands of other entrepreneurs, the Fadrnys began the manufacturing business in their garage. Kennedy says the Czech company's biggest problem is taking on too many different projects, ranging from crafting wooden playground equipment to making metal dumpsters.

"I wrote a business plan for them. They were very responsive to all the suggestions," Kennedy says. "They were interested in how things work in America."

Although the Fadrnys spoke no English, they relied on an interpreter and managed to establish a friendly rapport with the Kennedys. "They are very warm and considerate people," says Kennedy. "They took us on trips to small villages so we could get acquainted with their culture."

Kennedy says the Czech people are dedicated to becoming an industrial nation again.

Meanwhile, Marty Stein hopes to sign up more volunteers because "if you have freedom without economic freedom, you've got no freedom at all."

TIP

The CDC was formed in 1990 to foster democracy and free-market economies in Eastern Europe. The Agency for International Development (AID) provides a portion of the funding for CDC's estimated $5 million budget. The majority of its funding, however, is provided by corporate and private contributions. John J. Murphy, chairman of Dresser Industries, serves as its chair. Board members include former secretary of state Henry Kissinger, Drew Lewis, chairman and chief executive of Union Pacific Corp., and Lane Kirkland, president of the AFL-CIO. For information on volunteering for the business entrepreneur program, call: (800) 394–1945.

Doing Business in Japan: One Woman's Story

Knowing how tough it is for big business to crack the Japanese market, is there any hope for a small business? The answer is yes—if you are patient, flexible, and willing to learn how business is really done in Japan.

"In the United States, buyers and sellers are pretty much equal in social status, but in Japan the customer is God," says Christopher Engholm, author of *When Business East Meets Business West*, published by John Wiley & Sons.

Another key difference: While price is king in America, the relationship between two companies is more important in Japan. American business people don't realize that Japanese business relationships are carefully forged to last a long time. According to Engholm, changing suppliers is a major decision for a Japanese company, even if what you are offering is cheaper and better.

The Japanese also believe in keeping as much business at home as possible.

Cheryl Rowley, a West Los Angeles interior designer, learned this the hard way when she was hired to take over the furnishing of the 600-room Yokohama Grand Inter-Continental Hotel after another design firm washed out.

"All of our design specifications were written for U.S. goods," Rowley says. "But countless times, the Japanese owners made decisions to use Japanese-made products even though they cost more and were not always the highest quality."

After much discussion, she was permitted to order American-made furniture for the hotel's public areas and buy American accessories and lighting fixtures. Rowley also insisted that a San Francisco company be permitted to install the mural that is the centerpiece of the grand ballroom. However, the carpets were Japanese-made, and all the guest-room furniture she designed was produced by Japanese craftspeople.

In addition to the pressure of a tight deadline and the need to greatly increase her staff, Rowley soon realized she was the only female consultant assigned to the hotel project—and an American one, at that. Once she proved her competence, she says she was treated with respect and cooperation.

One of the most challenging aspects of the project, which brought in a six-figure fee to her small firm, was dealing with strict chains of command. "The people I worked with were terrified by my need to make a decision right away," says Rowley, who adjusted to her client's decision-making style.

American business owners who have been successful in Japan say although details—such as the right way to present a business card (facing the recipient and held with both hands)—are important, the key thing is to realize that creating a a relationship with an Asian firm takes time and patience.

One of the easiest ways for a small business to gain a toehold in Japan is to find a distributor or agent there, according to Engholm, author and principal of Pacific Rim Ventures in Rancho La Costa, California.

"Try to sign a performance contract to test your product in their market for a short time," Engholm advises. Many Japanese companies are also interested in investing in American companies, offering a cash infusion as well as valuable business connections.

Another tip: If you want to pitch a product or service to Japan, you don't have to speak fluent Japanese. Knowing a few polite phrases is helpful, but English is widely spoken. In fact, the big rage in Japan is to learn how to speak English at one of scores of private language schools opening up across the country.

If you are ready to test the Japanese market, which is flooded with about 30,000 new products a year, do your homework first.

Honoring the Customer—Marketing and Selling to the Japanese, by Robert March (John Wiley & Sons), is packed with interesting anecdotes and suggestions.

If you can afford it, attend the annual conference on doing business in Asia sponsored by the U.S. Department of Commerce and the University of Southern California. Every March, USC brings together the senior commercial officers from fifteen U.S. embassies in the Asia/Pacific region with scores of experts and hundreds of business owners from across the country. The fee is about $850. For registration information, call (213) 740-7132 or fax a request to (213) 740-7559.

The Japan External Trade Organization (JETRO) and the Greater Los Angeles World Trade Center Association also offer seminars and classes on doing business in Japan.

For further information, call JETRO at (213) 624-8855 or the World Trade Center Association at (213) 680-1888.

International Business Tips and Resources

Savvy small-business owners are thinking globally, but with nineteen different federal agencies and departments dealing with exports, getting started can be tough. But now, the U.S. Small Business Administration has a new system to help you figure out which countries want to buy what you have to sell. The new Automated Trade Locator Assistance System or SB-Atlas, as it is known, generates two types of valuable reports. One report focuses on an individual country and lists the top twenty products or services imported into or exported from that country in the past three years. The second report focuses on the products or services you have to offer. It comes up with about thirty-five countries looking to buy what you have to sell. Tapping into this resource is easy.

Just contact your local U.S. Small Business Administration field office, or a small-business development center. The offices are listed in the white pages, or you can call (800)-8-ASK-SBA [827-5722].

Conclusion

Since 1988, when I began writing my syndicated Succeeding in Small Business® column, I've met with thousands of entrepreneurs across the country and abroad.

In every conversation, I always try to find out exactly which qualities distinguish the successful entrepreneur from the person who never really achieves success.

I thought I had the answer before I began the research for this book. But to be sure, I wanted to cast a wider net by developing and distributing a totally unscientific, anecdotal survey. My survey, distributed around the country by business groups and during an eight-city speaking tour sponsored by IBM, asked business owners to reveal the smartest and dumbest business decisions they ever made. Members of the San Diego–based The Executive Committee (TEC), an executive self-help group, National Small Business United, and the Valley Economic Development Center in Van Nuys, California, participated in the survey.

The secret to entrepreneurial success was simple:

Surround yourself with good people. Work hard. Love what you do.

The people part is where we started this book a few hundred pages ago.

The 300 or so entrepreneurs who responded to my survey said their smartest decisions involved hiring talented people and getting out of their way. Their dumbest decisions were hiring their girlfriends or unqualified spouses, their inexperienced children, neighbors, or people who drifted into their offices.

Many people said the dumbest thing they did was not get rid of problem employees, dishonest partners, and aggravating associates faster. Although making changes may be painful, the results are usually positive. The clear message from the surveys was: Always take action sooner rather than later.

Many regretted not taking risks, such as buying new equipment to expand a product line, buying their business property, or acquiring another business. It's easy to keep the status quo, but in business, opportunities not taken are truly lost.

While all of the TEC members had mentors within their group, about half of the non-TEC people said they had mentors as well. Many sought the advice and counsel of older business owners in their community. Several relied on their fathers, wives, and mothers for outside advice.

Many who said they didn't have mentors wished they had.

It surprised me that very few mentioned money as a problem, since access to capital is supposed to be the number-one small-business problem in America. It seems that successful entrepreneurs, at least this group, found it easy to attract bank financing or private investors or were fueling their growth through cash flow.

I also asked people what advice they would give young entrepreneurs. In virtually every case, they recommended being honest, being aggressive, being straight with people, and starting your business sooner rather than later. Many said they wished they had had the guts to start their businesses ten years before they did. They also recommended taking advantage of technology. Today, with $5,000 to $10,000 worth of equipment including a computer, a printer, and a few telephones, you can set up or grow virtually any small business.

Another strong theme among the respondents was achieving a balance between the demands of their companies and the demands of their families.

The surveys were heavy with regret. Regrets about broken marriages and neglected children. One man's greatest regret was not "learning to appreciate sushi at an earlier age." Several people wished they had learned to play the piano.

This self-selected batch of successful people felt badly about missing too many family vacations, soccer games, school plays, birthday parties, picnics, church services, and weddings. They looked back on their busy lives and saw too many late nights at the office and too few days on the beach.

The truly successful business owners I've met and interviewed work hard to achieve a balance between work and family. They know that without strong support from their families, they won't have the emotional stamina needed to ride the entrepreneurial roller coaster. Achieving a balance is tough, especially in the beginning, when you have to work so hard to keep the lights on and the customers coming in the door.

But if you want to succeed in the long run, you have to keep your business from devouring your time, your family, and your spirit.

My solution is trying to divide a sixteen-hour day into blocks of work time, family time, and personal time. (I need my eight hours of sleep.) I take a long break in the late afternoon and early evening to spend time with my children, Jeanne and Evan. In those hours, I help them with their homework, catch up on what's happened that day, and enjoy our meal together.

Then, fortified with their love, a few laughs and a cup of tea, I head back down the driveway, into my office for the night shift. I stack up my Beatle CDs and settle in to write my *Working Woman* magazine column, my newspaper column, or my radio or television reports. Most Saturday or Sunday mornings, I spend a few hours recording my radio reports. But nearly every weekend afternoon and evening is set aside for family time. Friday or Saturday night is popcorn night, with salty, buttery popcorn and a rented video.

My personal time for reflection, planning, and dreaming is stolen, hour by hour, during the week, between projects or on airplanes, en route to speaking engagements.

Once in a while, when I've been away for more than three days, Evan scrunches up his face and tells me to "quit my job!" I tell him that I don't have a job, I have a company and I love what I do. I also explain that because my office is at home, I'm with him more now than when I commuted to the *Los Angeles Times* office all those years. He still manages to make me feel guilty, which six-year-old boys with teary blue eyes can easily do.

I can't give you percentages and statistics based on my survey. I can tell you that success is more than making lots of money and having lots of things. It's having control over your life and your time. It's being free to pursue a personal dream, even when everyone tells you it's a stupid idea and you shouldn't quit your job. You'll never work harder than when you work for yourself, but you know it's worth it when your passion for the work counteracts the exhaustion.

To help you remember the key points of this book, I've come up with an easy formula called the "Five P's of Success."

The first P is *passion*. If you don't love what you are doing, think seriously about doing something else. Every successful entrepreneur I've met would keep working at their business even if they won a $10 million lottery prize tonight.

The second P is *people*. Surround yourself with bright, energetic and upbeat colleagues. Never work with anyone who gives you a stomachache or a headache.

The third P is *planning*. Successful business owners rely on a clear, detailed business plan. They frequently update their plan, making changes as the market and the world change.

The fourth P is *persistence*. Maintaining your physical and emotional stamina is essential to your success. When you feel that you just can't go on, take a break and give it just one more day.

The fifth P is *profits*. If you commit yourself to the first four P's, profits will eventually follow.

To your success in life and business!

Resource Section

"The most valuable commodity I know of is information."
—Corporate raider Gordon Gecko in the film *Wall Street*

Newsletters, Newspapers, and Magazines

Biz (newspaper)
342 Madison Avenue, #2001
New York, NY 10173
(212) 573-6015

Pr/Ink (newsletter)
594 Broadway, Suite 809
New York, NY 10012
Subscription, 12 issues: $195

Talking to the Boss (Chicago area newspaper)
(708) 933-9659
$18 per year

Coleman Report (newsletter)
P.O. Box 5401
Pasadena, CA 91117
Subscription, 24 issues: $395

Home Office Computing (magazine)
411 Lafayette Street
New York, NY 10003
Subscription, 12 issues: $19.97
(800) 288-7812

Consultants Roundtable News
(newsletter)
The Southern California
Organization of Professional
Consultants
P.O. Box 6159
Torrance, CA 90504
(310) 517-7958

Barter News (magazine)
Corporate and Editorial Offices
P.O. Box 3024
Mission Viejo, CA 92690
(714) 831-0607
Subscription: $40

Retirement Watch (newsletter)
c/o Kaleidoscope Publishing,
Ltd.
1420 Spring Hill Road
McLean, VA 22107
(703) 821-0571 or (800)
820-0422
Subscription: $99

The Accidental Entrepreneur
(newsletter)
3421 Alcott Street
Denver, CO 80211
(303) 433-0345
Subscription, 6 issues: $24

The Do-able Marketing Plan
Workbook by Adrienne Zoble
$42.95 plus $6.75 shipping and
handling

Unconventional Wisdom
by Adrienne Zoble
Adrienne Zoble Associates, Inc.
P.O. Box 130
Somerville, NJ 08876
(908) 685-8008
Subscription, one year, six issues:
$89.95 plus sales tax (NJ only).

The Art of Self-Promotion
(newsletter)
302 Garden Street
Hoboken, NJ 07030
(201) 653-0783 or
(800) 737-0783
Subscription, one year, four
issues: $25. A sample issue is $1.

Professional Services Guide for
Minority-Owned Businesses
(quarterly magazine)
714 W. Olympic Boulevard
Suite 714
Los Angeles, CA 90015
(213) 748-2215

California Business Incubation
Network (CBIN)
c/o Coopers & Lybrand
350 S. Grand Avenue
Los Angeles, CA 90071

Business Trends Report
(newsletter)
537 Newport Center Drive,
Suite 355
Newport Beach, CA 92660
Phone/Fax (714) 644-8818
Subscription, one year: $29.

Lesko's Info-Power Newsletter
Information USA
P. O. Box E
Kensington, MD 20895-0418
(301) 924-0556
(800) 955-POWER
$33.95 plus $4.00 shipping and
handling

*Bootstrappin' Entrepreneur: The
Newsletter for Individuals with
Great Ideas and a Little Bit of
Cash* (quarterly newsletter)
Research Done Write!
Suite B261
8726 South Sepulveda Boulevard
Los Angeles, CA 90045-4082
(310) 568-9861
Subscription, one year: $24.

Entrepreneur (magazine)
2392 Morse Avenue
Irvine, CA 92714
Subscription, one year: $19.97
P. O. Box 50368
Boulder, CO 80321-0368

Booklets

*100 Tips for Small Business Owners: How to Get the Coverage You
Need.*
For a free copy, send a self-addressed, stamped #10 envelope to:
　　The Society of CPCU
　　720 Providence Road
　　P.O. Box 3009
　　Malvern, PA 19355-0709

151 Travel Tips
Send $4.00 and a self-addressed, *double*-stamped business envelope
to:
　　K.M. Enterprises
　　P.O. Box 774
　　Dept. LATS
　　Centuck Station
　　Yonkers, NY 10710
　　(914) 961-3906

Disability Etiquette: Interacting with People with Disabilities
Send a self-addressed, stamped envelope to:
 Access Resources
 340 West 28th Street, Suite 6J
 New York, NY 10001
 (212) 741-3758 (Voice/TTY)

Consumer Information Center (directory)
Send name and address for a free copy to:
 Consumer Information Center
 Department KO
 Pueblo, Colorado 81009

70 Steps to Speaking Success
Send $5 and a self-addressed business envelope with 58 cents postage
to:
 HCG, Inc., Dept. LATS
 1954 First Street, #103
 Highland Park, IL 60035

Managing Employees
For free sample guidelines, send a self-addressed, stamped #10
envelope to:
 Easy Street Publishing, Dept. MEPR
 2261 Market Street, #333
 San Francisco, CA 94114

123 Great Marketing Ideas to Grow Your Business
Send $5 and a business envelope with 58 cents postage to:
 Barbara Leff
 The Marketing Menu, Dept. JA
 70 W. Burton, Suite #1804
 Chicago, IL 60610

Books

Finding, Hiring, and Keeping the Best Employees by Robert Half, John Wiley & Co., $22.50. 1 (800) 225-5945.

How to Hire the Right Person by Denis L. Cauvier, HRD Press, $24.95. (800) 822-2801.

Effective Interviewing, Every Manager's Guide to Selecting High Performers by Richard Beatty, John Wiley & Co., $17.95. (800) 225-5945.

The AMA Handbook for Employee Recruitment and Retention by Mary F. Cook, AMACOM, $75.00. (800) 262-9699.

Extraviewing: Innovative Ways to Hire the Best by Arthur H. Bell, BusinessOne Irwin, $24.95. (800) 634-3966.

The Employee-Selection Workshop, HRD Press, $99.95. (800) 822-2801.

The Zen of Hype: Creative Tactics and Advice for Anyone with a Business, Product or Talent to Promote by Raleigh Pinskey, $10.95. (310) 998-0055. (Audio tapes also available.)

The U.S. Asian Market, a Practical Guide to Doing Business, Pacific Heritage Books, P.O. Box 3967-J94, Palos Verdes, CA 90274-9547, $32.00. (310) 541-8818.

Books of Interest to Women

A Few Good Women: Breaking the Barriers to Top Management by Jane White, Prentice Hall. (800) 288-4745.

Body and Soul: Profits with Principles by Anita Roddick with Russell Miller, Random House. (800) 726-0600.

Exceptional Entrepreneurial Women: Strategies for Success by Russel R. Taylor, Greenwood Publishing Group. (800) 225-5800.

Hers: The Wise Woman's Guide to Starting a Business on $2,000 or Less by Carol Milano, Allworth Press. (800) 247-6553.

National Directory of Woman-Owned Business Firms, Business Research Services. (800) 845-8420.

On Your Own: A Woman's Guide to Building a Business by Laurie B. Zuckerman, Upstart Publishing. (800) 235-8866.

The Purple Rose Within: A Woman's Basic Guide for Developing a Business Plan by Millicent G. Lownes, Business of Your Own. (615) 646-3708.

Regional Directory of Minority and Woman-Owned Business Firms, Business Research Services. (800) 842-8420.

The Woman Entrepreneur: Out of Your Mind . . . and into the Marketplace by Linda Pinson and Jerry Jinnett, Upstart Publishing. (800) 235-8866.

Women Entrepreneurs, Networking & Sweet Potato Pie: Creating Capital in the 21st Century by Dolores Ratcliffe, Corita Communications. (213) 624-8639.

A Woman's Guide to Starting a Business by Claudia Jessup and Genie Chipps, Henry Holt and Co. (800) 488-5233.

Our Wildest Dreams: Women Entrepreneurs Making Money, Having Fun, Doing Good by Joline Godfrey, HarperCollins. (800) 242-7737.

Recommended Books

Fax-Ready Guerrilla Grams: Instant Tear-out, Feed-in Business Faxes with a Mission, Distributed by The Globe Pequot Press, $8.95 plus shipping. (800) 243-0495.

Endless Referrals: Network Your Everyday Contacts into Sales by Bob Burg, McGraw-Hill, $14.95.

Save Your Business a Bundle: 202 Ways to Cut Costs and Boost Profits Now—for Companies of Any Size by Daniel Kehrer, Simon & Schuster, $22.00.

Managing Employees: A Step-by-Step Guide to Personnel Procedures for the Small Business in California, Easy Street Publishing, $159.00. (415) 863-3917. National edition, Adams Blake Publishing, $69.00. (415) 241-3061.

All publications below are products made available by Raphel Publishing. There are three ways to order them:
Mail: Raphel Publishing, 12 South Virginia Avenue, Atlantic City, NJ 08401. Phone: (609) 348-6646; fax: (609) 347-2455.
Add $3.50 for first item and $1.00 for each additional item for shipping.

Customerization by Murray Raphel. 180 rules to increase your business by using radio, TV, newspaper, direct mail, promotions . . . and more! $19.95.

How to Find, Capture and Keep Customers by Stan Golomb. Thousands of businesses have hired Stan Golomb. Now you can find out Stan's secrets of business success. $19.95.

Tough Selling for Tough Times by Murray and Neil Raphel. Marketing ideas of successful business people including Listen! Sell! and Reward! $19.95. Cassette companion to *Tough Selling for Tough Times,* $9.95

The Do-It-Yourself Direct Mail Handbook by Murray Raphel and Ken Erdman. Totally revised 1992 edition. Everything you need to know to start producing direct mail for your business. $19.95.

Mind Your Own Business by Murray Raphel. Promotions that work in business. Lots of stories and ideas in this book. $19.95.

Network Your Way to Success by Ken Erdman and Tom Sullivan. Proven networking strategies. $19.95.

Crowning the Customer by Feargal Quinn. Customer-service tips from a leading Irish supermarket-chain owner. $19.95.

Videotapes and Audiocassettes

What You Need to Know about Business Law. A six-tape series of audiocassettes released by the Santa Monica–based Business Advisement Center. Features invaluable tools for anyone who is involved in business. Includes tax, shipping and handling. $79.95.

Entrepreneurship for Women: Escape from the Pink-Collar Ghetto by Charlotte Taylor, Center on Education and Training for Employment.

The Power of Family Business, National Education Center for Women in Business. (412) 830-4625.

The Women Entrepreneur Series, National Education Center for Women in Business. (412) 830-4625.

How To Legally Hire, 40-minute videotape produced by The Friedman Group, Culver City, CA, $95.00. (800) 351-8040.

Women's Business Associations

American Business Women's Association. (816) 361-6621. Offers leadership training, conferences, and conventions.

American Women in Enterprise. (800) 222-2933. Provides publications, an advice hotline and meeting space in major cities.

American Woman's Economic Development Corporation. (800) 222-2933. Counsels women on starting and managing businesses.

An Income of Her Own. (800) 350-2978. Volunteers provide entrepreneurial education, a newsletter, and networking for teenage girls.

Association of Black Women Entrepreneurs. (213) 624-8639. Offers education, counseling, publications and a hotline.

Mothers' Home Business Network. (516) 997-7394. Provides information for mothers with home-based businesses. Members receive quarterly newsletter.

SBA Office of Women's Business Ownership. (202) 205-6673. Offers information and programs to assist women business owners.

National Association of Women Business Owners (NAWBO), based in Silver Spring, Maryland. (301) 608-2590. Offers workshops on issues affecting female owners.

National Foundation for Women Business Owners. (301) 495-4975. This arm of NAWBO offers an annual leadership conference for female owners and sponsors research on women's economic issues.

Women in Franchising. (800) 222-4943. Provides training and networking to women.

Powerlink. (412) 563-1542.
Helps female owners establish a board of directors. Applicant firms must be at least two years old, with $150,000 in annual sales.

American Women's Economic Development Corporation (AWED, D.C.).
1250 24th Street NW, Suite 120
Washington, DC 20037
(202) 857-0091
Offers training and support services.

AWED (Southern California)
230 Pine Avenue, Third Floor
Long Beach, CA 90802.
(310) 983-3747

The National Education Center for Women in Business,
Seton Hill College
Greensburg, PA 15601-1599
(412) 830-4625 or (800) NECWB-4-U.

Mothers on the Move, An Alliance of Entrepeneurial Mothers
P.O. Box 64033
Tucson, AZ 85728-4033
(602) 628-2598

General Associations

The Institute for Crisis Management
710 West Main Street, Suite 210
Louisville, KY 40202
(502) 584-0402; fax (502) 587-6132

National Association for the Self-Employed (NASE)
P.O. Box 612067
DFW Airport, TX 75261
(800) 232-6273

Corporation Against Drug Abuse.
Provides information on employee-assistance programs. Call (800) 678-0654 to receive a free Drug-Free Workplace and Assistance Service package.

Institute for a Drug-Free Workplace
1301 K Street, N.W., East Tower, Suite 1010
Washington, DC 20005
(202) 842-7400

Owner Managed Business Institute
(800) THE-OMBI [843-6624]
Offers a course on business development.

KIDI
Kansas Innovation Development, Inc.
12 West 6th
Topeka, KS 66603
A new way to create jobs, develop technologies, and generate business.

Direct Marketing Association, Inc.
11 West 42nd Street
New York, NY 10036-8096
(212) 768-7277

The American Franchise Association
53 West Jackson Boulevard, Suite 205
Chicago, IL 60604
(312) 431-0545

American Vendors Association
Penthouse Suite 930
Benjamin Fox Pavilion
Jenkintown, PA 19046
(215) 887-5700

Dinah Adkins
National Business Incubation Association
20 East Circle Drive
Suite 190
Athens, OH 45701
(617) 593-4331

The Product Development & Management Association
International nonprofit organization for people with a professional
interest in product innovation. Contact John Moran at (805)
495-9927 or the PDMA national office at (800) 232-5241.

Promotional Products Association International
3125 Skyway Circle North
Irving, TX 75038-3526
(214) 252-0404; fax (214) 594-7224

Small Business Administration Answer Desk
409 Third Street SW
Washington, DC 20416
(800) 827-5722
A one-stop source for recorded information on the SBA's national and
local services and programs.

National Marketing Federation, Inc.
324 Pinewood Avenue
Silver Spring, MD 20901
(800) 2 SOLVE IT [276-5834];
(301) 681-6626; fax (301) 681-0227
Provides guidance for small and home-based business owners.

National Federation of Independent Business
53 Century Boulevard, #300
Nashville, TN 37214
(800) 634-2669
A national advocacy group, the NFIB also provides employers with information on what the state legislature is doing and how it will affect independent business owners.

National Small Business United
1155 15th Street NW, #710
Washington, DC 20005
(202) 293-8830 or (800) 345-NSBU
A small-business advocacy organization that offers information on legislation concerning small-business owners. Priority issues include health care reform, banking reform, and taxes.

On-line Resources

For a geographical directory of computer bulletin board systems, send $39.95 to:
    National Directory of Bulletin Board Systems
    Meckler Corporation
    11 Ferry Lane
    Westport, CT 06880
    (203) 226-6967

SBA Online
(800) 697-4636
(900) 463-4636
The toll-free 800 number offers information on the SBA's loans and business development programs. The 900 number is 30 cents for the first minute, 10 cents for each additional minute, and allows users to communicate with each other and download information directly to their own computers.

President's Committee Job Accommodation Network
Bulletin Board
(800) DIAL JAN [342-5526]

Organizations

The Alternative Board
185 East 85th Street, Suite 35B
New York, NY 10028-2150
(800) 727-0126

Scripps Center for Quality Management, Inc.
9747 Business Park Avenue
San Diego, CA 92131
(619) 566-3472

Telephone Effectiveness Institute
Research Training Consultation
631 West Broadway
Glendale, CA 91204
(818) 244-TELL [8355] (800) 451-TELL

Dr. Leon Danco
The Center for Family Business
P.O. Box 24268
Cleveland, OH 44124
(216) 442-0800; fax: 442-0178

American Society for Training and Development
1640 King Street
Box 1443
Alexandria, VA 22313-2043
(703) 683-8100

American Disabilities Act (ADA) Resources

President's Committee Job Accommodation Network
1 (800) 526-7234 or (800) ADA-WORK [232-9675]

Guidance/Consulting

American Management Association
The American Management Association Building
135 West 50th Street
New York, NY 10020-1201
(212) 586-8100

The Business Network International
268 South Bucknell Avenue
Claremont, CA 91711-4907
(909) 624-2227; fax (909) 625-9671

Experts Reference Guide
Office of External Affairs
School of Business Administration
University of Southern California
Los Angeles, CA 90089-1421
(213) 740-6411

Venture Capital

National Association of Small Business Investment Companies
(NASBIC)
1199 North Fairfax Street
Suite 200
Alexandria, VA 22314
(703) 683-1601

National Venture Capital Association
1655 North Fort Myer Drive, Suite 700
Arlington, VA 22209
(703) 351-5269

Financial Assistance—Women

National Federation of Business and Professional Women's Clubs
(202) 293-1100.
Offers personal loans up to $10,000 and home-equity loans up to
$100,000.

Women's World Banking
(212) 768-8513.
Finds financial and technical help for female owners.

Microloan Intermediaries

A program that offers small business people an opportunity to obtain
needed capital in small amounts.
   Call ASBA at 800-ASBA-911 [272-2911] for a copy of the original
list of Microloan Intermediaries.
   Call 800-827-5722 for more information about the microloan
program.

Shipping Smarter

Powership 3 (Federal Express's Automated Shipping and Tracking
System) provides big business advantages for small business needs.
For information on obtaining a Powership 3, call (800) 817-8300.

Roadway Package System, Inc.
A leading business-to-business air and small package ground and
second-day air carrier. RPS shippers can now receive same-day
delivery information, including delivery time and receiver's name, as
a standard service on every package shipped, at no extra cost.
   For more information on RPS's complete services, call (800)
ROADPAK [762-3725].

Transportation Options, a free booklet published by Ryder.
Call (800) RYDER-OK.

Air Transport Association of America
(202) 626-4000

American Trucking Association
(703) 838-1700

Council of Logistics Management
(708) 574-0985

National Association of Freight Transportation Consultants
(505) 299-0615

National Industrial Transportation League
(703) 524-5011

National Private Truck Council
(703) 683-1300

Transportation Brokers Conference of America
(703) 329-1894

International Resources

State Committee for Cooperation and Investment
56 Quoc Tu Giam Street
Hanoi, Vietnam
(844) 254970; 253666
Publishes books on foreign investments and partnerships with
Vietnam; also has copies of the country's foreign investment laws.

U.S. Committee for Scientific Cooperation with Vietnam
1300 University Avenue
Madison, WI 53706
Helps facilitate meetings and guides U.S. firms through the
Vietnamese business licensing process.

Winning in Foreign Markets: Your Global Guide
by Michele Forzley, Crisp Publications, $9.95. Available from:
Forzley & Co., "Your Global Guide," 3 Hanover Square, New York,
NY 10004. Phone: (212) 943-0270.

Export Profits: A Guide for Small Business
by Jack S. Wolf, Upstart Publishing, $19.95. Available from: Upstart
Publishing, 12 Portland Street, Dover, NH 03820. Phone: (800)
235-8866.

Vietnam Today
Global Directions, Inc.
P.O. Box 471553
San Francisco, CA 94147-1553
(415) 333-3800
Subscription, one year: $64
A bimonthly (soon to be monthly) English-language magazine
published in Singapore and distributed in the United States.

William Cherkasky
International Franchise Association (IFA)
1350 New York Avenue, N.W.
Suite 900
Washington, DC 20005
(202) 628-8000

Organizations

The University of Southern California's International Business
Education and Research Program (IBEAR)
(213) 740-7140;
fax (213) 740-7559

U.S. Chamber of Commerce
1615 H Street, N.W.
Washington, DC 20062
(202) 463-5600

The U.S. Commerce Department
Offers a variety of resources for business owners interested in
exporting. To request a list of subjects available, call (202) 482-5745.

The Small Business Foundation of America operates the Export
Opportunity Hot Line, Mondays through Fridays, between 9 A.M. and
5 P.M. EST. The hot line provides a variety of free export information
and referrals to entrepreneurs as well as data base services for a
modest fee. Phone: (800) 243-7232. In Washington, D.C., call: (202)
223-1104.

  The Foundation also publishes an excellent exporting guide,
Exportise: An International Trade Source Book for Smaller Company
Executives. The cost is $49.50. For ordering information, call: (202)
223-1103.

Home Business Institute (HBI)
A White Plains, New York, organization that can achieve the same bulk buyer cost reductions as larger companies. For example, 1,000 customized brochures at 50 cents each. For HBI's brochure describing membership benefits (fee: $49 a year), write to P. O. Box 301, White Plains, NY 10605, or call (914) 946-6600; fax (914) 946-6694.

Hotlines

Export Hotline
Free exporter's kit and 24-hour fax retrieval (sponsored by AT&T with seven other organizations and U.S. Department of Commerce) (800) USA-XPORT [872-9767]

Trade Information Center
U.S. Department of Commerce (export assistance programs) (800) USA TRADE [872-8723]

Office of International Trade
U.S. Small Business Administration
409 Third St. SW
Washington, DC 20416
(800) U-ASK-SBA [827-5722]
Small Business Answer Desk for prerecorded information; or contact the SBA office nearest you, listed in U.S. government pages of telephone books.

U.S. Export–Import Bank
(Eximbank)
811 Vermont Avenue NW
Washington, DC 20571
(800) 565-3946

Venture Link USA, Inc.
13101 Washington Boulevard
Suite 242
Los Angeles, CA 90066-5125
(310) 822-5628; fax (310) 822-2175

U.S. Department of Commerce, Office of Canada (DOC-OOC)
Flash Facts Hotline. (202) 482-3101.

Canada Customs Automated Information Service
This service offers information about shipping goods into Canada. It
also includes a recorded update on the monetary exchange rate. Call
(416) 973-8022.

NAFTA Facts
(202) 482-4464 is a seven-day-a-week, 24-hour-a-day hotline fax
service provided by the U.S. Department of Commerce, Office of
Mexico.

NAFTA Update, a four-page monthly newsletter published by Price
Waterhouse, free on request. Call (800) 568-8949 or contact your
local Price Waterhouse branch.

Four federal agencies have joined forces to open a new Export
Assistance Center in Long Beach. The Small Business
Administration, Department of Commerce, U.S. Export–Import Bank,
and the U.S. Agency for International Development are now located
at the center at One World Trade Center, Long Beach. For
information call (310) 980-4550.

The Greater Los Angeles World Trade Center Association
publishes a terrific newsletter called *Tradelinks*. For $50 you can
receive a one-year's subscription to the monthly publication, plus a
copy of the group's International Resource Guide.

To order, call (310) 499-7070 or (213) 680-1888.

Index

DUTTON **PLUME**

THE LATEST WORDS ON BUSINESS

☐ **WINNIE-THE-POOH ON MANAGEMENT** *In which a Very Important Bear and his friends are introduced to a Very Important Subject.* **Roger E. Allen.** Using the characters and the stories of A.A. Milne to illustrate such principles as setting clear objectives, strong leadership, the need for accurate information, good communication, and other neglected basics of prudent management, the author offers sensible, time-honored advice in a captivating style.
(938982—$17.95)

☐ **FROM HERE TO ECONOMY** *A Shortcut to Economic Literacy.* **by Todd G. Buchholz.** With refreshing wit and irreverence, the author takes readers by the hand and reveals the basic rules behind everything from food prices to trade deficits. He gives us a precise and accessible understanding of economic ideas, actions, and consequences as they actually exist in the here and now.
(939024—$21.95)

☐ **SIX STEPS TO FREE PUBLICITY** *And Dozens of Other Ways to Win Free Media Attention for You or Your Business.* **by Marcia Yudkin.** Whether you want to pull in new business, establish yourself as an expert, or introduce a new concept to the community, free publicity is the cheapest, most credible way to do it. This is the savvy, start-to-finish guide that shows you how to make your message a worthy event.
(271924—$9.95)

☐ **JANE APPLEGATE'S STRATEGIES FOR SMALL BUSINESS SUCCESS** America's top small-business management expert shares her practical knowledge to help you avoid the pitfalls and tap the full potential of starting and running your own enterprise. This uniquely valuable guide is written in a lively, no-nonsense style, and enriched by scores of interviews with people who have made being their own bosses pay off.
(273528—$12.95)

Prices slightly higher in Canada.

Visa and Mastercard holders can order Plume, Meridian, and Dutton books by calling
1-800-253-6476.
They are also available at your local bookstore. Allow 4-6 weeks for delivery.
This offer is subject to change without notice.